THE BIG BOOK OF
Preserving
THE Harvest

Carol W. Costenbader

A Storey Publishing Book

STOREY

Storey Communications, Inc.
Schoolhouse Road
Pownal, Vermont 05261

The mission of Storey Communications is to serve our customers
by publishing practical information that encourages personal independence
in harmony with the environment.

Edited by Pamela Lappies and Julia Rubel
Cover and text design by Cynthia McFarland
Front and back cover photographs by Nicholas Whitman
Text production by Erin Lincort and Susan Bernier
Expert review by Lynda Spivey
Chapter opener art by Carolyn Bucha
Illustrations by Alison Kolesar, except pages 325, 326, 327, and 328 by Wendy Edelson; pages 83 and 290 by
    Judy Eliason; pages 13, 113, and 287 by Brigita Fuhrmann; page 91 (top) by Charles Joslin; pages 28 (top
    and center), 31 (left and center), 116, and 245 by Doug Merrilees; and pages 35 (top), 38 (left), 39 (top), 42
    (top left and top right), 43 (top left, top right, and bottom right), 44 (bottom), 79, 80, 88 (top), 120, 250,
    251 (top left and bottom left), 310, and 312 by Elayne Sears.
Indexed by Susan Olason, Indexes + Knowledge Maps

The information in this book is true and complete to the best of our knowledge. All recommendations are
made without guarantee on the part of the author or Storey Communications, Inc. The author and publisher dis-
claim any liability in connection with the use of this information. For additional information please contact Storey
Communications, Inc., Schoolhouse Road, Pownal, Vermont 05261.

Storey Publishing books are available for special premium and promotional uses and for customized editions.
For further information, please call the Custom Publishing Department at 800-793-9397.

Printed in the United States by R.R. Donnelley
Printed on recycled paper

10 9 8 7 6 5 4 3 2

LIBRARY OF CONGRESS CATALOGING-IN-PUBLICATION DATA

Costenbader, Carol W.
     The big book of preserving the harvest / Carol W. Costenbader.
        p.   cm.
     "A Storey Publishing book."
     Includes bibliographical references (p.   ) and index.
     ISBN 0-88266-800-5 (hardcover : alk. paper) — ISBN 0-88266-978-8 (pbk. : alk.
paper)
     1. Canning and preserving.   I. Title.
   TX603.C67   1997
   641.4—dc21
                                                                    97-22704
                                                                       CIP

Contents

Acknowledgments

Special thanks to Lynda Spivey, Family and Consumer Educator,
North Carolina Cooperative Extension Service;
Lane W. Byrd, a typist who is also a great cook;
my husband, the gardener in the family;
Pamela Lappies — my editor;
Julia Rubel, production editor;
and Nancy Ringer, editorial assistant.

Deo Sit Gloria.

ONE OF MY FONDEST MEMORIES of childhood is playing in my grandmother's pantry — the smell of the onion bin; the way the air stayed cool, even in the hot summertime. Sometimes the mouthwatering aroma of ham from Sunday dinner wafted out to greet you when you opened the door. The floor space under the bottom shelf made a great cubbyhole for hiding away. There were endless rows of pickles — watermelon rind, green tomato, bread and butter — stacks of colorful jam jars, and rows of mixed vegetables. Granny must have felt rich. In those times preserving was a necessary economy.

In earliest history a new age began with the discovery of drying as a way of preserving. How revolutionary to be able to save meat and produce from a time of abundance into the leaner winter months. Around 3000 B.C. the Egyptians preserved herbs in their precious olive oils. Fishermen in Biblical times dried their catch in the hot, dry open air. In colonial times, Native Americans shared their methods of drying corn and meat with early European settlers. That help meant the difference between living and dying as winter took its toll.

In 1809, Frenchman Nicolas Appert devised a way to preserve food by heating it in a sealed container. From there Louis Pasteur, another Frenchman and scientist, documented sterilization as a way to destroy dangerous microorganisms that spoil food. In the 19th century, pre-serving food had become a science instead of folklore. The metal can and the glass canning jar were improved.

Introduction

To avoid frustrating delays, gather together all the equipment before starting your recipe.

Electricity and the advent of refrigeration soon revolutionized food storage. Refrigeration became so popular that the old methods of preserving the harvest were not widely used.

Today's families often turn to food preservation as an inexpensive and time-saving way to have chemical-free food that captures the abundance and flavors of summer. Because I have preserved much of the harvest of seasons past, I can serve almost any condiment, relish, chutney, or fancy pickle from my own pantry — and for far less than the cost at expensive specialty food stores.

The Big Book of Preserving the Harvest considers all forms of food preservation for today's busy families. We seldom rely on the methods our grandmothers used because of what we now know about the dangers of bacteria. But we have at our disposal an array of new appliances that make the job of preserving healthy, safe, and simple. Here are the best of Granny's offerings updated into safe, creative, good-tasting recipes everyone can use.

As you might guess, my kitchen is set up for almost any food preservation method, and having the proper equipment makes getting started that much easier. Nothing is more frustrating than realizing in the middle of a recipe that you are lacking a key piece of equipment. The beginner need not invest in every single piece of equipment mentioned in this book, but it's a good idea to purchase everything you will need for the particular method you choose. The good news is that many of the items mentioned are standard kitchen equipment.

When the harvest is rolling in, my philosophy is to gather either enough produce for one recipe of a canned product — usually four to eight jars, or two recipes of a frozen product — one for dinner that night and one for the freezer. Preserving in small batches does away with the long hours of preparation, and frequently you can complete that evening's dinner at the same time. Picking small batches assures impeccable freshness.

I hope this idea of preserving in small batches will motivate even the most timid or inexperienced cook to try food preservation. Small batches make more sense for families that may not have the room to store great quantities of preserved food or that may not even own a large freezer.

TIP

......

Try preserving in small batches, particularly if you are a beginner.

TIP

......

Start as early as possible in the day and allow plenty of time.

CHAPTER 1

Choosing Ingredients

ONE OF THE GREATEST JOYS of growing your own produce is to stand in your garden as you are harvesting, in the midst of all your labor, and eat a just-picked tomato still warm from the sun. Nothing compares, whether because of the time you've put into it, the experience of seeing something grown out of almost nothing, or the incomparable flavor and juiciness. The same is true of harvesting strawberries and other fruit, sun-sweet, ripe, and ready for shortcake. The flavor and nutritive value of just-picked garden vegetables is far superior to what you encounter in most supermarkets, and the goal of preserving food you've grown yourself or purchased from a local farmer is to lock that flavor in so that you can enjoy it during off seasons.

Nothing compares to the satisfaction of growing your own fruits and vegetables, but looking at pantry shelves stocked with preserved produce, ready for the the cold season ahead, certainly comes close.

Starting out with the very best ingredients is absolutely essential. Choosing the freshest produce, spices, and herbs helps ensure that your final product will be of the highest quality. I check the garden early every morning to see what is ready. Harvesting early in the day before the sun warms the garden heightens the freshness of your produce and gives you plenty of time to start whatever preserving process you choose. Time is of the essence between the harvest and processing, though, so getting organized before you pick your fruits and vegetables is important.

Only the Freshest Produce

No book on food preservation would be complete without a word about handling the harvest. You'll want to use only the very best-quality fruits and vegetables, since no recipe, however elaborate, can make up for ingredients that are inferior in taste or freshness.

Whether you get them from your garden or a farm stand, choose vegetables that are still young and tender. The older they are, the more fibrous and tough they're likely to be. Once again, no amount of processing can change the basic qualities of the original produce.

Vegetables and herbs undergo change immediately after they are picked. Their vitamin C content, for instance, begins to decline. If you must wait several hours between harvesting and starting the preserving process, refrigerate your unwashed bounty. If you pick tomatoes or herbs, however, keep them at room temperature — they actually lose flavor at lower temperatures. Stand herbs in a "vase" of water like flowers until you can use them.

An alternative to refrigerating produce is to submerge it in water and ice cubes in your kitchen or laundry sink. This works especially well for short periods of time (one or two

Stand freshly picked herbs in water until you are ready to use them.

Fruit for Preserving

● ● ● ● ● ● ● ● ● ● ● ● ● ● ●

Pectin, the naturally occurring substance found in the skins and cores of fruit, produces a gel when combined with sugar and additional fruit. While commercial pectin can be added to recipes, the natural pectin in fruit can sometimes produce enough of a gel for jams and jellies. Underripe fruit contains more pectin than ripe fruit. Listed below are fruits that when underripe contain enough pectin to produce a proper gel.

Sour apples	*Currants*	*Loganberries*
Blackberries	*Gooseberries*	*Plums*
Crab apples	*Eastern Concord grapes*	*Raspberries*
Cranberries	*Lemons*	*Quince*

hours). When you're ready to begin preserving, drain the water and rinse off any garden dirt. Several sinkfuls of rinse water may be necessary to get your produce perfectly clean and ready for processing. For winter squash, cucumbers, and other thick-skinned vegetables, you may need to use a soft scrub brush. When you're sure your bounty is clean and ready, dry it on clean towels.

FARMER'S MARKET PRODUCE

Most cities and towns have farmer's markets that provide fresh produce to urban and suburban dwellers. I find walking the aisles of a farmer's market in spring, late summer, or fall one of life's greatest pleasures. Each time I do, I'm reminded of the bounty of blessings we have in this country. (If you're tired of gardening, you can doubly

Community Supported Agriculture

• •

One wonderful solution to the dilemma of how to obtain fresh produce without actually gardening yourself is Community Supported Agriculture. This began 30 years ago in Japan when a group of women realized that more and more of their food was being imported. They organized a group that bought directly from a farmer, inaugurating the system that came to be known as Community Supported Agriculture (CSA). The Japanese word for CSA is teikie, which means "putting the farmer's face on food."

Most CSAs begin with a farmer and sometimes a core group of members, who draw up a budget that includes all farm production costs, including salaries and overhead, for one year's operation. The total cost is divided by the number of families the farm will provide for, and that determines the cost of one share of the harvest. Each week, shareholders go to the farm to collect their produce, with one share's worth enough to feed a family of four for a week. Most CSAs offer half shares, as well, and make arrangements for installment payments. The risk of the harvest is shared by the farmer and the members.

The first CSA in the United States began in Massachusetts in 1985, and since then six hundred more have come into being, almost all using organic methods. Not only do they foster a sense of community in the region, but they also encourage good environmental practices and a strong local economy.

appreciate how much effort has gone into growing the piles of spring asparagus or the mountains of ripe summer tomatoes.) The produce at a farmer's market is usually better than most grocery store fare because it's grown locally (or at least regionally), and therefore less time has elapsed between harvest and purchase. I like to eat "close to the earth" and always try to buy produce in season for the region.

Using In-Season Produce
. . . .

When you plan menus, try to keep in mind when different fruits and vegetables mature. For example, in a recipe that calls for green spring onions and butternut squash, which mature in autumn, something has come from cold storage or isn't locally grown. An eggplant purchased in October in the South or a strawberry in February in the Northeast has been grown in another part of the world. Some of this produce could possibly be acceptable for eating, but not for preserving. When you buy locally grown fruits and vegetables, you know you are buying fresh, in-season produce.

Never go to the farmer's market in the hottest part of the day, load up your car with beautiful fruits and vegetables, and continue running errands. Produce in a hot car will wilt very quickly, and you'll defeat your original purpose of preserving fresh foods. If schedules are tight, try taking a cooler with you, pre-iced for storing produce until you can get home.

Fortunately, some produce cellars, or stores, very nicely. Many root crops such as carrots, onions, sweet potatoes, and white potatoes, because of how easily they can be stored, are perfectly good much of the year (see chapter 8 on root storage). Do experiment, and you'll learn the difference in the taste of a new-crop spring potato and a cold-storage or root-cellared potato.

TIP
. . . . . .

Call ahead to reserve just the fresh produce you need for the exact time you need it. Produce stand owners are often glad to cooperate.

To keep fruits and vegetables fresh in a hot car, pack them in a cooler.

● ● ● ● ● ● ● ● ● ● ● ●

Fruits ripen at their own pace, and you pretty much have to strike at the decisive moment. However, if you know in advance when you will be on vacation, try planting your vegetables so that they will reach maturity when you return from your trip.

SUPERMARKET PRODUCE

Big business has forever changed the world of agriculture, and the same is true of the way food is marketed. While common sense supports the notion that locally grown food is the best quality and least expensive, big business has created wholesale markets that buy in huge quantities and then distribute to chain supermarkets throughout the country.

In "supermarket mentality," foreign-grown produce travels long distances to appear in the bins of your supermarket, while fresh, locally grown produce is left out. In the United States, food travels an average of 1,300 miles from its origin before it reaches supermarket shelves, and most U.S. grocers purchase 85 to 90 percent of their food from out-of-state sources. Aside from the loss of freshness, foreign-grown fruits and vegetables are often grown under less stringent controls regarding the use of pesticides.

Another reason for choosing locally grown produce is the higher nutrient content of fresh food. Fruits and vegetables begin to lose vitamins and minerals the moment they are picked. Food that must be shipped thousands of miles contains fewer nutrients by the time it reaches your table than food that was picked 12 hours ago. You can also be more confident that lettuce or apples grown by a local farmer who prides himself on his organic methods is indeed chemical-free than you can from a sign in a grocery store. While organically grown produce has not been proven to contain more nutrients than that grown with chemical pesticides, no one can deny that it's best to consume untreated food.

Aside from economics and nutrition, the difference in taste, appearance, and scent between fresh-picked fruits and vegetables and those sold in the supermarket is the most persuasive reason to avoid supermarket produce. No one benefits from unappealing produce that lies uneaten in the refrigerator bin. When you consider all the arguments for eating locally grown food, you wonder why anyone would chose the alternative.

Much of the produce sold in supermarkets is coated with a protective wax to help prevent mold during shipping. If produce has wax on it, you can be sure it wasn't grown locally. Unfortunately, the wax makes it impossible to properly clean the fungicides off the skins. Before you eat or process such foods, always peel off the skin.

TIP
• • • • • •

Avoid using waxed supermarket produce for preserving.

Caution! Waxed Produce

One supermarket in North Carolina has a sign over the produce section that reads:

Coated with Food Grade Vegetable, Petroleum, Beeswax, and/or Shellac-based Wax or Resin:

Apples	Lemon	Peppers
Pears	Limes	Tomatoes
Oranges	Cantaloupes	Squash
Peaches	Honeydews	Asparagus
Plums	Grapefruit	Eggplant
Tangelos	Passion Fruit	Turnips
Mangoes	Pineapples	Parsnips
Apricots	Nectarines	Beans
Avocados	Tangerines	Yucca Root
Star Fruit	Rutabagas	Jicama
Cucumbers	Sweet Potatoes	

QUANTITY PER QUART

FRUIT	QUANTITY PER QUART CANNED	VEGETABLE	QUANTITY PER QUART CANNED
Apples	2½–3 lbs.	Artichokes, globe	6–10 whole
Apricots	2½–3½ lbs.	Artichokes, Jerusalem	¾–1½ lbs.
Blackberries	1½–3 lbs. or 1–2 qt. cartons	Asparagus	2½–4½ lbs.
		Beans — bush green	1½–2½ lbs.
Blueberries	1½–3 lbs. or 1–2 qt. cartons	Beans — bush yellow	1½–2 lbs.
		Beans — lima, in pod	3–5 lbs.
Cherries	2–2½ lbs.	Beans — pole	1½–2½ lbs.
Figs	2–2½ lbs.	Beets	2–3½ lbs.
Grapes	4 lbs.	Broccoli	2–3 lbs.
Lemons and limes	8–16 fruits	Brussels sprouts	2 lbs.
Oranges	8–12 fruits	Cabbage	2 lbs.
Peaches	2–3 lbs.	Carrots	2–3 lbs.
Pears	2–3 lbs.	Cauliflower	3 lbs.
Plums	1½–2½ lbs.	Corn	3–6 lbs.
Raspberries	1½–3 lbs. or 1–2 qt. cartons	Cucumbers	6–12 whole
		Eggplant	2 medium whole
Rhubarb	2 lbs.	Kale	2–3 lbs.
Strawberries	1½–3 lbs. or 1–2 qt. cartons or 6–8 cups	Mushrooms	1½–3 lbs.
		Okra	1½ lbs.
		Onions	3–8 whole
		Peas	3–6 lbs.
		Peas, snap	2–2½ lbs.
		Peppers	2 lbs.
		Spinach	2–3 lbs.
		Squash, summer and winter	2–4 lbs.
		Swiss chard	2–4 lbs.
		Tomatoes	2½–3½ lbs.

Notes about Other Ingredients

Fruits and vegetables aren't the only ingredients used in canning, freezing, or drying. Salts and spices provide the extra zing and variety that makes preserving a creative endeavor.

Salt

Salt added to canned foods acts as a flavoring. When used for cured meats and seafoods, it is added as a preservative. Be sure to choose the right kind of salt, for many are unacceptable for food preservation.

Canning salt. Pure sodium chloride, it is the preferred salt to use for processing. You will usually find it in the canning section of hardware and grocery stores. It is also called pickling salt.

Kosher salt. Originally used in the Jewish ritual of food cleaning, it is also acceptable for food preserving. Today kosher salt is frequently labeled as gourmet salt and is usually coarser in grain than table salt. One pound of kosher salt can measure anywhere from 1½ cups to 1⅔ cups.

Table salt. This is not the best choice to use for preserving food. It contains a filler that makes it pour easily out of the shaker but will cause cloudiness in the canning process. Also, the iodine in table salt can darken foods being canned.

Sea salt. Although it is considered food grade, it is not recommended for preserving food because of its high cost and possible mineral content, which can affect the color of preserved foods.

There are many other kinds of salt on the market, and most should be avoided for food preservation. *Solar sea salt* should never be used for food preservation. It is produced for use in water purification systems and is not food grade. If used for curing meat, it will actually promote spoilage. *Dairy salt* is used as a supplement for animal feed and not

TIP
......

Salt is perhaps the only ingredient in your kitchen that can benefit from being stored over or on the stove. Particularly in a humid climate, the warm, dry air from a heated oven will prevent the salt from caking.

for human consumption. *Halite salt,* used for melting ice and snow, is also not food grade. Also avoid *salt substitutes* for food preservation; they cause preserved food to have an unpleasant aftertaste. Salt substitutes are best suited for use at the table.

SPICES AND HERBS

As with the produce itself, you'll want to choose the finest, freshest, most aromatic herbs and spices available for canning so the final product will be the best.

Spices

Spices age quickly, and using old spices in food preservation is a complete waste of energy. Whole, fresh allspice or this season's fragrant cinnamon bark enhance the flavor of a splendid jar of watermelon rind pickles, while old spices would add little. Mail-order sources offer an excellent selection of spices and herbs, especially for difficult-to-find varieties. Health food stores frequently sell dried herbs and spices in bulk at prices much lower than those the supermarket charges for small cans and jars.

Whole spices are generally preferred for pickling, although a ground spice may be used for some chutneys and relishes. Generally, canned products with clear liquids call for whole spices because ground spices can cloud the finished product. Whether whole or ground, spices left in canning liquid or vinegar continue to intensify the flavor of the preserved food. Sometimes this is desirable, as well as pretty to look at. As the cook, you'll have to decide how strong you want the final flavor to be. (See chapter 7 for more on how to decide this.)

Herbs

Nothing is quite as appealing as a sprig of rosemary or thyme suspended in a bottle of vinegar, or chopped mint leaves in a jar of jelly. Using herbs to ornament and flavor preserved food allows a personalized touch that will

TIP

Tie spices in a cheesecloth or muslin bag so they can be removed after the cooking process and before canning, to prevent darkening of the produce and intensifying of the flavor after it's bottled and sealed.

distinguish your canned goods from others. Fresh herbs impart less intense flavors than dried ones, but a fresh dill sprig or a plump garlic clove looks great in a jar of pickles.

You can find fresh herbs in most supermarkets, but don't forget that you can easily grow them, outdoors or on a sunny windowsill. Growing them indoors in the winter can be very satisfying. I like to use a huge terra-cotta pot and plant several different herbs together, such as chives, parsley, oregano, and thyme. These seem to winter over particularly well in a south- or west-facing window. The large pot keeps the soil from drying out as quickly as it does in the little pots you find in sets of three for hanging in your kitchen window. When warm weather returns, you can move the pot outdoors in the sun or plant the herbs directly in soil in a sunny location.

Herbs for preserving can be fresh or dried, but don't use dried herbs that have been on your shelf for more than six months to a year. Dried herbs lose their flavor quickly when exposed to air, so keep them in airtight containers. (See chapter 3 for herb-drying instructions.)

TIP
· · · · · ·

Dried herbs and spices are best kept in a cool, dark place. Heat will make their flavors evaporate very quickly. A bouquet of delicate tarragon might look great hanging in your kitchen window, but its essence will dissipate quickly.

Mint
· · · ·

Mint is a prolific grower and one the easiest herbs to grow outdoors. It doesn't require a lot of sun and thrives in a damp area, for instance under an outdoor faucet or in a low area of your garden. My mother used to place a brick soaked in water next to a newly planted mint cutting to keep the plant moist until it got over transplant shock. Plant mint in a submerged clay pot outdoors to prevent it from spreading too far and wide.

Whether you grow your own herbs or purchase fresh herbs at the market, be sure to choose the best and use them right away. If you pick herbs in the morning, when they are covered with dew, you may wash them right away and then lay them on a towel to dry. Herbs grown with heavy mulch may not even need washing. If that's the case, wait until later in the day to pick them to allow the dew to dry. To choose the freshest herbs in the food market, pick packages that have no condensation to ensure that no mold has formed. Use purchased herbs immediately when you get home.

Choosing Herbs. The herbs that you most like to use in cooking are the herbs to use as flavorings when you preserve other foods. Since the taste of the herb will intensify the longer the preserved food sits, you don't want to rely on herbs you don't enjoy. Experiment with an herb by using it in fresh food before you commit your hard-won harvested produce to it.

One of the favorite herbs for flavoring preserved foods, especially cucumbers, is dill. While it is subtle when used fresh in cooking, preserving allows the flavor of dill to emerge and permeate other food around it. The dill plant produces a light yield, but both foliage and seeds can be used for flavoring. The dill flower, or head, can be used in salads or as a garnish.

Use basil in combination with tomatoes for a somewhat sweet flavor. Other herbs that blend well with tomatoes are parsley, oregano, garlic chives, and cilantro, which is especially good in salsas.

Almost any herb can be used alone or in combination with other herbs and spices to flavor vinegar. A simple process, making flavored vinegars requires little in the way of equipment, and the end result makes a stunning gift. Creating your own blends is fun to do, and anyone who dines with you will appreciate the results. See chapter 7 to learn how to make flavored vinegars.

Sweeteners

Sugar helps the color, texture, and flavor of foods when used in small amounts for canning, curing, or freezing. With only 16 calories per teaspoon, it is the ingredient almost always called for in the recipes in this book. You'll want to use "table" sugar, white and refined, from cane or beets. Sugar is a preservative and is used to help form a gel for jams, jellies, and preserves. You may, however, wish to substitute other forms of sugar or sweeteners. The chart below gives substitution measurements that do not affect consistency or texture.

Artificial Sweeteners

Aspartame. This is most commonly known by the brand name NutraSweet. Because heat destroys the components of this artificial sweetener, it is suitable only for uncooked freezer fruit recipes. (See chapter 4.)

Saccharin. This is used in commercially canned products. It carries a Food and Drug Administration (FDA) warning label as a possible health hazard. It is not recommended for use in home food preservation.

Chart of Sugar Substitutes

Item	Substitution	Variation	Calories
Brown sugar	packed equal parts for equal parts	could change color of food and impart a distinct flavor	17 per teaspoon
Light corn syrup	replace 25% of sugar called for with this canning syrup	increases richness of color; in jelly helps coat fruits	19 per teaspoon
Fructose (granulated)	use ⅓ less for same sweetening power	much sweeter than table sugar (sucrose)	18 per teaspoon
Honey (mild flavor)	replace up to ½ of sugar called for with honey	has double the sweetening power of sucrose	21 per teaspoon

Thickeners

Flour. Some recipes call for flour as a thickening agent. The drawback in using flour as a thickener when canning is that the sauce can be runny if it's heated too long.

Agar. This natural seaweed product can be used for thickening uncooked sauces. It's available from health food stores and Asian markets and comes in flakes, powder, or packages of long, thin strands.

Clearjel. This new cornstarch can be used as a thickener. A modified waxy food starch, when used in canned foods it produces a smooth, heavy-bodied sauce that does not set to a gel upon cooling. Clearjel is resistant to breakdown under high temperatures and low pH conditions. It has no starchy taste and makes a clear thickening agent that gives an excellent sheen to the finished sauce. Clearjel contributes to the shelf life stability of canned foods: They retain a smooth texture and show no liquid separation upon storage. Although Clearjel is not recommended for frozen food applications, it is perfect for canned cream-style corn, soups, sauces, gravies, and pie fillings. Use and handle it like regular cornstarch, knowing the finished product won't become thin in the canning process or if it's overcooked.

Water

Heavy amounts of minerals in your water supply can change the finished product of your preserved food. Sulfur and iron will darken foods. Hard water caused by calcium or magnesium carbonate toughens and shrivels vegetables. Don't ever assume that the heat in a canning process will destroy microorganisms in a questionable water supply. Always have the health department test your water for bacterial levels and mineral content. It may be possible to purify your water supply by boiling, but I prefer to purchase distilled water by the gallon if in doubt. Using purchased distilled water shortens and simplifies the purification step, and rarely is more than a gallon of water needed.

TIP
● ● ● ● ● ●

Don't use potato or wheat flour or regular cornstarch for thickening sauces that you intend to can, freeze, or refrigerate unless a recipe specifically calls for it. They can make the sauce very liquid.

Choosing the Preservation Method

Those who are new to food preserving sometimes find that choosing a method is as difficult as the process. Is there a reason to freeze berries but not potatoes? Why go through the bother of pressure canning for tomatoes? Can you dry potatoes?

The method you choose depends on a number of factors, with flavor being among the most important. While nothing can top the taste of a freshly picked strawberry, the preserving method that comes closest is freezing. The same, however, is not true of apples, which are much better when kept in a root cellar. Determining how a preserving method affects flavor is a very important consideration.

Safety, of course, is the primary consideration. The acidity of a food will be a determining factor in which process you use. The more acidic a food, the more options you have from which to choose. Most fruits are acidic enough to allow canning using the boiling-water-bath canner, while vegetables canned without the acidity of vinegar will need to be canned with the pressure canner to kill bacteria that could otherwise grow to potentially harmful levels.

The charts on the next pages list most fruits and vegetables, the proper time to harvest, and the preferred method of preservation for each. Throughout the book, each food has been included in the chapter that recommends its best preservation technique. For instance, potatoes are a wonderful root-cellar candidate but a poor choice for canning. Therefore, I've included no instructions for canning potatoes in chapter 2. If you don't see a particular food on the chart in the canning chapter, it probably isn't ideally preserved in that particular fashion. On the other hand, some vegetables such as carrots are good root-cellar candidates as well as excellent for canning and freezing. You'll find carrots in all three chapters.

PRESERVING METHODS FOR FRUITS & VEGETABLES

FRUIT & BEST VARIETY	BEST METHODS	WHEN TO HARVEST/WHAT TO LOOK FOR
FRUITS		
Apples, most varieties	cold storage	Late summer or fall. Deep color, firm flesh.
Jonathan, Stayman Winesap	freeze, cold storage, cider, juice, sauce	
McIntosh, Red Rome	cold storage, cider, juice, sauce	
Whitney Crab	pickle, jelly, sauce	
Apricot, most varieties	fruit spreads, can, dry	Summer and fall. Deep color, firm but soft.
Goldcot	fruit spreads	
Blackberries, most varieties	can, freeze, fruit spreads	Mid- to late summer. Deep color, sweet, soft.
Blueberries, most varieties	can, freeze	Spring to early summer. Deep color, sweet, soft.
Cherries, bush and sour	can, freeze, fruit spreads, dry	Spring and summer. Deep color before fully ripe but softening.
Sweet	can, freeze, fruit spreads, dry	Deep color, sweet, soft as they begin to fall.
Figs, most varieties	can, freeze, dry	Late or early summer. Pick before ripe, let soften on counter. Skins can split.
Grapes, most varieties	fruit spreads, juice, dry	Aromatic, soft and sweet but firm.
Lemons and limes, most varieties	fruit spreads, dry, freeze the juice	Year-round for lemons, winter for limes. Deep color, juicy in subtropical climates.
Melons, most varieties	cold storage	Late summer. Deep color, mature on vine, sweet odor, blossom end springy to touch on some melons.
Oranges, most varieties	freeze, fruit spreads, dry, juice	Check year-round in your region. Tree ripened.
Peaches, most varieties	can, freeze, dry	Late summer and early fall. Deep color, tree ripened, soft, firm and aromatic.
Balmer, Golden Jubilee	can, freeze, pickle	
Stark Earliglo	can, freeze, fruit spreads	
Summer Pearl	can, fruit spreads	
Pears, most varieties	can, dry	Late fall. Pick before ripe but fully grown, ripen on the counter.
Colette, Duchess, Kieffer, Seckel, Starking Delicious	can, fruit spreads	

FRUIT/VEGETABLE & BEST VARIETY	BEST METHODS	WHEN TO HARVEST/WHAT TO LOOK FOR
Plums, most varieties	can, fruit spreads, dry	Late summer. Deep color, soft, sweet.
Raspberries, most varieties	can, freeze, fruit spreads, dry	Midsummer, some fall producers as well. Deep color, firm, sweet.
Rhubarb, most varieties	can, freeze	Harvest stalks only in spring. Tender, 1–2'-long stalks.
Strawberries	freeze, fruit spreads, dry	Late spring to early summer. Vine ripened, deep color, aromatic, soft but firm.
Pocahontas, Dunlap, ... Superfection	can, freeze, fruit spreads	
Premier, Sunburst, ... Surecrop, Trumpeter	can, freeze, fruit spreads	

VEGETABLES

Artichoke, globe	pickle	Spring. Tender, fully grown, before flowering.
Artichoke, Jerusalem	cold storage, pickle	Dig in late summer or fall after frost.
Asparagus, Jersey Knight	can, freeze	Spring. 5–10" stalk with closed "rooster head."
Beans: Bush green, and . . . . . . yellow, most varieties	can, freeze	Summer. Thin, pencil-like rods, seeds immature.
Lima, most varieties . . . . (except Jackson Wonder and King of the Garden)	dry, can, freeze	Summer. Tender, green seeds inside, outside is plump.
Pole, most varieties	freeze	Summer. Tender, green.
Blue Lake	can, freeze	
Selma Zebra	dry, freeze	
Black Turtle, Fava, ... Garbango, Great Northern, Kidney, Maine Yellow Eye, Mung, Navy, Pinto, White Marrow	dry	Fall. Dry on vines until seeds inside are dry, pick before wet weather of fall sets in — no pretreatment, shell when beans are shriveled and seeds rattle, freeze 48 hours to kill insect eggs.
Beets: Detroit Dark Red, ... Sweetheart	can, freeze, cold storage	Summer. Dig when 1½–2" in diameter or pull by hand.
Dark Red Canner, ... Perfected Detroit	pickle	

Vegetable & Best Variety	Best Methods	When to Harvest/What to Look For
Vegetables (continued)		
Broccoli, most varieties	freeze	Spring or fall, cool weather. Deep color but closed flower heads.
Brussels sprouts	freeze, pickle, cold storage	Fall or spring, cool weather. Deep color, firm, no yellowing.
Cabbage: green, most varieties	freeze, pickle, cold storage, kraut	Spring or fall, cool weather. Firm heads, mature size.
Red, Red Acre	cold storage	
Red Danish	cold storage, kraut, relish	
Red Root	pickle	
Carrots, most varieties	can, freeze, pickle, cold storage	Fall, cool weather. 3–8" spears, dark brown, deep root color.
Redca, Scarlet Nantes	juice	
Cauliflower, most varieties	freeze, pickle	Spring or fall, cool weather. Sun blanch the almost mature heads by tying outer leaves over the heads for 5–12 days; heads should be 2–3 inches when picked.
Celery	pickle, cold storage, dry	Cool weather. Pull whole plant when mature, roots and all.
Corn, most varieties	freeze, pickle, dry	Mid- to late summer (when silks turn brown twist off ears from stalks).
Marcross Hybrid, Stowell's Evergreen, Stylepak	can	
Cucumbers, most varieties	pickle	Mid- to late summer. Small, deep color, firm.
Eggplant	freeze	Mid- to late summer. Small, deep color, glossy.
Little Fingers, Pirouette	pickle	
Endive — Neos	cold storage	Fall. Tie outer leaves over 12–19" plant, wait 2–3 weeks for sun blanching until outer leaves are dry, cut entire head.
Kale, most varieties		Harvest as needed through winter.
Kohlrabi	freeze	Fall and spring, cool weather. 2–3"-wide stem.
Leeks, most varieties	cold storage	Leave in ground as needed or harvest all at once in cool weather.
Mushrooms	freeze, pickle, dry	Spring. Harvest when moist, not dried out.
Okra, most varieties	can, freeze, pickle	Small pods, not tough or fibrous.
Onions, most varieties	cold storage	Spring. Harvest green shoots to thin crop, when tops turn brown in fall dig bulb.
Vidalia	freeze	
Quicksilver	can, freeze, pickle	
White Portugal	pickle	

Vegetable & Best Variety	Best Methods	When to Harvest/What to Look For
Parsnips	cold storage	Harvest as needed through the winter, leave in ground.
Peas, most varieties	can, freeze, dry	Deep color in summer. Firm pods well filled out.
Snap	freeze	Spring. Deep color, not full size.
Peppers: Ace hybrid, Big Bertha,	freeze	Early to late summer. Deep color, young green or very mature; deep red, green, or yellow for sweetness; hot peppers should be thin stemmed in late summer.
Burpees Early Pimento,		
Golden Bell, Twiggy		
Napels Stallion, Spartan Garnet,	can	
Super Italian Shepherd		
Cherry Sweet, Hungarian Wax,	pickle	
Serrano, Sweet Variegated		
Early Jalapeño	pickle, dry	
Potatoes, most varieties	cold storage	New crop when vines flower in spring, for cellaring when vines die back and potato skins are hardened off.
Pumpkin, most varieties	cold storage	Deep color in fall. Fully vine ripened.
Big Max, Big Moon,	can	
Early Sweet Sugar		
Radishes	cold storage	Early to late summer. Small globes about 1".
Rutabagas	cold storage	4" bulbs after a light frost in fall.
Spinach, most varieties	freeze	Pull whole plant before plant bolts or when leaves are tender; pick leaves one at a time in early to late spring or plant as a fall crop; hates hot weather.
Squash, fall and winter, most varieties	cold storage	Deep color before heavy frost of fall. Ripen on vine, hard.
Golden Delicious, Hungarian, Mammoth	can, freeze	
Golden Hubbard	can, freeze, cold storage	
Summer, zucchini, most varieties	freeze, pickle	
Sweet potatoes, most varieties	cold storage	Dig in fall near first frost.
Swiss chard, most varieties	freeze	Fall, cool weather, but more heat tolerant.
Tomatoes, most varieties	can	Mid- to late summer. Firm, deep color, before they split.
Bellstar	can, juice, paste, sauce	
Nova	can, paste, sauce	

CHAPTER 2

Canning

SINCE THE DAWN OF TIME, people have wanted to preserve food to stave off hunger when fresh food was not available. For hunter-gatherers, a successful hunt meant food for the moment, but keeping a supply at hand was difficult during the warm weather. Necessity caused prehistoric families to invent an organized approach to smoking, salting, and drying to preserve their food.

A BRIEF HISTORY OF CANNING

For centuries the ancient Egyptians preserved foodstuffs in olive oils and made precious, soothing cosmetics from herbs to protect their skin from the power of the sun. Fruits such as figs, abundant in Mediterranean civilizations, were left in the hot sun. Under hot, dry conditions, moisture in the figs evaporated rapidly, and someone noticed that the figs that were dried out didn't spoil as quickly. Today we know that low levels of moisture in foods limit the growth of bacteria and microorganisms that cause spoilage.

In 1791, when France was in economic and military shambles, the lack of supplies and fresh food for the troops caused scurvy and malnutrition. In 1795, the French government announced a prize of 12,000 francs to any patriot who could invent a new way of preserving food for longer periods of time. Nicolas Appert, a chef, winemaker, brewer, distiller, and confectioner by trade, took up the challenge and experimented with various methods and equipment. It took him 14 years of experimentation, but in 1810, Appert accepted his prize from the French army for inventing a safe and practical method of preserving food. He stressed the use of airtight glass containers and insisted that applying heat to the filled container eliminated the air, essentially creating a vacuum that kept food from spoiling. He sealed his widemouthed glass containers with corks and placed them in boiling water. Although he did not know why this method worked, he was successful in preserving more than 50 types of food. His thesis, entitled "The Art of Preserving All Animal and Vegetable Substances for Several Years," was published in 1810 and translated into English in 1811. He was the first to can food commercially, but his factory near Paris was destroyed during the Napoleonic wars.

Peter Durand, an Englishman who had access to Appert's thesis, obtained a patent for using iron and tin to make cans for preserving food. By 1818, the British navy and army utilized the method, which Durand patented under the name "tin canister." Later refinements were made, and "tin canister" was shortened to "can."

In America in 1858, John Mason invented the glass jar with a threaded top, which replaced the cork-stoppered jars. The early history of home canning culminated in 1874, when A. J. Shriver invented a pressure canner for home use, also in America.

Pasteurizing Foods

When Louis Pasteur refined the process of preserving food in 1857 by applying heat to destroy the microbes that caused spoilage, he accomplished the same thing that home canners do today. Regardless of which canning method you use, the principle behind it is the same: to destroy microorganisms that cause food to spoil and to create a vacuum in which remaining bacteria cannot grow.

Clostridium botulinum grows in the absence of air (oxygen 2%) and the absence of acidity in a moist environment between 40° and 120°F. Although *Clostridium botulinum* is present on fresh food, the conditions are not right for it to be harmful while the food is still fresh. But when the fresh food is canned and the proper conditions do exist for the bacteria to grow, the food could be harmful *if the canning process was not properly carried out.*

This is the axis upon which all canning principles turn. The acidity of produce is the determining factor in which final canning process (boiling-water bath or pressure canner) must be used to make the food safe to eat. See the discussions of canning safety found on pages 29, 31, 35, and 47.

Containers and Equipment

The cork-stoppered, widemouthed, handblown canning jars used by Nicolas Appert in 1810 have been replaced by a wide variety of jars. You can choose half-pint, pint, and quart jars; widemouthed pickle and jelly jars; small-mouthed jars for mixed vegetables, soups, and main dishes. Whether you are using large widemouthed jars for canning whole cucumbers or small jars for grape jelly, you need to use the right kind of jars and lids.

Jars and Lids

Recycling commercial glass jars such as mayonnaise or pickle jars for use in home canning may sound practical, especially with today's emphasis on conserving resources, but if you do, you're jeopardizing the preserving process and risking injury. Jars containing commerical products are not the same sturdy quality as jars made specifically for canning and may not be able to withstand the lengthy exposure to the high temperatures of the boiling-water bath or the high pressure of pressure canning methods.

TIP

• • • • • •

Never use recycled commercial jars for canning. They are not strong enough and can easily break in the canning process.

Commercial jars can shatter, destroying your food and possibly causing you or others in your kitchen injury. Although the United States Department of Agriculture (USDA) allows the re-use of commercial jars in boiling-water-bath processing, I do not recommend it. The last thing you want is to risk ruining the fruits or vegetables by placing them in jars that might break.

Clean, glass canning jars, free of chips and cracks, are the only containers you should use for canning. Each jar must have a two-piece lid that consists of a new metal vacuum lid and a new or used metal screw-ring. These are the only acceptable lids to use. Mason jars and lids, manufactured by Ball and Kerr, fill this requirement.

Although jars of other sizes are available, the half-pint, pint, and quart-size jars are the ones most recipes call for and fit best into most home canners. Make certain you match your recipe requirements with the jar size before you get started. This affects quantity-to-jar ratio as well as processing time. Half-gallon jars can be used for juice canning, and you can consult your county agent for processing times for them.

Your finished product will determine the kind of jar to use. Widemouthed jars are absolutely essential for foods that are packed whole, like pickled peaches or cucumbers, whereas relishes or jams can easily be ladled into the small-mouthed jars. Follow recipe requirements for jars carefully and use good judgment.

Avoid using recycled commercial glass jars for canning.

Appropriate canning jars must be free of chips and cracks.

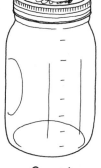

Half-pint jar   *Pint jar*   *Quart jar*

TIP

Be sure to choose the correct-size jar for your recipe, as processing time and quantity-to-jar ratio can be affected.

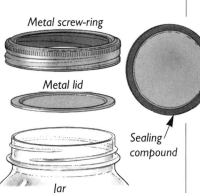

Metal screw-ring

Metal lid

Sealing compound

Jar

Components of a canning jar lid

TIP

• • • • • •

Use antique jars to enhance your kitchen or pantry or as canisters for storing pasta, dried beans, or rice — but don't use them for canning!

In canning, the screw-ring holds the vacuum lid in place and, unlike the vacuum lid, it can be used year after year. Twenty-four hours after the canning process, when the jars have thoroughly cooled, remove the metal screw-rings from the jars before storing your canned goods in the pantry. Metal screw-rings left on jars may rust. If a screw-ring is stuck or stubborn, don't force it and risk breaking a seal, but rather leave the ring in place. *Under no circumstances should you tighten the screw-ring further after processing.* This action could break the seal and leave the food vulnerable to spoilage.

There are new jars available with differently styled lids, which can be used for home canning. While some are quite attractive, don't buy any of these unless they include specific processing instructions that meet USDA guidelines.

Antique jars with porcelain-lined zinc caps are available at flea markets, and new rubber rings to fit them are available commercially. However, I don't recommend using these for modern home canning. It is heartbreaking to have half your recipe not seal properly because of the equipment. Rather than taking a chance, use new canning jars or re-use last year's jars, but always buy new lids.

Old glass jars with bailed-wire seals and rubber rings with glass lids, which look pretty, are also not recommended for use in boiling-water baths or pressure canning. If they are clean, in good condition, and free of chips, these jars can be used for refrigerator storage of fancy sauces and fruits, or for dried products.

Tin cans are not widely used today, as they are difficult to find and unwieldy to use. Special sealing equipment for the cans is also required. The commercial cans we now call "tin" are really made of aluminum.

Regardless of which type of canning jars you use, they must be short enough for the water bath to cover them by 2 inches before the water boils. An additional 2 inches of "pot space" is needed after the boiling begins, so plan to use jars that are at least 4 inches shorter than the height of your canner.

BOILING-WATER BATH

The boiling-water bath is a process that submerges packed canning jars of highly acidic, raw, or blanched food in boiling water long enough for every particle of food to reach a certain temperature. Jars of food are often densely packed, and unless the jars are exposed to the high temperatures of the boiling water long enough, the food in the centers of the jars won't reach the same temperature as food closer to the outsides of the jars. The food needs to reach a temperature that is high enough to kill the molds, yeasts, and bacteria that cause food to spoil. The boiling-water-bath method also drives out any air in the jar, including air in the food itself, creating a vacuum that causes the rubber-coated lid to form a seal.

Only food that is highly acidic can be canned with a boiling-water bath. *Clostridium botulinum*, the bacterium that causes botulism, the lethal food poisoning, exists in the soil and is always on fresh foods, though not in dangerous quantities. For this bacterium to grow to a potentially fatal level, it requires a vacuum and a nonacidic environment. It becomes harmful only when food is improperly canned. Among the highly acidic foods that are suitable for canning using the boiling-water-bath method are pickles, relishes, chutneys with vinegar, most fruits, and heavily sweetened spreads like jams, jellies, butters, and preserves.

Boiling-Water-Bath Equipment

Ideally, a newly purchased 21- or 33-quart boiling-water-bath canner with lid and jar rack is the piece of equipment of choice. The better ones are made of aluminum or porcelain-covered steel. The most expensive but durable ones are made of stainless steel. There are also many appropriate alternatives. Any large pot with a lid can be substituted as long as it is at least 4 inches higher than the jars (deep enough to allow 1 to 2 inches of water to

Standard Equipment for Canning
• • • • • • • • • •

Having all the equipment on hand and ready to use will make canning easier and help you feel more confident. If you have extras of standard kitchen equipment such as measuring cups and spoons, keep them on the counter, just in case.

Canning jars with screw-rings
New rubber-edged vacuum lids
Jar lifter or tongs
Boiling-water-bath canner or
    pressure canner
Widemouthed canning funnel
Kitchen timer
Teakettle
Clean kitchen towels
Large wooden and slotted
    spoons
Nonmetallic spatula or wooden
    chopstick
Soft scrub brush
Sieve
Colander
Paring and chopping knives
Measuring cups and spoons
Large bowls
Food processing equipment
    (grinders, slicers, blender, or
    food processor)
Heavy potholders or mitts

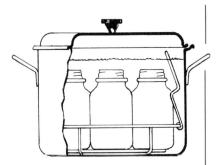

A boiling-water-bath canner

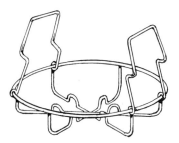

Wire rack used in boiling-water-bath canner

Pressure canner

cover the jars plus the 2 inches of "boiling room"). You will need a wire rack for the bottom to hold jars away from the direct heat and from each other to prevent cracking. In lieu of a rack, you can use towels between the jars to prevent breakage during the canning process, just as Nicolas Appert did in 19th-century France. Connect metal screwrings with twist-ties to lift the toweled jars off the bottom of the pot.

A pressure canner, although usually small, can also be used for a boiling-water-bath canner. When using it for the boiling-water-bath process, however, do not lock the lid and make sure the petcock is wide open.

Pressure Canning

Because some foods lack high acidity, the bacteria are free to grow in the vacuum created by canning. Using a pressure canner exposes these low-acid foods to high temperatures (240°F), which will sterilize the food by destroying the toughest microorganisms, including the bacteria that cause botulism. Low-acid foods include all vegetables (except tomatoes), meats, seafoods, and all mixtures such as soups. Only vegetable products with a high vinegar content, such as pickles and sauerkraut, do not require processing with a pressure canner.

Pressure Canner Equipment

Don't confuse a pressure canner with a pressure cooker. A pressure cooker is not as reliable as a pressure canner in maintaining proper pressure and is not recommended for use in canning.

A 16- to 22-quart-size pressure canner is ideal. Check the petcock and safety valve opening of your pressure canner before each canning season begins. You can clean the petcock and safety valve easily by passing an ice pick or string through the holes to free them of food bits and other matter. Wash the valve in hot soapy water and set it out to dry.

Unsafe Canning Methods

You may hear of canning methods used by previous generations that are no longer recommended. They may not produce tainted food every time, but even a small risk should be avoided. After all, the consequences could prove deadly. Do not use the following canning methods.

*   ***Atmospheric Steam Canner.** This is not considered proper equipment in the canning process. It cannot produce the high temperatures necessary to destroy dangerous bacteria.*

*   ***Open-Kettle Canning.** Once the preferred method, open-kettle canning is now considered dangerous. If an old recipe calls for packing boiling-hot foodstuffs in clean sterilized jars, beware. Bacteria and mold can get inside the food or the jar at any point in the process. Even if the jars should seal, the temperatures are often not raised high enough for long enough periods of time to create the vacuum and properly process the food. Unfortunately, jams and jellies are still being processed in open-kettle canning, in combination with paraffin wax seals, in many parts of the world. The USDA recommends that a boiling-water bath be used for processing all jams and jellies.*

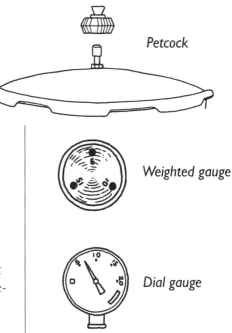

Petcock

Weighted gauge

Dial gauge

There are two types of pressure canners, weighted and dial gauge. Weighted gauge models regulate pressure precisely, and they don't need to be checked annually for accuracy, as dial gauge canners do. They are also less fragile than dial gauge canners.

The single advantage of dial gauge over weighted gauge canners is that because each pound of pressure is marked on the dial, you can increase the pressure in increments of 1 pound. This is essential for pressure canning at high altitudes.

Dial gauge canners should be checked annually for accuracy. If the gauge is high by more than 1 pound at 5, 10, or 15 pounds of pressure, overprocessing can result. It also indicates that the overall accuracy of the gauge is unreliable. Dial gauge canners may be checked at most Cooperative Extension offices.

Converting Granny's Recipes

. . . .

If your favorite recipe is left over from Granny's time, it is still possible to enjoy it safely today if you use modern methods. Frequently that simply means adjusting the pack method from merely hot packing and hoping jars will seal to adding a short boiling-water bath as is done in some pickle recipes. As long as the product is acidic enough, as in pickles with plenty of vinegar, this is possible. But never rely on this method with low-acid foods, including all seafoods, vegetables (except tomatoes), and meats. They must be canned in a pressure canner even if there is one low-acid ingredient in the recipe — tomato soup, for instance, that has corn in it.

All canning revolves around the axis of acidity — low or high. Low-acid food, as stated — all seafoods, vegetables, and meats or combinations — must be pressure canned to kill harmful bacteria. See pages 24, 28, and 33 for discussions of this. High-acid foods like pickles, fruit spreads, relishes, and chutney can be canned in a boiling-water-bath canner. The vinegar and fruit acid in these foods make them acidic enough for the boiling-water-bath canner.

You can also get information on canning from the county Cooperative Extension office. In some cases, if you add enough vinegar to a low-acid food like black-eyed-pea salsa, it can be safe to use the boiling-water-bath canner. (If you put it in a pressure canner to kill bacteria, you would have mush, or at best baby food.) Consult your local Cooperative Extension office before adapting old recipes for today's methods.

A foolproof method to test acidity is to use the paper strips available at drugstores that test the pH of liquids. These are called litmus papers. A reading of below 4.0 is required to ensure proper acidity and canning safety. It is better to overcompensate than undercompensate where acidity is concerned.

The lids of both types of pressure canners should be handled and stored carefully to prevent dents or warping that could compromise the seal. Clean canner lids and gaskets according to the manufacturer's directions. To protect the accuracy of a dial gauge, never immerse it in water, but clean the lid carefully with a cloth.

OTHER EQUIPMENT FOR CANNING

To remove the hot jars from the boiling-water-bath or pressure canner, you'll need either a pair of home-canning tongs or a jar lifter. You'll also need a timer and wide-mouthed funnel. Most other equipment is already on hand in a well-stocked kitchen. A large supply of clean dish or tea towels is essential.

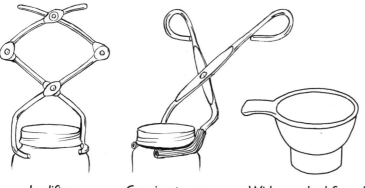

Jar lifter   Canning tongs   Widemouthed funnel

THE IMPORTANCE OF SAFE CANNING METHODS

Safety in canning cannot be overstressed. Fresh food contains high percentages of water, active food enzymes, bacteria, molds, and yeast, all of which cause spoilage. *Clostridium botulinum* exists in the soil and is always on fresh foods, though not in dangerous quantities. Because this bacterium grows to a potentially fatal level only in a vacuum, it becomes harmful only when the food is improperly canned. (See General Principles of Safe Canning on page 35.) The correct canning process sterilizes the food with heat and holds it in a sterile state in the canning jar until you are ready to eat it.

SIGNIFICANT TEMPERATURES FOR PRESERVING

TEMPERATURE	WHAT HAPPENS
240°F	• Minimum temperature for pressure canning.
212°F	• Boiling point (sea level).
165°–240°F	• Temperature range that destroys most bacteria. Kill time decreases as temperature increases.
170°F	• Air exhausts from jars and cans in raw-pack method.
140°–165°F	• Bacterial growth stopped but some survive.
120°–140°F	• Bacteria may grow; many survive.
60°–120°F	• Danger zone: allows rapid growth of bacteria and toxins.
40°–60°F	• Food-poisoning bacteria may grow. Store meat, fish, and poultry no more than a week.
32°–40°F	• Some food-spoilage bacteria will grow slowly. • Chill meat, fish, game, and poultry under 40°F and as close to freezing (without freezing) as possible.
32°F	• Freezing point for most liquids and foods.
0°–32°F	• Bacteria stop growing but may survive.
0°F	• Store frozen food.
-10°F	• Minimum for fast freezing.

Partially based on USDA Home & Garden Bulletin No. 162.

Tomatoes Are a Special Case

New information has caused food scientists to disagree about acidity of some tomatoes and the proper method of processing them. To ensure complete safety in preserving tomatoes, use the pressure canner method. This method also results in higher quality and nutritional value since less processing time is required in a pressure canner than a boiling-water bath. However, the boiling-water-bath method can be safely used provided more acidity is added to the tomatoes. To acidify and thereby ensure safety when using the boiling-water-bath canners for tomatoes, use 2 tablespoons of bottled lemon juice or ½ teaspoon of citric acid per quart of whole, crushed, or juiced tomatoes. It is possible to use 4 tablespoons of vinegar, but the vinegar may impart undesirable flavors to the tomatoes.

The safest way to can all tomatoes is by using the hot-pack method instead of the raw-pack method. (See Raw Pack versus Hot Pack, page 36.)

High- and Low-Acid Foods

Choose your canning method carefully, based on the acidity of the food and the actual food type. Always follow recipe directions and use the canning method prescribed.

High-acid foods, such as most fruits and pickles, can be processed by the boiling-water-bath method. Because of their acidity, they do not provide an environment conducive to the growth of Clostridium botulinum, the bacterium that causes botulism.

Low-acid foods, such as most vegetables, meats, and seafood, need canning temperatures higher than that of boiling water to destroy the deadly bacteria so that they won't grow in the vacuum created by canning. These foods must be processed by the pressure canner method.

TIP

Simplify the cooking time for thick tomato-based sauces and avoid burning by using a slow-cooker. A less labor-intensive procedure, and my favorite to avoid stove-top burning, is to use an oven for slow, long cooking. Use an ovenproof container, uncovered, in a 350°F oven, stirring occasionally until the sauce is thickened (about one to three hours).

Regardless of which method you use to process tomatoes, be sure to choose only vine-ripened, undamaged fruits. Do not pick from dead vines or from frost-killed vines. The tomatoes that have fallen from a vine may have already begun to spoil.

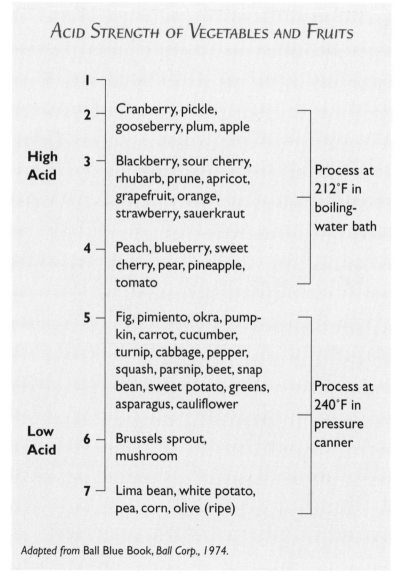

ACID STRENGTH OF VEGETABLES AND FRUITS

1

High Acid

2 — Cranberry, pickle, gooseberry, plum, apple

3 — Blackberry, sour cherry, rhubarb, prune, apricot, grapefruit, orange, strawberry, sauerkraut

4 — Peach, blueberry, sweet cherry, pear, pineapple, tomato

Process at 212°F in boiling-water bath

5 — Fig, pimiento, okra, pumpkin, carrot, cucumber, turnip, cabbage, pepper, squash, parsnip, beet, snap bean, sweet potato, greens, asparagus, cauliflower

Low Acid

6 — Brussels sprout, mushroom

7 — Lima bean, white potato, pea, corn, olive (ripe)

Process at 240°F in pressure canner

Adapted from Ball Blue Book, Ball Corp., 1974.

General Principles of Safe Canning

Perhaps the most important step in canning food occurs before you even begin. Preparation can make or break a canning session. Before you begin, line up your equipment on the counter and read through the recipe. Mentally check off each ingredient and piece of equipment called for. Canning is a precise science, and keeping the time from the harvest to processing short is important. This method will ensure that there will be fewer surprises, especially for the beginner.

Preparing Food for Canning

Always start with clean hands, equipment, and food. You can thoroughly scrub sturdy produce with a soft vegetable brush using warm water. Delicate fruit, however, fares better when soaked in several sinkfuls of water, lifting the fruit out each time with a strainer or colander so the grit sinks to the bottom. Be certain all the food you are going to preserve is properly washed or peeled and is free of grit. You don't want gritty tomato sauce!

Pit or peel the produce if necessary (potatoes must be peeled) and cut into pieces of uniform size. Keep prepared raw fruits and vegetables from acquiring unsightly dark spots by submerging them in a gallon of water with either 1 teaspoon of ascorbic acid or 1 teaspoon of lemon juice added. This acidified water will also prevent cut fruits and vegetables, especially potatoes and apples, from darkening.

Prewashing Jars

Start with clean jars. If the recipe calls for a processing time of less than 10 minutes, you must use a boiling-water-bath canner to sterilize the prewashed jars. If the processing time is longer than 10 minutes, a wash in the

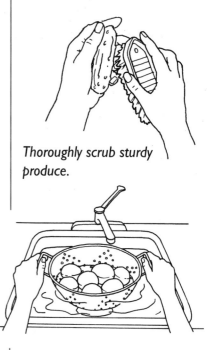

Thoroughly scrub sturdy produce.

Rinse delicate produce in several sinkfuls of water.

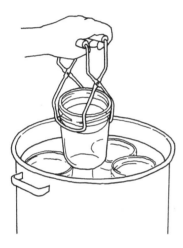

Sterilize jars in boiling water.

dishwasher or hot soapy water will be sufficient to process your produce with either the pressure canner or boiling-water-bath method. Be sure to thoroughly rinse the jars taken from a dishwasher or dishpan and be careful to remove all traces of soap before filling. Keep the lids hot in a large saucepan of gently boiling water. However, you should always read the manufacturer's directions and follow them to the letter.

STERILIZING EMPTY JARS

Sterilize clean prewashed jars for processing times under 10 minutes in a boiling-water bath. Fill the clean jars with hot water and lower them, right-side up, onto the rack in the water-filled pot, making sure that there is at least 1 inch of water above the rims of the jars. At sea level, boil the jars for 10 minutes. At higher elevations, boil them 1 additional minute for each 1,000 feet of altitude. Remove the sterilized jars one by one as you need them, using the jar lifter, and fill them immediately with foodstuffs. Quickly top each jar as it is filled with the lid and metal screw-ring. (Save the boiling water for the canning process.)

CLEANING OTHER EQUIPMENT

Make sure the boiling-water-bath canner or the pressure canner gauge and petcock are clean and unclogged. Be certain you are organized and have everything you need ready to complete the process before you actually get started.

RAW PACK VERSUS HOT PACK — WHICH TO USE?

Many foods can be packed in their canning container raw, or cold. This method, called the *raw-pack method,* is sometimes also referred to as cold pack. Cleaned, trimmed, peeled raw produce is packed into a warm jar and hot liquid is added. Then the jar is sealed and is ready for processing in a warm, not-yet-boiling water bath.

In the *hot-pack method,* hot vegetables are added to a clean, warm jar and hot liquids are added. The lids are sealed and the jars are ready for processing.

Raw Pack. In the raw-pack method, which is used mostly for high-acid foods including delicate fruits — apricots, berries, grapes, peaches, plums, and pears — and pickled foods, jars are packed *firmly* allowing, of course, for headspace. (See the sections on headspace and altitude, pages 39–41.) The raw, room-temperature food is cut up uniformly and cleaned. Pack one jar at a time, allowing for headspace (see the chart on page 50). Add very hot liquid. Generally add 1 to 1½ cups of liquid for each quart jar and ½ to ¾ cup of liquid for each pint jar. Apply the lid and secure it with the screw-ring. Raw-pack foods usually have longer processing times. You will put the filled jars in hot, but not boiling, water one at a time and bring the water to a boil. This will help to prevent cracking the jars.

One disadvantage of using the raw-pack method is that in two to three months the upper inch or so of food may become slightly discolored (gray or brown), possibly because of minerals in the water or on cooking utensils. As unappealing as this may be, it does not affect the quality or safety of the food. Another drawback of the raw-pack method is that fruit frequently floats to the top of the canning liquid.

Raw pack is also suitable for some vegetables processed in a pressure canner. Consult the chart on page 50 to determine which vegetables can be raw packed for pressure canning.

Hot Pack. The hot-pack method is required for low-acid foods such as vegetables, meats, and seafoods. It is the safest method because it kills the bacteria with heat, and more and more authorities are recommending its use. When using the hot-pack method, prepare the food as with other methods: Place it in a pan, cover with water, and bring to a boil. Reduce heat and simmer for two to five minutes. Pack the food loosely in warm jars, allowing for headspace (see the chart on page 50 or refer to your

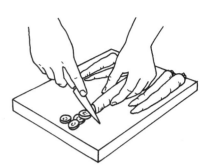

Cut up food in uniform pieces.

Finding Your Local Cooperative Extension Office

Look in the telephone directory under "local government" or call the nearest land-grant university. The national office is the Cooperative State Research, Education, and Extension Service, U.S. Department of Agriculture, Washington, D.C., 20250-0900; Internet address http://www.esusda.gov

Filling the jars using the hot-pack method.

Run a spatula along the sides of the jar to remove bubbles.

recipe). Add boiling liquid, generally 1 to 1½ cups for quarts and ½ to ¾ cup for pints, put on the lid, and secure with a screw-ring. Processing time for hot-pack foods in a pressure canner will be the same as for raw-packed foods. There's no need to worry about cracking jars, since the food will not be cold as it is for the raw-pack method.

FILLING THE JARS

When you have chosen the method and prepared the equipment and food, fill the jars, one at a time. The wide-mouthed funnel and a ladle are invaluable for this stage. Be careful of drips when you remove the funnel from each filled jar. Drips can burn the cook, but they also can spoil a seal if left on the mouth of the jar. Precision is the word here. Be sure to pack each jar for the proper density and headspace according to your chosen processing method (see page 39).

If bubbles appear in the liquid, gently tap the side of the jar with a nonmetallic knife handle to help settle the contents. Or run a clean plastic spatula along the sides in several places to help remove bubbles between pieces of the food. Don't stir, which creates more bubbles.

I like to use a clean, thin, wet tea towel over my index finger to rub around the rim of each jar — it picks up the smallest drip of food or liquid. (You will be able to feel the slightest chip on the rim as well. If the jar is chipped, discard it and choose another. The chance of contamination is too great.) A wet paper towel works for this job, also. Place the lid and the metal screw-ring on the jar and secure. Then begin on the next jar. Put each jar to the side until they have all been filled. Then process together.

Wipe the rim of the jar with a clean, damp towel.

HEADSPACE

Regardless of whether you use raw pack or hot pack, it is important to leave a space between the jar lid and the level of the food liquid. This headspace is necessary because the heat of the canning process expands the food and allows a vacuum to form, thereby sealing the jar.

Too *much* headspace can cause foods to discolor on the top level of food. Too *little* headspace will cause the food to be forced out of the jars during processing and prevent sealing. (See the chart on page 50.) Consult your local county agent, especially if you are a high-altitude cook, and always follow the recipe carefully. Remember that density of food plays an important role in headspace.

Seal the jar securely.

Headspace

. . . .

In a pressure canner for low-acid foods, leave 1 to 1 1/4 inches of headspace. In a boiling-water-bath canner, leave 1/3 inch for jams and jellies, 1/2 inch for fruits, tomatoes, and pickles.

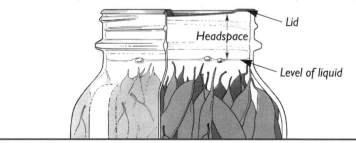

Lid

Headspace

Level of liquid

ALTITUDE ADJUSTMENTS FOR BOILING-WATER-BATH CANNING

When stating processing time for boiling-water-bath canning, all recipes assume an altitude of less than 1,000 feet. If you live higher than 1,000 feet, you must adjust your processing time as shown.

ALTITUDE IN FEET	PROCESSING TIMES OF 20 MINUTES OR LESS, ADD	PROCESSING TIMES OF MORE THAN 20 MINUTES, ADD
1,000	1 minute	2 minutes
2,000	2 minutes	4 minutes
3,000	3 minutes	6 minutes
4,000*	4 minutes	8 minutes
5,000*	5 minutes	10 minutes

*At this altitude you may want to consider pressure canning, which will accomplish the same thing without overcooking your food.

ALTITUDE AND BOILING-WATER-BATH CANNING

Water boils at 212°F at sea level. As altitude increases, water boils at *lower* temperatures (which is less effective for killing bacteria). Therefore, you must determine your local altitude and increase the processing time as given above. Consult your canner instructions or your county agent for information specific to your area if you have questions.

ALTITUDE ADJUSTMENTS AND THE PRESSURE CANNER

At higher altitudes steam expands more in the headspace of the canning jar as it sits in the pressure canner. To allow for this expansion, some sources advise increasing the headspace by ⅛ inch for every 1,000 feet of altitude above sea level, not to exceed ¾ inch for a half-pint jar, 1 inch for a pint jar, and 1¾ inches for a quart jar. The chart on page 50 specifies the headspace at sea level. You may wish to adjust headspace for your altitude accordingly.

TIP

. . . . . .

Even though the water is rapidly boiling away in your canner at higher altitudes, it is boiling at a *lower* temperature. You will need to adjust your processing time upward at higher altitudes.

SELECTING THE CORRECT PROCESSING TIME

When you're canning in a boiling-water-bath canner, you'll need more processing time for most raw-packed foods or quart jars than you need for hot-packed foods or pint jars.

To destroy microorganisms in low-acid foods processed in a boiling-water canner, you must:

- Process jars for the correct number of minutes in boiling water.
- Cool the jars at room temperature.

The food may spoil if you fail to add extra processing time for the lower boiling-water temperatures that occur at altitudes above 1,000 feet, if you process for fewer minutes than specified, or if you cool jars in cold water.

To destroy microorganisms in low-acid foods processed with a pressure canner, you must:

- Process the jars using the correct time and pressure specified for your altitude.
- Allow the canner to cool at room temperature until it is completely depressurized.

Your canned food may spoil if you fail to select the proper processing times for specific altitudes, fail to allow the canner to exhaust properly before weighting or closing the petcock, process at a lower pressure than specified, process for fewer minutes than specified, or cool the canner with water.

Two serious errors in temperatures obtained in pressure canners occur because:

1. The internal temperatures of canners are lower at higher altitudes. To correct this error, canners must be operated at the increased pressures specified for appropriate altitude ranges.

2. Air trapped in a canner lowers the temperature obtained at 5, 10, or 15 pounds of pressure and results in underprocessing. The highest volume of air trapped in a canner occurs in processing raw-packed foods in dial gauge canners. These canners do not vent air during processing. To be safe, all types of pressure canners must be vented 10 minutes before they are pressurized.

Preparing Food and Jars for Processing

1. Clean food and, if needed, cut it into uniform pieces. For raw-pack method, set prepared food aside. For hot-pack method, place food in large saucepan, cover with water, and bring to a boil. Simmer 2 to 5 minutes.

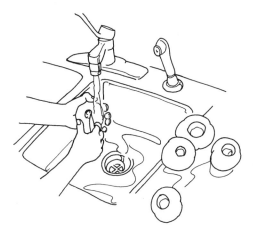

2. Sterilize the clean jars by filling them with hot (not boiling) water and lowering them onto rack in a water-filled pot. Make sure there's at least 1 inch of water above the rims. Bring the water to a boil and boil for 10 minutes (see altitude chart on page 50). Keep jars hot.

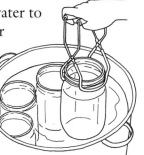

3. Remove a jar and fill it immediately with food. If using raw-pack method, pack it tightly. If using hot-pack method, fill the warm jar loosely.

4. Add very hot water, syrup, or juice, according to the recipe, to the jar until it covers the food. Allow for proper headspace (see chart on page 50).

5. Remove air bubbles by inserting a nonmetallic utensil and firmly pressing food.

6. Using a clean towel, carefully wipe the jar rim to allow a good seal.

7. Apply the lid and secure it with the screw-ring.

8. Repeat steps 3, 4, and 5 until all jars are filled. Reserve the water used to sterilize jars for the canning process. Continue on page 44 for boiling-water-bath canning or page 45 for pressure canning.

Boiling-Water-Bath Canning

The steps below are based on USDA recommendations.

Place the jars in the canner.

1. After packing the jars and fitting them with lids and screw-rings, fill the canner halfway with water (or use half the water reserved from sterilizing jars) and heat it to 140°F for raw-packed food, or to 180°F for hot-packed food.

2. You may either put the empty rack in the canner and then load the jars into the rack with the jar lifter, or place the packed jars on the canner rack first and then, using the handles, lower the rack into the hot water.

Add hot water until the water level is at least 1 inch above jar tops.

3. Check the water level to make sure it is at least 1 to 2 inches above the lids of the jars. Add more hot water if necessary.

4. Heat the water to a full boil.

5. Once the water is rapidly boiling, set a timer for the number of minutes specified in your recipe. Cover with the lid and reduce the heat enough to keep the water at a gentle boil during the processing. Be sure to allow for altitude.

6. Check the canner to make sure the water level is still 1 inch above the jars, and add boiling water if necessary.

7. When the specified time is over, turn off the heat and remove the lid, keeping your face back to avoid the hot steam that will escape.

8. Place a folded towel on the counter near the canner. Use a jar lifter to remove the jars, placing them on the towel. Keep them at least 1 inch apart to allow air to circulate.

Remove jars from the canner to a clean towel.

Pressure Canning

• • • • • • • • • • • • •

The steps below are based on USDA recommendations.

1. After packing the jars and fitting them with lids and screw-rings, put the rack in the canner and fill with 2 to 3 inches of water. Place the filled jars in the rack with the jar lifter. You may fill the rack before placing it in the canner, if you like. Put the lid on the canner, fastening securely.

2. Open the petcock or remove the weight. Heat on high until steam flows out.

3. Continue to heat on high for 10 minutes before closing the petcock or placing the weight on the vent port. During the next 3 to 5 minutes, the pressure will build.

4. When the dial gauge shows the recommended pressure, or when the petcock begins jiggling or rocking, set the timer for the time specified in the recipe. At high altitudes, increase the pressure 1/2 pound for each 1,000 feet above sea level.

5. Maintain a temperature at or just above the specified gauge pressure. Weighted gauges will jiggle two or three times per minute or rock slowly, depending on the brand. Avoid large variations in temperature, which may cause liquid to be forced from jars, jeopardizing the seal.

6. When the time is up, turn off the heat, remove it from the burner if possible, and let the canner depressurize. Do not use cold water to speed depressurization. This risks losing liquid from the jars, breaking the seals of the jars and, in some models, warping the canner lid. Don't open the vent port. Let the canner sit 30 minutes if loaded with pints, or 45 minutes with quarts. Newer models cool more quickly and have vent locks that indicate when pressure is normal.

7. When the pressure is normal, remove the weight or open the petcock. Let it sit for 2 minutes before unfastening the lid and removing it. Keep your face back to avoid escaping steam.

8. Using the jar lifter, remove the jars and place on a folded towel, allowing at least 1 inch of air to circulate.

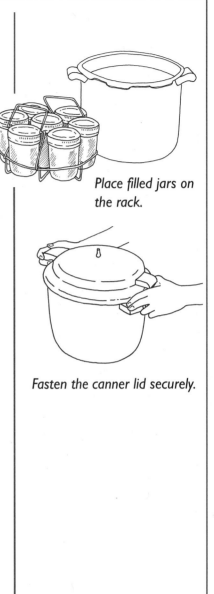

Place filled jars on the rack.

Fasten the canner lid securely.

CHECKING THE SEALS

After the filled and finished jars of canned goods have cooled, in 12 to 24 hours, use your thumbs to test the seal of the metal lids. Press hard on the center of one. If the lid does not move downward or give, your jar is complete. If one or two aren't sealed, you can refrigerate these faulty jars and consume within a day or two.

Another method for checking the seals is by lifting your newly canned jar by its lid without the screw-ring, using the weight of the jar to test the strength or weakness of the seal. (Protect yourself and the jar by doing this over a sink prepared with a towel to pad the possible fall.)

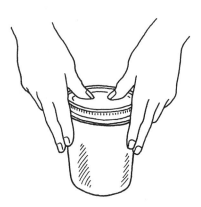

Check the seal on a jar by applying pressure to the center with your thumbs. It should not give at all.

Questions to Ask Yourself

1. Did I execute the processing method called for in the recipe properly?

2. Did I fill the canner with the correct amount of water to cover jars properly?

3. Did I figure the altitude adjustment and headspace correctly?

4. Did I check to make sure that the jar rims were free of cracks and chips, and did I use new lids?

5. Did I fill the jar to the proper density and cap it in the prescribed method?

6. Did I cool the jars naturally at room temperature and in a reasonable amount of time, about 12 to 24 hours?

7. Did I remove the screw-rings before storing? If they could not be removed, did I avoid tightening them, which could disturb the seal?

STORAGE

Home-canned foods do not require special storage equipment, just a cool shelf in a dry, dark place. You can tuck canned foods in all sorts of nooks of your house or apartment. Just don't forget where you stored them! Keeping a location chart is a good idea: I tape mine to the inside of a kitchen cabinet door.

The best temperature for storing canned goods, and the one recommended by the USDA, is between 50° and 70°F.

Canning can be a source of safe, economical, chemical-free, quality food all winter long. You'll want your labor to be efficient and precise to fully enjoy the bounty of all your efforts. Attributes of home canning are lost when food spoils, jars break or don't seal, or poor-quality food is used.

CANNING SAFETY

Examine jars carefully using the guidelines on the next page to detect signs of spoilage. If you suspect that canned food has spoiled, don't hesitate to throw it out, but be careful about how you dispose of the spoiled jar and contents. If you flush it down the drain or toilet, it could contaminate the water supply. To protect you, your household, and your pets, detoxify the jar and its contents before you dispose of them.

DISPOSING OF SPOILED FOOD AND EQUIPMENT

To detoxify a jar of spoiled food, place it unopened in a pot of boiling water for 30 minutes, then put it in a garbage bag, and bury it or dispose of properly.

If the jar has been opened already, remove the lid and empty the contents into one saucepan. Place the empty container, the lid, and the ring (if it remained on the jar during storage) in a second pan that is filled with water. Bring both pans to a boil. If the spoiled food is thick, thin

TIP

· · · · · · · · ·

Keep a chart that gives the location of canned goods posted on the inside of your kitchen cabinet or pantry door.

Warning

· · · · · · · ·

Clostridium botulinum — the bacterium that causes botulism — grows in the absence of air. It is deadly. Never taste even a tiny bit of canned food you suspect may be spoiled.

**Look First:
A Warning List
for Spoiled Food**

. . . .

1. The jar has mold on it
and/or food has leaked out
during storage. The lid has
mold inside.

2. The food in the jar is completely and very darkly discolored. (Uniform light gray
or brown discoloration may
be caused by minerals in
the water, in which case the
food is safe to eat.)

3. The food looks shriveled,
spongy, slimy, or cloudy.

4. The liquid in the jar is not
static and seems to bubble.

5. The jar's contents "shoot"
out when the lid is opened.

6. The food has an "off" odor.

with water to make it boil more easily. Add to the pot of water any other equipment that has come into contact with the food. Make sure all items are completely covered by at least 1 inch of water. (The jar can lie on its side.)

When both pans have been brought to a boil, boil hard for 30 minutes. While they boil, gather any sponges, towels, rubber spatulas — anything that has touched the spoiled food and can't be boiled — and wrap them in a heavy plastic bag.

When the contaminated items have boiled for 30 minutes, place them in the garbage bag with the other things and tie tightly. Dispose of it on the day your county collects hazardous materials or bury it deep in the ground. Call your county agent if you have any questions or need further guidance.

Remember to wash your hands thoroughly with hot, soapy water immediately after you have contact with any spoiled food or contaminated item.

SERVING LOW-ACID HOME-CANNED FOOD

The traditional safety precaution when heating home-canned, low-acid food before eating was to boil it for 10 minutes to eliminate the possibility of dangerous bacteria. The USDA now says that is no longer necessary as long as the following guidelines were observed when the original canning took place.

1. You processed the food in a pressure canner.

2. You checked the gauge of the pressure canner for accuracy.

3. Times and temperatures for processing were correctly used for the size jar, method of packing, and food canned.

4. You made proper altitude adjustment for your recipe's pressure and processing time.

5. The jar lid passed all the seal tests.

6. The contents have not leaked from the jar.

7. No unpleasant odor can be detected.

8. No liquid shoots from the jar when opened.

Canning Meats and Poultry

The scope of this book does not deal with canning wild game, duck, bear, and so forth, but I have included several recipes for today's cook that use meats generally available in the supermarket. Detailed instructions are given with each recipe.

Successful home-canned meat-only recipes can only be hot packed then processed in a pressure canner. Fifteen pounds per square inch (psi) is recommended to be certain all bacteria are killed. It is most convenient to use wide-mouthed jars for this.

If you are starting with fresh-killed meat from your own stock and have a large supply for canning, refrigerate immediately whatever portion of meat you are not canning right away. Bacteria start to grow immediately on fresh meat.

Recipes that contain meat products in combination with produce will still need to be pressure canned, but may require less processing time in the canner than meat-only recipes, depending on the acidity of the added produce (as in tomato sauce with meat, for instance). Combination meat-and-produce recipes may require 10 psi. Always follow canning directions carefully.

LOW-ACID FOODS FOR THE PRESSURE CANNER

Unless otherwise indicated, all vegetables are to be processed with 10 pounds of pressure.

PRODUCE	PACK	PROCESSING TIME (MINUTES*)		HEADSPACE (INCHES*)
		Pint	Quart	
Artichoke	hot	25	30	½
Asparagus	raw	25	30	½
	hot	25	30	½
Beans — bush and pole	raw	20	25	½
Yellow, green, wax	hot	20	25	¼
Beets	hot	30	35	½
Carrots	raw	25	30	I
	hot	25	30	½
Corn — cream style	raw	95	no quarts	I
	hot	85	no quarts	I
Whole kernel	raw	55	85	I
Okra	hot	20	40	I
Peas — green	raw	40	40	I
	hot	40	40	I
Snow	raw	20	25	I
Peppers — Sweet**	hot	50	60	½
Spaghetti sauce — no meat	hot	20	25	I
With meat	hot	60	70	I

*At sea level.
**5 pounds pressure.

Vegetables for Pickling

• • • • • • • • • • • • • • • • • • • •

Not all vegetables are suitable for canning. Cucumbers, eggplants, and hot peppers, for example, lose their crunch and flavor when exposed to the high temperatures of pressure canning. Pickle them instead. The addition of vinegar provides enough acidity for these vegetables to be processed at lower temperatures than those required for standard pressure canning.

HIGH-ACID FOODS FOR THE BOILING-WATER BATH

PRODUCE	PACK	PROCESSING TIME (MINUTES*)		HEADSPACE (INCHES*)
		Pint	**Quart**	
Apple	hot	15	20	½
Apricot	raw	25	30	½
	hot	20	25	½
Berries — black, blue, and raspberry	raw	15	20	½
	hot	15	15	½
Cherries	raw	25	25	½
	hot	15	20	½
Currants and grapes	raw	15	20	½
	hot	10	10	½
Figs (use 2 tablespoons lemon juice per 1 quart)	hot	85	90	½
Grapefruit, oranges, tangerines	hot	10	10	½
Peaches	raw	25	30	½
	hot	20	25	½
Purees — fruit applesauce, baby food	hot	20	20	¼
Plums	raw	20	25	½
	hot	20	25	½
Pears	raw	25	30	½
	hot	20	25	½
Rhubarb	hot	15	15	½
Stawberries (see chapter 5, Jams & Jellies)				
Tomatoes** — juice	hot	35	40	½
Juice and flesh blend	hot	35	40	½
Crushed, no liquid added	hot	35	45	½
Sauce	hot	35	40	¼
Halved or whole, in juice	raw or hot	85	85	½
Halved or whole, no liquid	raw	85	85	½

*At sea level.

**Add 1 tablespoon lemon juice per pint, 2 tablespoons per quart. If even one other vegetable is added (potato, squash, peppers, etc.), pressure canning is required.

Recipes for Canning

Easy Autumn Apple Cider

Green Tomato Dip

Pepper and Eggplant in Garlic Oil

Green Chile Salsa

Corn and Zucchini Salsa

Easy Tomato Ketchup

Barbecue Sauce

Chile Sauce

Cabbage Borscht

Tomato Sauce

Spaghetti Sauce with Meat

Mother's Chicken à la King

Chili con Carne

Vegetable Beef Stew

Spicy Asparagus

Pungent Green Beans

Carrots in Honey and Vinegar

Stewed Tomatoes

Marinated Mushrooms

Mixed Vegetables

Pineapple Spears

Orange Syrup

Apple Pie Filling

Peach Pie Filling

Cherry Pie Filling

Easy Autumn Apple Cider

* * * * * * * * * * *

*Not only is this recipe an easy beverage, but just ¹/₂ cup can add zip to
pumpkin soup, cooked beets, or beef stew.*

Boiling-water-bath canner; six 1-quart jars

Purchase cider fresh from the mill in apple
season. I like to process this in quart-size
jars — 6 quarts or 1½ gallons at a time.
Strain it through a dampened jelly bag.
Please read about jelly bags on pages
182–184.

1. Bring to a slow simmer in a large
kettle, but not a hard boil.

2. Pour into hot, clean jars leaving
½ inch headspace.

3. Cap and seal and process in a
boiling-water-bath canner 30 minutes.
May be packed in pints or quarts.

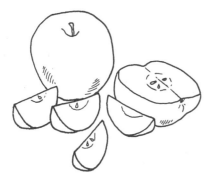

* *

YIELD: 6 QUARTS (TWENTY-FOUR 1-CUP SERVINGS)
NUTRITION PER SERVING

Calories	117	Total fat	<1g
% from fat	2	Saturated	0g
Carbohydrates	29g	Cholesterol	0mg
Fiber	<1g	Sodium	7mg

* *

Green Tomato Dip

Is it a dip for fresh vegetables, a salad dressing for mixed greens, or a sandwich spread? Any way you use it, it is remarkable.

Boiling-water-bath canner; four 1-pint jars

8   green tomatoes, washed and cored

4   red bell peppers, washed, halved, and seeded

4   large onions, peeled, cut in half

3   cucumbers, peeled, cut in chunks

½   cup pure granulated pickling salt

2   teaspoons celery seed

1   teaspoon dry mustard

¼   teaspoon freshly ground black pepper

1   cup sugar

2½ cups white wine vinegar

1   teaspoon mixed pickling spice

2   eggs

½   cup flour

¾   cup vegetable oil

YIELD: 4 PINTS (THIRTY-TWO 2-OUNCE SERVINGS)
NUTRITION PER SERVING

Calories	108	Total fat	6g
% from fat	44	Saturated	<1g
Carbohydrates	14g	Cholesterol	11mg
Fiber	2g	Sodium	1,608mg

1. Grind the vegetables coarsely, using a hand-turned grinder or pulsating motions in a food processor. You may also chop the vegetables by hand. Sprinkle them with the salt.

2. Cover and let stand at least 8–12 hours to allow the vegetables to "sweat."

3. Drain vegetables and combine them with celery seed, mustard, pepper, sugar, and 2¼ cups vinegar. Add pickling spice tied in a cheesecloth bag.

4. Pour vegetables and seasonings into a nonreactive saucepan. Cook, simmering over low heat 30 minutes. Combine eggs, flour, and ¼ cup vinegar in food processor. With motor running, add oil by droplets in a steady stream until the mixture is thick and smooth.

5. Remove the spice bag from the vegetables and stir in the egg mixture. Cook, simmering over low heat until thick. This should take 5–10 minutes.

6. Ladle into hot, clean jars, leaving ½ inch headspace.

7. Cap and seal, and process in a boiling-water-bath canner 10 minutes.

Pepper and Eggplant in Garlic Oil

Serve this delicate dish between split slices of focaccia smeared with goat cheese.

Boiling-water-bath canner; two 1-pint jars

5 small eggplants, unpeeled, sliced ½ inch thick

4 large red bell peppers

2 large yellow bell peppers

1 cup olive oil

3 cloves garlic, peeled and sliced

¼ teaspoon dried red pepper flakes

½ teaspoon pickling salt

¾ cup cider vinegar

10 large basil leaves

1. Broil eggplant circles on a greased cookie sheet about 4 inches from flame, turning once, until they are lightly browned, about 15–20 minutes.

2. Broil whole bell peppers on cookie sheet 4 inches from the flame, about 30 minutes, until they are soft and collapsed. Turn them occasionally while they're cooking.

3. Place the peppers in a paper grocery bag to trap heat. When cooled, peel off outer skins, quarter, and remove seeds.

4. Heat oil, garlic, red pepper flakes, salt, and vinegar. Simmer 4–5 minutes.

5. Alternate layers of eggplant circles, bell pepper quarters, and basil leaves in two clean, hot pint jars.

Layer the ingredients in the jars.

6. Top off with the hot, seasoned oil, leaving ½ inch headspace.

7. Cap and seal jars and process 15 minutes in a boiling-water-bath canner. Let flavors marry 10 days–2 weeks before using.

YIELD: 2 PINTS (EIGHT ½-CUP SERVINGS)

NUTRITION PER SERVING

Calories	324	Total fat	28g
% from fat	72	Saturated	4g
Carbohydrates	21g	Cholesterol	0mg
Fiber	7g	Sodium	142mg

Green Chile Salsa

Poblano chiles give this recipe a mild heat but mellow flavor. If poblano chiles are not available, you may substitute Anaheim chiles, or even green bell peppers and 1 jalapeño, seeded and chopped.

Boiling-water-bath canner; eight 1-pint jars

18 poblano chiles

10 cups (about 80 medium tomatillos, or 4 pounds) coarsely chopped, husked tomatillos with juice

2 cups coarsely chopped onions

1 cup chopped cilantro

1½ cups fresh lime juice

1 cup water

6 cloves garlic, minced

2 teaspoons salt

1. Place peppers on greased cookie sheet and broil until skins blister, about 15 minutes.

2. Peel membranes and seeds from chiles. (Wear gloves to prevent pepper oils from burning skin.) Chop skins coarsely and combine in heavy nonreactive saucepan with tomatillos.

3. Bring mixture to a simmer and add onions, cilantro, lime juice, water, and garlic. Cook over medium heat, stirring occasionally, 10 minutes.

4. Add salt. Stir well.

5. Ladle into hot clean jars, cap, and seal.

6. Process in a boiling-water-bath canner 20 minutes.

YIELD: 8 PINTS (SIXTY-FOUR 2-OUNCE SERVINGS)
NUTRITION PER SERVING

Calories	17	Total fat	<1g
% from fat	13	Saturated	0g
Carbohydrates	4g	Cholesterol	0g
Fiber	<1g	Sodium	69mg

Corn and Zucchini Salsa

• • • • • • • • • • •

Serve this remarkable salsa with corn chips or use it to top off grilled chicken breasts.

- 3 medium zucchinis, cleaned, trimmed, and diced
- 1½ teaspoons salt
- 2 ears yellow corn, husked, silk removed
- 4 tablespoons olive oil
- ½ cup cider vinegar
- 2 jalapeño peppers, seeded and minced (use rubber gloves)
- 2 large tomatoes, seeded and chopped
- 1 cup fresh lime juice
- 3 cloves garlic, minced
- ¼ cup finely chopped scallions with tops
- ¼ teaspoon pepper

1. Toss zucchini with salt and "sweat" 3 minutes in a nonreactive colander. Rinse and dry on paper towels.

2. Coat corn with 2 teaspoons oil and roast on a cookie sheet in 400°F oven 30–40 minutes. Cool. Cut off kernels and scrape cobs.

3. Combine corn, zucchini, 3½ tablespoons oil, vinegar, chiles, tomatoes, lime juice, garlic, scallions, and pepper in heavy saucepan. Bring to a boil and cook 2–3 minutes.

4. Ladle into hot clean jars, cap, and seal. Process in a boiling-water-bath canner 15 minutes.

Handling Chile Peppers

• • • • • • • • • • • • • • • • • •

The same oils that give chile peppers their heat and spice can cause skin irritation and burning. When preparing chiles for cooking, wear rubber gloves, especially when handling the really fiery peppers like jalapeños and habañeros. And always keep your hands away from your eyes and face.

If you cannot wear gloves, try coating your hands with cooking oil, which can provide a protective shield.

If you do suffer from contact with chiles, wash your hands with soap, or try soaking the burning area in milk to relieve the irritation.

When you wash or immerse dried chiles, always start with cold water. Pouring hot water on dried chiles can create strong fumes that may irritate your eyes and nose.

YIELD: 2 PINTS (SIXTEEN 2-OUNCE SERVINGS)
NUTRITION PER SERVING

Calories	61	Total fat	4g
% from fat	47	Saturated	1g
Carbohydrates	8g	Cholesterol	0mg
Fiber	<1g	Sodium	202mg

Easy Tomato Ketchup

• • • • • • • • • • •

This recipe eliminates the need for grinding the tomatoes.
Not only is it easy, but it is also fresh and delicious.

Boiling-water-bath canner; two 1-pint jars

24	medium-size tomatoes, about 8 pounds
1	medium onion, chopped
1	cup sugar
1	cup white distilled vinegar
4	teaspoons salt
¼	teaspoon cayenne pepper
1½	teaspoons whole cloves
1½	inches cinnamon stick
2	tablespoons dry mustard
1	teaspoon celery seed

1. Wash tomatoes, then dip in boiling water 60 seconds until the skins split. Transfer to cold water, then slip off the skins. Core and quarter tomatoes. Squeeze out some of the seeds and juice and discard. This prevents the ketchup from being too runny.

2. Process the tomatoes and onions in a food processor.

3. Simmer mixture in a heavy kettle until it is reduced by half. (Or you may cook the mixture in the oven at 375°F, which can help prevent burning.) Stir frequently and watch the pot! This will take 1–2 hours.

4. Add sugar, vinegar, salt, and spices tied in a cheesecloth bag, and continue boiling until the sauce "rounds up" on a spoon. There will be no separation of liquids.

5. Remove and discard spice bag.

6. Fill clean, hot jars. Cap and seal, leaving ⅛ inch headspace.

7. Process in a boiling-water-bath canner 15 minutes.

• •

YIELD: 2 PINTS (THIRTY-TWO 1-OUNCE SERVINGS)
NUTRITION PER SERVING

Calories	30	Total fat	<1g
% from fat	4	Saturated	0g
Carbohydrates	7g	Cholesterol	0g
Fiber	<1g	Sodium	267mg

• •

Barbecue Sauce

Delicious with pork or beef, this barbecue sauce, adapted from the Ball Blue Book, should be a staple for your pantry shelf.

Boiling-water-bath canner; four 1-pint jars

24 large red-ripe tomatoes

3 stalks celery, chopped

2 medium onions, chopped

2 medium red bell peppers

1 teaspoon whole, black peppercorns

2 hot serrano peppers, seeded and chopped (wear rubber gloves*)

1 cup firmly packed brown sugar

2 cloves garlic, minced

1 tablespoon dry mustard

1 tablespoon paprika

1 tablespoon salt

1 teaspoon hot pepper sauce

1/8 teaspoon cayenne pepper

1 cup white distilled vinegar

Use rubber gloves to prevent burning hands when cutting any hot pepper. Don't touch eyes or face after handling hot peppers. The hot oils on your hands will cause eyes and face to burn as well. See page 57.

1. Blanch tomatoes by plunging them into boiling water for 1 minute, then rinse with cold water. Remove the skins, core, and chop.

2. Combine tomatoes, celery, onions, and bell peppers in a large saucepan. Cook until vegetables are soft, about 30 minutes.

3. Press through a fine sieve or food mill and return to pan. Continue cooking on low heat until mixture is reduced by about one-half, about 45 minutes. Stir often and be careful not to burn.

4. Tie peppercorns in a cheesecloth bag; add with remaining ingredients and cook slowly until mixture is the consistency of ketchup, about 1½ hours. As mixture thickens, stir frequently to prevent sticking. Remove spice bag. Pour hot into hot jars, leaving ¼ inch headspace.

5. Adjust caps. Process in a boiling-water-bath canner 20 minutes.

YIELD: 4 PINTS (THIRTY-TWO 2-OUNCE SERVINGS)
NUTRITION PER SERVING

Calories	61	Total fat	<1g
% from fat	3	Saturated	0g
Carbohydrates	15g	Cholesterol	0mg
Fiber	2g	Sodium	215mg

Chile Sauce

· · · · · · · · · · · ·

This recipe is adapted from the Ball Blue Book. *Watch it disappear when served with burgers, or add it to sautéed hamburger along with several varieties of canned beans for an appetite-provoking chili.*

Boiling-water-bath canner; six 1-pint jars

24 large red-ripe tomatoes

3 medium onions, chopped

4 medium red bell peppers, seeded and chopped

2 jalapeño peppers, seeded and finely chopped (wear rubber gloves)

1 cup sugar

3 tablespoons salt

3 tablespoons mixed pickling spice

1 tablespoon celery seed

1 tablespoon mustard seed

2½ cups white distilled vinegar

1. Combine tomatoes, onions, bell and hot peppers, sugar, and salt in a large saucepan. Cook over low flame 45 minutes.

2. Tie spices in a cheesecloth bag and add to tomato mixture. Cook until mixture is reduced by one-half, about 45 minutes. As the mixture thickens, stir frequently to prevent sticking.

3. Add vinegar and cook slowly until desired thickness. Remove spice bag.

4. Pour into hot jars, leaving ¼ inch headspace. Adjust caps. Process 15 minutes in boiling-water-bath canner.

· ·

YIELD: 6 PINTS (FORTY-EIGHT 2-OUNCE SERVINGS)

NUTRITION PER SERVING

Calories	41	Total fat	<1g
% from fat	9	Saturated	<1g
Carbohydrates	10g	Cholesterol	0mg
Fiber	1g	Sodium	407mg

· ·

Cabbage Borscht

This soup recipe makes a meal that is hearty and low in calories. It can be served either hot or cold, with just a dollop of sour cream.

Pressure canner; four 1-quart jars

5   pounds tomatoes, washed, peeled, cored, and quartered

8   cups red cabbage, shredded coarsely

6   cups water

4   medium onions, chopped (about 4 cups)

3   small tart apples, peeled and sliced

2   tablespoons instant beef bouillon granules (or substitute 2 all-natural vegetable cubes available at health food stores)

2   tablespoons lemon juice

1   teaspoon salt

Freshly ground black pepper to taste

Shred the cabbage coarsely.

1. Combine all ingredients in Dutch oven, and gently boil uncovered 5 minutes.

2. Ladle hot soup into hot, clean jars, leaving ½ inch headspace.

3. Cap and seal jars and process 55 minutes in a pressure canner. If you're using a dial gauge canner, process at 11 pounds pressure. If you're using a weighted gauge canner, process at 10 pounds pressure.

YIELD: 4 QUARTS (SIXTEEN 1-CUP SERVINGS)
NUTRITION PER SERVING

Calories	39	Total fat	<1g
% from fat	4	Saturated	0g
Carbohydrates	9g	Cholesterol	0mg
Fiber	2g	Sodium	510mg

Tomato Sauce

*With this sauce on your shelf, you will be a wealthy homemaker. Add sautéed meat
if you wish or serve it over summer squash topped with cheese.
It's also a great sauce for baked chicken.*

**Pressure canner; ten 1-pint jars or
five 1-quart jars**

30 pounds farm-ripe tomatoes (½ bushel),
    peeled, cored, and quartered

2 tablespoons olive oil

1 pound mushrooms, sliced

2 medium onions, chopped
   (about 1 cup)

2 stalks celery, chopped

4 cloves garlic, minced

2 tablespoons dried basil

2 tablespoons dried oregano

2 tablespoons dried parsley flakes

2 bay leaves

½ cup firmly packed brown sugar

**YIELD: 10 PINTS OR 5 QUARTS (TWENTY 1-CUP
SERVINGS)**

NUTRITION PER SERVING

Calories	179	Total fat	4g
% from fat	16	Saturated	<1g
Carbohydrates	37g	Cholesterol	0mg
Fiber	8g	Sodium	63mg

1. In a 16-quart heavy nonreactive
saucepan, bring the tomatoes to a boil,
stirring often. Reduce heat and simmer,
uncovered, for 20 minutes, stirring often.
Process tomato sauce through a food mill
and return to pan.

2. Heat the oil in a heavy skillet and add
mushrooms, onion, celery, and garlic.
Sauté, stirring often, until soft, about 8–10
minutes.

3. Add garlic, herbs, sugar, and
mushroom mixture to the tomatoes, and
simmer uncovered until sauce is thick. Stir
often and be careful not to burn the sauce.
This will take about 4–6 hours. Remove
bay leaf before canning. You may simplify
this process by placing the pot uncovered
on the bottom rack of a 350°F oven for
several hours. Remove and stir every 30
minutes to prevent sticking.

4. Fill clean hot jars, leaving 1 inch
headspace, cap, and process. If you're using
a dial gauge canner, process at 11 pounds
pressure. If you're using a weighted gauge
canner, process at 10 pounds pressure. If
you can this recipe in pint jars, process for
30 minutes. If you can it in quart jars,
process for 35 minutes.

Spaghetti Sauce with Meat

. . . .

No pantry should be without this recipe, adapted from the USDA. A great standby, this sauce requires a very big saucepan and rewards with more than a gallon of sauce.

Pressure canner; nine 1-pint jars

30	pounds tomatoes
2½	pounds ground beef
5	cloves garlic, minced
2	medium onions, chopped (1 cup)
2	stalks celery, chopped, or 1 large green pepper, chopped (1 cup)
1	pound fresh mushrooms, sliced
4½	teaspoons salt
2	tablespoons fresh oregano
4	tablespoons minced fresh parsley
2	teaspoons black pepper
¼	cup brown sugar

Do not change the amounts or ratio of peppers, onions, and mushrooms in this recipe, as it may change the final product, both for acidity and canning safety and for taste.

1. Dip tomatoes in boiling water 30–60 seconds. Plunge into cold water and slip off skins. Core and quarter.

2. In a very large saucepan, boil the tomatoes 20 minutes, uncovered.

3. Meanwhile, sauté beef until brown. Add garlic, onion, celery, and mushrooms. Cook until vegetables are tender.

4. Add to cooked tomatoes. Stir in salt, spices, and sugar. Bring to a boil.

5. Reduce heat and simmer, uncovered, until thick enough for serving. At this time initial volume will have been reduced to approximately one-half. Stir frequently to avoid burning.

6. Fill jars, leaving 1 inch headspace.

7. Adjust lids and process in a pressure canner for 60 minutes. If you're using a dial gauge canner, process at 11 pounds pressure. If you're using a weighted gauge canner, process at 10 pounds pressure.

. . . .

YIELD: 9 PINTS (EIGHTEEN 1-CUP SERVINGS)
NUTRITION PER SERVING

Calories	401	Total fat	18g
% from fat	38	Saturated	7g
Carbohydrates	50g	Cholesterol	54mg
Fiber	8g	Sodium	645mg

. . . .

Mother's Chicken à la King

Childhood memories of great comfort food include this recipe. In the 1940s, it was made with heavy cream! Try adding a can of drained sliced mushrooms at serving time for a special treat.

Pressure canner; one 1-quart jar

1 stewing chicken (7 pounds)

2 stalks celery, coarsely chopped

1 carrot, peeled and cut in 1-inch chunks

1 medium onion, chopped

6 whole, black peppercorns

2 whole allspice

2 bay leaves

2 teaspoons salt

¼ cup butter or margarine

½ cup flour

4 stalks celery, chopped

1 tablespoon chopped fresh parsley

½ red bell pepper, seeded and chopped

½ teaspoon salt

1. In a stewpan place chicken along with celery, carrot, onion, peppercorns, allspice, bay leaves, and salt. Add water to cover. Cover and simmer 2½ hours. Turn off heat and allow chicken to cool in the broth.

2. Defat broth. Remove chicken from the bone and cube. Strain broth.

3. Melt butter and add flour, stirring until smooth. Cook 3 minutes. Slowly pour in 5 cups of the chicken broth, stirring until it begins to thicken. If there is any broth left over, freeze it for another use. Add chicken cubes, celery, parsley, red pepper, and salt. Simmer 3–5 minutes.

4. Ladle into hot, clean jars. Allow 1 inch headspace. Can and seal.

5. Process in pressure canner 1 hour 15 minutes at 10 pounds pressure.

YIELD: 1 QUART (EIGHT ½-CUP SERVINGS)
NUTRITION PER SERVING

Calories	792	Total fat	59g
% from fat	67	Saturated	19g
Carbohydrates	15g	Cholesterol	250mg
Fiber	3g	Sodium	946mg

Chili con Carne

* * * * * * * * * * *

*A great one-dish meal to stock your pantry, this modified USDA classic
is tried and true.*

Pressure canner; nine 1-pint jars

3 cups dried pinto beans, or dried red
   kidney beans, rinsed and picked over

5½ cups water

5 teaspoons salt, divided

3 pounds ground beef

3 medium onions, chopped

1 large green bell pepper, chopped
   (about 1 cup)

1 teaspoon black pepper

3 tablespoons chili powder

2 quarts crushed or whole tomatoes
   (15–18 medium tomatoes, about 5
   pounds)

1. Place beans in a 2-quart saucepan. Add cold water to a level of 2–3 inches above the beans and soak 12–18 hours. Drain and discard water.

2. Combine beans with 5½ cups fresh water and 2 teaspoons salt. Bring to a boil. Reduce heat and simmer 30 minutes. Drain and discard water.

3. Brown beef, onions, and peppers in a skillet. Drain off fat and add 3 teaspoons salt, pepper, chili powder, tomatoes, and drained cooked beans.

4. Simmer 5 minutes. Adjust seasonings.

5. Fill jars, leaving 1 inch headspace. Adjust lids.

6. Process in a pressure canner 75 minutes. If you're using a dial gauge canner, process at 11 pounds pressure. If you're using a weighted gauge canner, process at 10 pounds pressure.

* *

YIELD: 9 PINTS (EIGHTEEN 1-CUP SERVINGS)
NUTRITION PER SERVING

Calories	377	Total fat	21g
% from fat	50	Saturated	8g
Carbohydrates	28g	Cholesterol	64mg
Fiber	10g	Sodium	670mg

* *

Vegetable Beef Stew

*This Ball Blue Book adaptation of old-fashioned beef stew is difficult to improve!
It is very easy and delicious.*

Pressure canner; seven 1-quart jars

 4 pounds stew beef, cubed

 2 teaspoons vegetable oil

16 small carrots, scrubbed and sliced

 5 stalks celery, chopped

 3 medium onions, chopped

12 small potatoes, peeled and cubed

 1 teaspoon ground thyme

½ teaspoon salt

Freshly ground black pepper to taste

1. Brown the meat in oil in a large saucepan.

2. Add vegetables and seasonings.

3. Cover with boiling water and ladle into hot clean jars, leaving 1 inch headspace.

4. Process in a pressure canner 1 hour 15 minutes at 10 pounds pressure.

YIELD: 7 QUARTS (TWENTY-EIGHT 1-CUP SERVINGS)
NUTRITION PER SERVING

Calories	226	Total fat	6g
% from fat	24	Saturated	2g
Carbohydrates	26g	Cholesterol	36mg
Fiber	3g	Sodium	102mg

Spicy Asparagus

Wrap a crepe around these tangy asparagus pieces, or add them to your favorite green salad.

Boiling-water-bath canner; fourteen 1-quart jars

28 pounds asparagus, washed, trimmed, and cut evenly to fit into a 1-quart jar

1 quart water

3 quarts white wine vinegar

2 tablespoons sugar

Per Quart

¼ teaspoon freshly ground black pepper

⅛ teaspoon dried thyme

¼ teaspoon dried tarragon

¼ teaspoon celery seed

¼ cup olive oil

½ teaspoon salt

1. Blanch asparagus in boiling water 2 quarts at a time, about 5 minutes, and drain.

2. Bring water, vinegar, and sugar to a boil.

3. Fill hot clean jars with pepper, herbs, oil, and salt.

4. Evenly divide asparagus into jars and pour hot vinegar mixture into each, leaving 1 inch headspace. Adjust lids.

5. Process in a boiling-water-bath canner 30 minutes.

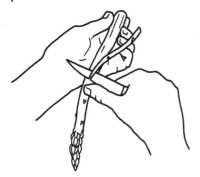

If your asparagus are mature and fibrous, peel from the stem end to make them more tender.

Yield: 14 quarts (one hundred twelve ½-cup servings)
Nutrition per Serving

Calories	79	Total fat	7g
% from fat	72	Saturated	<1g
Carbohydrates	5g	Cholesterol	0mg
Fiber	1g	Sodium	135mg

Pungent Green Beans

*Serve these surprising beans as a garnish for your favorite salad
or as a side dish for pork.*

Boiling-water-bath canner; five 1-pint jars

3 pounds green beans, washed and trimmed

1 large onion, minced

3 cloves garlic, minced

⅓ cup olive oil

3 cups white vinegar

¾ cup sugar

3 teaspoons celery salt

2 teaspoons salt

1 teaspoon pepper

4 cups water

1. Cut beans to uniform size. I like to cut them into pieces about 2½ inches long, but the length is a matter of personal preference.

2. Cook beans in boiling salted water until tender, about 5–6 minutes.

3. In a large saucepan, sauté onion and garlic in heated oil until soft.

4. Add vinegar, sugar, celery salt, salt, pepper, and water to onion mixture and boil until the sugar is dissolved.

5. Add beans and boil in the vinegar mixture 2 minutes.

6. Ladle into hot clean jars, leaving ½ inch headspace.

7. Seal and process in boiling-water-bath canner 10 minutes.

YIELD: 5 PINTS (TWENTY ½-CUP SERVINGS)
NUTRITION PER SERVING

Calories	89	Total fat	4g
% from fat	34	Saturated	<1g
Carbohydrates	15g	Cholesterol	0mg
Fiber	2g	Sodium	457mg

Carrots in Honey and Vinegar

Tender but crunchy, these carrots will be hard to resist as a side dish or as an hors d'oeuvre. Leaving a few inches of green tops makes a lovely presentation in the jar.

Boiling-water canner; two 1-pint jars

- 1 pound small carrots
- 1 cup white wine vinegar
- 1 cup water
- 2 teaspoons pickling salt
- ¼ teaspoon pepper
- 8 teaspoons honey
- 4 sprigs fresh dill

1. Scrub carrots and trim their green tops, leaving about 3 inches if desired. Remove root end. Blanch carrots in boiling water 2 minutes and drain well.

2. Combine vinegar, water, salt, pepper, and honey in a nonreactive saucepan and boil until honey is dissolved.

3. Evenly divide carrots into hot clean jars, wedging carrots in, stacking some upside down.

4. Fill jars with hot liquid, leaving ½ inch headspace.

5. Add 2 sprigs dill to each jar. Cap and seal.

6. Process 15 minutes. Let flavors marry 2 weeks before use.

Note: Widemouthed jars work well for this recipe.

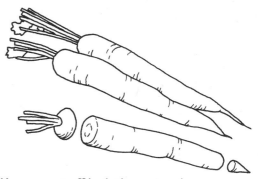

You can cut off both the root end and green tops of the carrots, or leave about 3 inches of green tops for show.

YIELD: 2 PINTS (EIGHT ½-CUP SERVINGS)
NUTRITION PER SERVING

Calories	48	Total fat	<1g
% from fat	2	Saturated	0g
Carbohydrates	13g	Cholesterol	0mg
Fiber	2g	Sodium	552mg

Stewed Tomatoes

. . . .

Use these tomatoes as a soup or sauce base, or serve them alone thickened with cornstarch and an added tablespoon of butter for richness.

Pressure canner; seven 1-pint jars

24 large ripe tomatoes, cored and quartered

2 stalks celery, chopped

1 medium onion, chopped

¼ cup chopped green pepper (about ½ pepper)

1 tablespoon sugar

2 teaspoons salt

1. Combine all ingredients in a large saucepan.

2. Cover and simmer 10 minutes, stirring frequently.

3. Uncover the pan and, using a fork, fish out the tomato skins.

4. Ladle mixture into hot clean jars, leaving ½ inch headspace. Cap and seal.

5. Process in a pressure canner 15 minutes at 10 pounds pressure.

. . . .

YIELD: 7 PINTS (TWENTY-EIGHT ½-CUP SERVINGS)
NUTRITION PER SERVING

Calories	29	Total fat	<1g
% from fat	10	Saturated	0g
Carbohydrates	7g	Cholesterol	0mg
Fiber	1g	Sodium	165mg

. . . .

Marinated Mushrooms

* * * * * * * * * * *

Serve this spicy side dish with chicken, beef, or pork, or as an hors d'oeuvre.

Boiling-water-bath canner; nine ½-pint jars

7 pounds small, whole, very fresh white mushrooms

½ cup bottled lemon juice, or the juice of about 4 medium lemons

2 cups olive oil

2½ cups white vinegar

1 tablespoon dried oregano

1 tablespoon canning or pickling salt

½ cup finely chopped onions

2 cloves garlic, quartered

25 whole, black peppercorns

1. Wash mushrooms and cut stems short. Add lemon juice and water to cover in saucepan.

2. Bring to a boil and simmer 5 minutes. Drain well.

3. Mix olive oil, vinegar, herbs, and salt in a saucepan.

4. Add onions and heat to boiling.

5. Divide peppercorns and garlic among jars.

6. Fill jars with mushrooms. Add hot oil-and-vinegar solution to each jar, leaving ½ inch headspace. Cap and seal.

7. Process in boiling-water-bath canner 20 minutes.

* *

YIELD: 9 ½-PINTS (EIGHTEEN ½-CUP SERVINGS)
NUTRITION PER SERVING

Calories	289	Total fat	25g
% from fat	72	Saturated	3g
Carbohydrates	17g	Cholesterol	0mg
Fiber	5g	Sodium	368 mg

* *

Mixed Vegetables

. . . .

These vegetables are not just pretty to look at, they're also versatile and tasty.

Pressure canner; seven 1-quart jars

6 cups sliced carrots (2 pounds, or 12–14 medium carrots)

6 cups cut green beans (3½ pounds)

6 cups shelled lima beans (6 pounds)

4 cups crushed tomatoes (2⅓ pounds)

4 cups diced zucchini (2 pounds)

6 cups sliced okra (2 pounds)

PER QUART

1 teaspoon salt

1 slice onion

1. Wash and prepare vegetables. Place them in a large pot and cover with water. Boil 5 minutes.

2. Place 1 onion slice and salt in each jar.

3. Ladle hot vegetables and liquid into jars, leaving 1 inch headspace. Cap and seal.

4. Process in a pressure canner 85 minutes. If you're using a dial gauge canner, process at 11 pounds pressure. If you're using a weighted gauge canner, process at 10 pounds pressure.

YIELD: 7 QUARTS (FIFTY-SIX ½-CUP SERVINGS)
NUTRITION PER SERVING

Calories	88	Total fat	<1g
% from fat	2	Saturated	0g
Carbohydrates	17g	Cholesterol	0mg
Fiber	5g	Sodium	277mg

Pineapple Spears

Garnish your next pork roast with this or serve it as a dessert.

Boiling-water-bath canner; three 1-pint jars

2 pineapples, peeled, cored, and quartered

2 cups thin Honey Syrup Blend (recipe on page 126)

1. Cut pineapple pieces about 1 inch shorter than the pint jars, or about 5 inches long.

2. Combine pineapple and syrup in heavy saucepan or Dutch oven.

3. Boil 7 minutes.

4. Divide fruit evenly, pack in jars, and cover with syrup, leaving ½ inch headspace. Cap and seal.

5. Process in a boiling-water-bath canner 30 minutes.

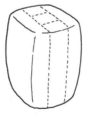

Core the pineapple by making the indicated cuts. Then slice the pineapple into spears.

YIELD: 3 PINTS (TWELVE ½-CUP SERVINGS)
NUTRITION PER SERVING

Calories	100	Total fat	<1g
% from fat	5	Saturated	0g
Carbohydrates	26g	Cholesterol	0mg
Fiber	2g	Sodium	3mg

Orange Syrup

· · · · · · · · · · ·

*Use this over buttermilk pancakes. Sprinkle fresh blueberries on top for
Sunday brunch. Or drizzle the syrup over an angel food cake and decorate it with the
blueberries or orange slices for a nonfat dessert.*

Boiling-water-bath canner; four 1-pint jars

Peel of 6 oranges, such as Valencia,
    cut into strips

4⅓ cups water

4 cups sugar

2½ cups fresh orange juice from oranges
    above, strained

2 tablespoons citric acid

1. Cook orange peel, water, and sugar until sugar dissolves, stirring constantly. Boil 3 minutes.

2. Remove from heat and cool. Strain through several layers of cheesecloth lining a strainer about 1–2 hours.

3. Add strained orange juice and citric acid. Mix well.

4. Reheat syrup and pour into hot clean 1-pint jars, leaving ½ inch headspace.

5. Clean jar rims, cap, and seal. Release jar ring half a turn.

6. Process in a boiling-water-bath canner 30 minutes.

Note: Syrup will keep 10 days unprocessed in refrigerator.

· ·

YIELD: 4 PINTS (SIXTEEN ½-CUP SERVINGS)
NUTRITION PER SERVING

Calories	213	Total fat	<1g
% from fat	<1	Saturated	0g
Carbohydrates	55g	Cholesterol	0mg
Fiber	<1g	Sodium	3mg

· ·

Apple Pie Filling

. . . .

When apples are abundant, this adapted USDA recipe fills a real need. You'll be thankful you planned ahead the first time you open a jar of this filling.

Boiling-water-bath canner; seven 1-quart jars

 6 quarts fresh tart apples, peeled and sliced

5½ cups sugar

1½ cups Clearjel (see page 16)

 1 tablespoon cinnamon

 1 teaspoon nutmeg

2½ cups cold water

 5 cups apple juice

 ¾ cup bottled lemon juice, or the juice of about 6 medium lemons

Note: Use firm, crisp apples.

1. Wash, peel, and core apples. Cut slices ½ inch thick and place in 1 gallon of water containing 1 teaspoon ascorbic acid to prevent browning.

2. Place 6 cups of fruit at a time in 1 gallon of boiling water.

3. Cook each batch 1 minute after the water returns to a boil. Drain, but keep fruit heated in a covered bowl or pot.

4. Combine sugar, Clearjel, cinnamon, and nutmeg in a large kettle with water and apple juice. Stir and cook on medium high heat until mixture thickens and begins to bubble.

5. Add lemon juice and boil 1 minute, stirring constantly.

6. Fold in drained apple slices immediately and fill jars with mixture without delay, leaving 1 inch headspace. Cap and seal.

7. Process in boiling-water-bath canner 25 minutes.

Note: This recipe makes enough filling for seven pies.

. . . .

YIELD: 7 QUARTS (FIFTY-SIX ½-CUP SERVINGS)
NUTRITION PER SERVING

Calories	131	Total fat	<1g
% from fat	1	Saturated	0g
Carbohydrates	33g	Cholesterol	0mg
Fiber	1g	Sodium	3mg

. . . .

Peach Pie Filling

. . . .

This version of a USDA favorite can't be beat.

Boiling-water-bath canner; seven 1-quart jars

6 quarts (44–48 medium peaches, about 11 pounds) fresh peaches, peeled and sliced

5¼ cups cold water

7 cups sugar

2 cups plus 3 tablespoons Clearjel (see page 16)

1 teaspoon cinnamon

1 teaspoon almond extract

1¾ cups bottled lemon juice, or the juice of about 14 medium lemons

1. Place peaches in water containing 1 teaspoon of ascorbic acid crystals or six 500-milligram vitamin C tablets per 1 gallon of water to prevent browning.

2. Place 6 cups of fruit at a time in 1 gallon boiling water.

3. Boil each batch 1 minute after the water returns to a boil. Drain, but keep heated fruit in a covered bowl or pot.

4. Combine water, sugar, Clearjel, cinnamon, and almond extract in a large kettle. Stir and cook over medium-high heat until mixture thickens and begins to bubble.

5. Add lemon juice and boil sauce 1 minute more, stirring constantly.

6. Fold in drained peach slices and continue to heat mixture 3 minutes.

7. Fill jars without delay, leaving 1 inch headspace. Cap and seal.

8. Process in boiling-water-bath canner 30 minutes.

Note: This recipe makes enough filling for seven pies.

. . . .

YIELD: 7 QUARTS (FIFTY-SIX ½-CUP SERVINGS)

NUTRITION PER SERVING

Calories	155	Total fat	<1g
% from fat	<1	Saturated	0g
Carbohydrates	39g	Cholesterol	0mg
Fiber	1g	Sodium	3mg

Peeling Peaches

. . . .

To peel peaches easily, submerge in boiling water 30–60 seconds. Immediately plunge in cold water 20 seconds. Slip off skins with knife and fingers. Slice ½ inch thick. This also works with apricots.

Cherry Pie Filling

* * * * * * * * * *

*An old tried-and-true favorite, this recipe continues to be good
as well as dependable, and is adapted from the USDA.*

3⅓ cups fresh sour cherries or
    unsweetened frozen sour cherries

  Ascorbic acid

 1 cup sugar

¼ cup plus 1 tablespoon Clearjel (see
   page 16)

1⅓ cups cold water

⅛ teaspoon cinnamon

¼ teaspoon almond extract

 6 drops all-natural red food coloring
   (optional)

 1 tablespoon plus 1 teaspoon fresh
   lemon juice

1. Wash and pit fresh cherries and use ascorbic acid dip to prevent darkening. If using frozen sweetened cherries, wash off the syrup.

2. Place cherries in 1 gallon boiling water. Boil 1 minute after water returns to a boil. Drain, but keep fruit hot and covered.

3. Combine sugar and Clearjel in a large saucepan and add water.

4. Add cinnamon, almond extract, and food coloring, if desired. Stir over medium heat until mixture thickens.

5. Add lemon juice and boil mixture 1 minute, stirring constantly.

6. Fold in the cherries.

7. Fill jars with hot fruit mixture leaving ½ inch headspace. Cap and seal.

8. Process in a boiling-water-bath canner 30 minutes.

Note: This recipe makes enough filling for one pie.

* *

YIELD: 1 QUART (EIGHT ½-CUP SERVINGS)
NUTRITION PER SERVING

Calories	158	Total fat	<1g
% from fat	2	Saturated	<1g
Carbohydrates	38g	Cholesterol	0mg
Fiber	1g	Sodium	4mg

* *

CHAPTER 3

Drying

WHILE CANNED FOODS SHINE with vivid colors that are beautiful to look at, dried foods are less glamorous but no less edible. Dried foods do have advantages. The reconstituted product can be quite tasty and convenient to use, and it contains more nutrients than canned foods.

Drying was one of the earliest methods of food preservation humans found to save food from times of bounty to use when food was scarce. As far back as pre-Biblical times, fishermen dried and smoked fish, and farmers dried olives and dates in the hot, dry climate of the Middle East.

Drying is by far the simplest and most natural way of preserving food. Little equipment is needed, but climate is everything. If you are fortunate enough to live in a warm, dry region, all you need is fresh food and a little time. The faster food can dry without actually cooking, the better its flavor will be when it's reconstituted. If you live in a relatively moist climate, you will want to learn to use one of the more active drying methods — a dehydrator, your oven, or, in some cases, the sun. As always, the finished product can be only as good as the original, so start with the very best fresh food.

The concept of drying food is quite simple. When all the moisture is removed from food, the growth of organisms that spoil food is stopped. Bacteria, molds, and yeasts can only be supported in an environment that has adequate water for them to grow. Properly dried fruits have about 80 percent of the water removed, and properly dried vegetables have about 90 percent of the water removed. Thus, you can count on keeping your home-dried foods about six months to two years, depending on the storage temperature. (See charts on page 86.) Remember that cooler storage temperatures are better. Food kept at 70°F does not keep as long as food stored at 52°F.

Food Preparation for Drying

Use only blemish-free perfect fruits and vegetables. Fruit should be *fully* ripe but not *overly* ripe. Save overly ripe fruit for sauces or for making fruit leathers (see pages 88–89). The smaller the piece of food to dry, the less time it will take to dry properly. Try to keep all the pieces about the same size so each piece will dry at the same rate.

Blanching

Proper blanching, which heats the food without actually cooking it, inactivates the enzymes that cause food spoilage. For use in the drying process, steam blanching is the only method recommended for vegetables.

The method of dipping produce in boiling water, used in many areas of the world, is not recommended because it adds more water to the produce and therefore increases drying time. Because the food is heated longer and hotter, it also robs the food of nutrients and does not fully protect the produce from spoilage organisms. If you must boil fruits or vegetables, use about 3 gallons of water to every 1 quart of food, then drain and chill the pieces in ice water to stop the cooking, and pat dry.

To blanch using the steam method, use a steamer, a large Dutch oven, or your canner with lid. Use a wire basket with legs, a basket that fits in the top of

TIP

· · · · · ·

Never use a microwave for drying food. You *can* use the microwave for blanching, however, before drying. If you try to use a microwave oven to dry your food, you'll find that your food will be cooked before it can dry.

TIP

· · · · · ·

A pretreatment, such as steam blanching, is optional for fruits that are to be dried, but for vegetables it is absolutely necessary.

Steam blanch produce before drying.

Cool blanched produce in ice water.

Dry blanched produce on towels.

the pot, or a colander that will allow 2 or more inches of water to boil without touching the produce. Steam 1 minute longer than the time given if you live 5,000 feet or more above sea level. (See chart on page 86 for steaming times.) After blanching, drain the food, then chill in ice water to stop the cooking. Drain again and dry on towels.

Blanching can be done in a microwave oven, but only in small quantities. Wattages vary, so consult the manufacturer's instructions.

Other Preparations for Drying

To improve the chances for good color retention, dip the fruit slices in other prepared solutions (see the dipping chart on the next page). This is, however, only partially effective. Steam blanching for both fruits and vegetables is still the best way.

For decades, many people used sulfur to pretreat dried fruit to preserve color. Fruit pretreated with sulfur must be dried by the sun method. Sulfuring of fruits is not a good practice for use with a home dehydrator.

While sulfuring preserves the color and vitamin C of many fruits, it may cause serious problems for people with allergies or asthma. Sulfur is now banned as a preservative for produce in supermarkets and salad bars in restaurants.

Four Types of Drying

Drying meat and produce involves the simple process of exposing the food to mild heat and moving air. This can be done by placing food in the sun, or in a dehydrator, in open air, or in an oven.

Air Drying

The process of air drying is very similar to sun drying. Puffs of dry air circulate around the food and absorb the

DIPPING

Dip	Ingredient	Time
Ascorbic acid/ all fruits	2 tbsp. ascorbic acid or 5 1-gram crushed vitamin C tabs and 1 quart water	Dip for 5 minutes, drain well, and pat dry.
Honey/bananas peaches, pineapples	3 cups water, 1 cup sugar; heat, then add 1 cup honey; stir well	Dip and remove immediately in batches, drain well, and pat dry.
Juice/apples, bananas, peaches	1 quart pineapple juice, 1 quart lukewarm water, ¼ cup bottled lemon juice	Dip no more than 5–10 minutes, drain well, and pat dry.
Pectin/berries, cherries, peaches	1 box powdered pectin, 1 cup water; boil together 1 minute, add ½ cup sugar, cold water to make 2 cups	Glaze fruit slices with thin coating, drain well, and pat dry.
Salt/all fruits	6 tablespoons pickling salt, 1 gallon water	Soak no more than 5 minutes, drain, and pat dry.

moisture and carry it away. Keep the food out of direct sun to prevent loss of color.

Try air drying steam-blanched green beans by stringing them on cotton thread and hanging them under the eaves of the house or porch, or in a well-ventilated attic. Depending on conditions, in two or three days you will have dried, pliable "leather britches," great for adding to soups. Bring the beans inside at night to prevent dew from collecting on them. Keep them out of direct sun; it will make them lose all color.

To dry mushrooms, wipe them clean, string using a needle and thread, and hang in an airy location. Or place clean mushrooms on several thicknesses of newspaper. Turn them several times as the day progresses, and change the newspapers as moisture is absorbed. Place the mushrooms in a dry, airy spot (in the direct sun if you wish, but don't forget to bring them in at night). In one or two days the mushrooms will be almost brittle.

After the drying process, both green beans and mushrooms must be heated in a 175°F oven for 30 minutes to

String the mushrooms on cotton thread.

destroy insect eggs. Condition the produce (see Post-Drying Methods, page 84) and then store in a cool, dry place for up to six months.

Sun Drying

Because sun drying takes more time, pretreating the produce by blanching or other methods is much more important. The ideal temperature is about 100°F with low humidity. If you are blessed with a climate like that, do try sun drying. In other climates, use caution. Low temperature and high humidity is the perfect combination for spoilage to occur before drying can be accomplished.

Sun-Drying Equipment

To make sun-drying equipment, I like to use old picture frames purchased from flea markets. First, clean the frames with a cloth dampened with soap and water. Then seal the frames with mineral oil. Stretch a clean, 100 percent cotton sheet or cheesecloth over the frames and secure with a staplegun. Some people use screens from their windows. This is fine, but don't use screens with galvanized wire, as it can impart "off" flavors to the food. Arrange the prepared produce on the cloth, then place the frames in direct sun, bracing them so that air can circulate on all sides. (Bring them in at night to prevent dew from collecting on them.) You can turn the produce over halfway through the drying process (after about two days). In about two to four days you will have leathery but pliable produce. This is great for Italian sun-dried tomatoes.

To destroy any pest eggs that may still be lurking in your homegrown foods, remove the produce from the frames and freeze it for two to four days below zero, or heat it on a tray in your oven 10 to 15 minutes at 175°F. (See Post-Drying Methods, page 84.) Whether you freeze or heat the produce, bring it to room temperature and then store in airtight jars for up to six months.

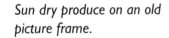

Sun dry produce on an old picture frame.

DEHYDRATOR

Using a food dehydrator is simple: You fill the trays with prepared produce, set the timer, turn on the dehydrator, and go about your business. Although a commercial dehydrator can be expensive, it can pay for itself over several seasons. Comparison shopping is difficult, since most commercial dehydrators are sold through mail order. Plan on writing for information before ordering. Many of these companies have Web sites on the Internet that can be accessed by searching "dehydrator" or "food drying." There are several features to consider before you buy.

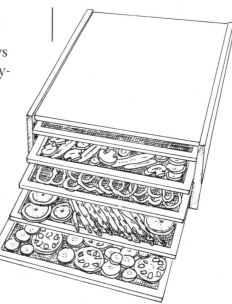

Commercial food dehydrators come in a variety of styles.

- The dehydrator should be approved for safety by Underwriters Laboratories (UL).
- Be sure you order a size that you can easily accommodate in your house and that will allow you to dry the right amount of produce or meat at a time.
- Trays should be lightweight and sturdy. Plastic screens are easier to clean and are better than metal. Metal screens can corrode, retain the heat longer, and can scorch food.
- If your model has a door, make sure that it opens easily and can be completely removed.
- The controls should be easy to read. Control settings to adjust vents for airflow and to regulate the heat are both important, and an automatice built-in timer is useful.
- The materials used in the outside cabinets vary greatly. Consider how easily you can move the cabinet, clean it, and store it. Look for double-walled insulation, also.
- Look for dehydrators that use less electricity.

An alternative to the cost of a dehyrator is to make your own. The basics include a heat source, a fan, and a food tray. See appendix A for instructions.

The most labor intensive of all the methods, oven drying is an effective (although possibly more expensive) process. In this method, place food directly on oven racks or cover the racks with clean, 100 percent cotton sheeting or cheesecloth.

Preheat your oven to 145°F. Using an oven thermometer, check the temperature periodically. Ovens vary, so you may need to experiment with a setting between 120° and 145°F. My gas oven dried produce best at 145°F. Use a wooden spoon to prop the door open to let the moisture escape. Be sure not to fill your oven too full, or the drying time will become quite long. Allow 4 to 12 hours, depending on the items and quantities being dried. Food should be dry but pliable when cool. (Test one or two pieces.)

While some authorities claim that it's possible to dry food in the microwave oven, I don't recommend it, because the microwave oven will cook your produce before it dries it. However, you can easily dry herbs in the microwave with good results.

POST-DRYING METHODS

After the food is dried, condition it by pouring it into a large open container such as a big enameled canner pot. Don't use a container that is aluminum or that is porous because it might affect the flavor or consistency of the dried food. Put the pot in a warm but dry and airy obvious place. For the next ten days or two weeks, stir it once or twice a day. Don't add newly dried food to the batch in the pot, as you want it to all finish drying at the same time.

PASTEURIZING

Pasteurizing is the partial sterilization of food. Since outdoor drying and oven drying are less exact, pasteurizing dried food is recommended.

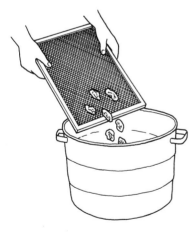

Pour sun-dried tomatoes into a large, open, nonreactive container.

The longer you wish to keep the dried food, the more the need for pasteurizing increases. Pasteurizing ensures that insect eggs and the organisms that cause spoilage are destroyed, allowing food to be stored for longer periods.

There are two ways to pasteurize:

Heat. Spread the dried produce on trays in a thin layer and leave in your 175°F oven for 10 to 15 minutes. Cool.

Freeze. Using plastic storage bags, place dried produce in a zero-degree freezer for two to four days. This destroys fewer vitamins than the oven method. The freezer *must* be at zero. A freezer compartment of a refrigerator will not do.

PACKAGING AND STORING

Dried food should be packed promptly in a "user-friendly" quantity ready for your meal preparation. Since light, moisture, and air are hard on dried foods, a cool, *dry,* dark place is best. (This does not necessarily mean the refrigerator, which is *moist* and dark.) Completely fill an airtight, clean glass container or a clean zip-seal plastic bag with all air squeezed out. Put the jars or plastic bags inside a brown paper grocery bag to protect them from the light. Label the dried food carefully, being certain to date it properly. Always use the oldest package first. If summer's heat becomes a problem, switch to the refrigerator but make certain the packaging is absolutely airtight to guard against moisture.

Rehydrating

To rehydrate dried produce, just cover it with boiling water. Let the produce stand for several hours to absorb the water, then cook the produce in the soaking liquid that is left. Vegetables take longer to rehydrate than fruits because they lose more water to dehydration. Cooking time will be much shorter than produce not rehydrated before cooking. In the case of dried beans, drain the rehydrated beans and cook them in fresh water because the nitrogen released by the beans in the soaking water is difficult to digest. Cook until tender.

TIP
• • • • • •
Rehydrate produce early in the morning. When your day is over and it's time to cook dinner, your reconstituted produce will be ready to go.

Squeeze the air in a packed zip-seal plastic bag from the bottom up.

Place the filled jars or plastic bags in a brown paper bag to protect the dried food from the light.

DRYING VEGETABLES AND FRUITS

BEST VEGETABLES/ FRUITS FOR DRYING	PREPARATION	PREFERRED PRETREAT METHOD
Vegetables		
Beans (green, wax, yellow)	trim or shell, string to air dry	steam blanch 4–6 minutes
Beans (all others)	shell, pick over mature beans	steam blanch 5 minutes
Corn	shuck, cut kernels off after blanching	steam blanch whole 10–15 minutes
Mushrooms	wipe clean, string to air dry or air dry on paper	steam blanch 3 minutes if not air drying
Okra	slice	steam blanch 5 minutes
Peas	shell	steam blanch 3 minutes
Peppers (chile)	string whole, air dry	not necessary
Peppers (bell)	slice or chop	not necessary
Tomatoes, Italian	slice in half lengthwise and remove seeds, air dry	not necessary
Fruits*		
Apples	peel, core, slice	juice or ascorbic dip, or steam blanch 5 minutes
Apricots	slice, pit	juice or ascorbic dip, or steam blanch 5 minutes
Bananas	peel, slice	honey, juice, pectin, or ascorbic dip, or steam blanch 5 minutes
Berries: blackberry, blueberry, cranberry	drop in boiling water to burst	honey or pectin dip
Strawberries	halve	honey dip
Cherries	pit	pectin, juice, or ascorbic dip
Figs	remove stem	not necessary
Grapes	remove from stem	break skin
Peaches	peel, pit, slice or halve	honey, pectin, juice, or ascorbic
Pears	peel, slice or halve	ascorbic dip, or steam blanch 2 minutes
Plums/prunes	pit, halve or leave whole	break skin

All can be pretreated by blanching or dipping as indicated.

Oven or Electric Dehydrator (Hrs.)	Sun/Air (Days)	Final Consistency	1 Cup Dry=Cups When Cooked	Cooking Time (Minutes)	Storage Time at 52°F (Months)
12–14	2–3	leathery	2½	45	8–12
48	4–5	hard		120–180	8–12
8–12	1–2	dry, brittle	2	50	8–12
8–12	1–2	leathery	1¼	20–30	4–6
8–12	1–2	dry, brittle	1½	30–45	9–12
12–18	2–3	shriveled	2	40–45	8–12
not recomm.	2–3	shriveled	1½	use directly	16–24
12–18	1–2	leathery	1½	30–45	
6–8	1–2	pliable, leathery	1½	30	6–9
6–8	2–3	pliable, leathery	1¼	30	18–24
8–12	2–3	pliable, leathery	1½	30–45	24–32
6–8	2	brittle		not recommended	12–16
12–24	2–4	hard		not recommended	18–24
8–12	1–2	hard		not recommended	18–24
12–24	2–4	hard	1½	30–45	36–48
36–48	5–6	shriveled		not recommended	18–24
24–48	3–6	shriveled		not recommended	18–24
10–12	2–6	leathery	1¼	20–30	18–24
12–18	2–3	leathery	1½	20–30	18–24
12–18	4–5	shriveled	1½	20–30	24–32

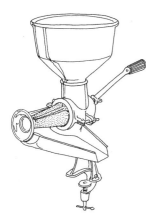
The Squeezo Strainer removes small seeds.

Spread the puree evenly over the lined cookie sheet to make fruit leather.

Fruit Leathers

Apples, bananas, peaches, and berries are perfect for fruit leathers. Many adventuresome people enjoy vegetable leathers as well. But the children's favorite, "fruit rolls" or "fruit taffy" as leathers are often called, have an incredible amount of concentrated natural sugar that frequently sticks to teeth. For that reason, dental health professionals suggest that teeth be cleaned soon after you eat this tasty treat.

Leathers from cooked fruits will be very vibrant in color.

Puree

The first step to make a fruit leathers is to pare and pit washed, ripe raw fruit and process it through a food mill. I like the Squeezo Strainer and the Victorio Strainer because they separate the small seeds and skins and leave you with a thick, rich puree. A blender or food processor can also be used for this. It may be necessary to add a small amount of liquid (juice or water will do) to reach a pouring consistency. There's no need to strain the fruit if a blender or processor is used. However, this is a matter of personal choice.

Another pureeing method, in which you cook the fruit, is to simmer clean, pared, and pitted fruit in a little water or juice for 10 to 15 minutes or until the mixture is broken down. Make sure you've added enough liquid to prevent it from burning. Then process as above in a food mill.

If you're using a food dehydrator to make your fruit leathers, follow the manufacturer's directions.

To dehydrate your puree in the oven, use 10½-by-15½-inch standard cookie sheets with sides. Line each cookie sheet with plastic wrap or freezer paper and then pour about 2 to 2¼ cups of puree onto each one. You'll want the puree to be about ⅛ to ¼ inch thick. Place the cookie sheets in a 120°F oven for 12 to 16 hours. Use an oven thermometer and set the door ajar with a spoon handle to maintain low heat and let the moisture escape. When the leather easily pulls away

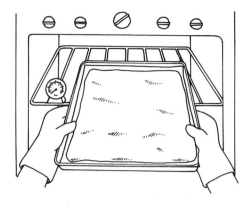

Use an oven thermometer to monitor the heat while dehydrating puree.

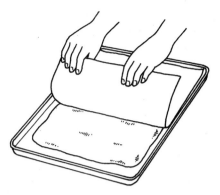

Turn the fruit leather over and remove the old wrap.

from the wrap after about six to eight hours, turn the leather over onto another prepared sheet, peel off the old wrap, and continue drying in the oven for another six to eight hours.

When it's done, remove the wrap and allow the leather to cool for several hours on a cake rack. Dust with cornstarch before rolling to prevent sticking. Roll the leather into a flute shape. Some people like to stack the layers, and with this method cornstarch dusting is a must. Store in an airtight container.

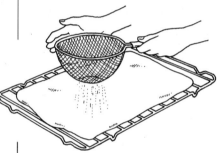

Dust the cooled leather with cornstarch to prevent sticking.

Drying Herbs

Dried herbs have been used since ancient times as medicines to remedy common ailments, to mask the taste of rancid food, or to elevate the simplest dish to a masterpiece. Low in fat and calories, they enhance almost any part of the meal and can be used in all kinds of foods — even desserts. With health-conscious people looking for ways to perk up flavor without using salt or fat, herbs have come into their own.

New research suggests that many herbs may be useful in treating physical and mental maladies. While the Food

Cut herbs 6 to 8 inches from the base of the plant.

and Drug Administration prohibits manufacturers from unsubstantiated medical claims, more people are looking to herbs as a natural alternative to prescription medicine. Herbs are being used more frequently for cosmetic purposes, also.

But by far the most common use of herbs is in the kitchen. With many herbs so easy to grow, either in a kitchen garden or on a windowsill, cooks are relying on them to add zest to our diets.

Preserving herbs and using them in combination with other foods makes sense, and the process of preserving herbs by drying is simple. While they do not exactly impart the same flavor as fresh herbs, dried herbs are a staple on any kitchen shelf and can be relied upon to spark the taste of any dish.

Be careful substituting dried herbs in a recipe that calls for fresh herbs. Adjust the amounts accordingly. A rule of thumb is that 1 teaspoon of chopped fresh herbs is equivalent to ¼ teaspoon of powdered dried herbs, or ½ teaspoon of crushed dried herb leaves.

For other methods of herb preservation, see chapter 4 on freezing and chapter 7 on vinegars.

HARVESTING AND AIR DRYING HERBS

Herbs should be harvested when their essential oils are at the highest level, usually right before flowering or bolting time when they form seeds. The best time of day to harvest them is *before* the hot sun wilts them but *after* the dew has evaporated. Cut them within 6 to 8 inches of the base of the plant. Some herbalists recommend not washing the leaves unless they are filled with grit or beaten down from rain, as washing depletes some of their essence.

To dry the cut herbs, tie small bunches of them together with garden twine and hang them with leaves pointed downward in an airy, warm, dry place that's not in direct sunlight. Gravity will force essential oils downward into the leaves.

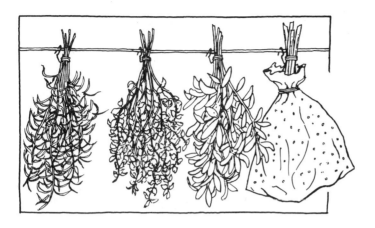

Hang herbs upside down to dry, drawing the essential oils downward into the leaves.

Never hang herbs over the stove, refrigerator, or freezer. Heat from these appliances causes deterioration. Also, don't store your purchased herbs and spices in cabinets above these appliances.

If you plan to use a dehydrator, consult the manufacturer's directions for drying herbs.

Before storing, test for remaining moisture. Put dried herbs, stems and all, in airtight containers in a warm place for a day or two. If there is moisture present on the *inside* of the container, it is better to take the herbs back to the drying process. When the herb leaves are completely dry, put them on a tray in a warm oven for two to three minutes to further dry them. Remove the leaves from the stem by stripping them off. Store the leaves undisturbed in a cool place with no direct sun, ideally in a dark glass container and/or inside your kitchen cabinet. Crush the leaves between your hands for cooking as needed; the crushing releases the pungent flavors and aroma. A mortar and pestle can be used to grind the leaves into powder. Either way, deterioration sets in within six months to a year, so plan on starting over with new batches the next season.

TIP

• • • • • •

Try suspending the fresh herb bunch inside a brown paper bag — either the lunch bag size or the grocery bag size. Prepare the bag by using a hole punch in a decorative pattern to allow air to circulate through the bag. Gather and tie off the top of the bag, securing the herbs as well, suspended upside down in the center. This method keeps dust off the drying herbs. Use colorful yarn for tying the bags, and stand them upright on a shelf in a warm, airy place. After a week or two give herbs as a gift, still in their brown bag, or use yourself.

Crush the herbs between your hands for cooking.

Oven-Dried Herbs

Start with herbs that are clean and, if washed, have been patted dry. Use a cookie sheet to spread the herbs in a single layer. Set oven to about 140°F and heat herbs for about 45 minutes. (This will not be exact, much like heating a room with a woodstove is not exact.) To allow the moisture to escape, prop the oven door ajar with a wooden spoon handle. Keep the temperature even by not opening the door farther to peek in too often. Better yet, use an oven thermometer to help you regulate the temperature. After 45 minutes, remove herbs from the oven and let them cool and then stand for about 12 hours, or overnight. To check for moisture, try the prestorage method of closing the dried, cooked herbs in a glass jar for 24 hours (page 91). If moisture appears on the inside of the glass, return herbs to the oven briefly. When they are completely dry, store in a cool, dark place in an airtight container.

Store dried herbs in airtight containers.

TIP
• • • • • •

Try hosing off the plants the night before you plan to pick them. Give them a good shake and make certain they are upright and not weighted down with water. The next day they will be grit-free and won't require washing after harvesting.

Bouquet Garni
• • • • • • • • • • • •

A classic French herb bouquet called bouquet garni is a combination of parsley, thyme, bay leaf, and lovage or celery leaves for soups, stews, sauces, and braised meat and vegetables. If you are using dried herbs, crumble them between your hands, then tie them in a wet cheesecloth pouch. (Wetting the cheesecloth prevents the oils from the herbs from being absorbed by the fibers of the cloth.) The cheesecloth pouch can easily be removed from the liquid after cooking. A tea ball also works well.

Drying Herbs in the Microwave

Microwaved herbs are labor intensive but the drying takes less time overall. All the herbs and seeds mentioned at the beginning of this section can be dried this way. Make sure you start with clean herbs. If necessary rinse until clean and pat dry with a paper towel. Just use leaves from the stems or pinch off small clusters of leaves to dry. There's no need to waste energy microwaving the stems, especially since they are thicker and would take longer to dry than the leaves. Work in small batches.

First, layer several thicknesses of paper towels in the microwave. Then spread the leaves or clusters in a single layer. Heat on high one to two minutes, depending on your oven. Then rotate the towels 180 degrees and repeat the one- to two-minute heating time. Times will vary for different ovens and herbs. By the end of the second microwave time you should have noticeably dryer leaves. Be careful here. You don't want to overdo it. Continue processing but only for about 30 seconds at a time. Test by removing one or two leaves and letting them cool completely to see if they're brittle. When they are, cool the whole batch on a wire rack and store them in dark airtight containers, giving them the moisture test described on page 91. If the container remains completely moisture-free, you are ready to store your herbs. They should retain their flavor for six months to a year.

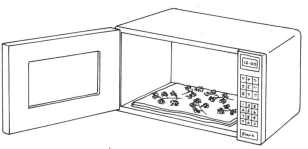

Spread the leaves over several thicknesses of paper towels in the microwave.

TIP

● ● ● ● ● ●

Dry meats at 140° to 150°F. If meat dries too slowly — at a lower temperature — there is a risk the meat will spoil before it can actually dry.

Drying Meats

Meats are dried in much the same way as fruits and vegetables, except that the drying temperature must be held at 140° to 150°F to prevent spoilage. Except when you're making meat jerky, all meats must be cooked before drying. To obtain the longest possible storage time, one year, use

TIP

• • • • • •

You'll get maximum flavor by drying meat over a longer time period at a lower temperature, but no lower than 140°F.

Meat Jerky

• • • • • • • • • •

The oldest method of preserving meat is to dry it in the sun and then store it on the shelf. This is, however, far from the safest method. For improved safety of dried meat jerky, store it in plastic bags in the refrigerator or freezer. Use frozen meat jerky within six months, refrigerated within two.

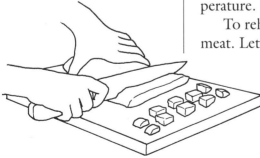

Cut beef into cubes.

only the freshest lean beef and store the finished product in zip-seal bags in the freezer. Dried meats will keep for two months in the refrigerator.

Meat jerky, which can be marinated before drying for flavor, has a much shorter shelf life than dried meat that is cooked first. It will keep two to six months, but it is easy to prepare and very convenient to use. I store jerky in the freezer in zip-seal bags.

Pork does not perform well because it contains more fat than lean cuts of beef, and the fat can turn rancid. Chicken should not be used either, because it also contains too much fat for successful drying, and it may present a health hazard. As stated, lean beef is the most reliable choice for dried meat.

Drying Beef

In a covered heavy saucepan, boil 2 pounds of lean beef cut into 1-inch cubes (lean lamb may be used) for about one hour in water to cover. Spread the pieces in a single layer on trays or cookie sheets and dry them in the oven at 140° to 150°F for four to six hours. Prop open the oven door with the handle of a wooden spoon to let moisture escape. To test, cool a cube and cut it open to check for moisture in the center. After four to six hours, continue drying the meat but lower the temperature to 130°F; dry until there is no moisture in the center of the cubes. An oven thermometer will help you maintain a stable low temperature.

To rehydrate, use 1 cup boiling water over 1 cup of meat. Let stand three to four hours. Use in stews, casseroles, or soups. Plan to marinate for flavor if necessary.

You can speed up the rehydrating process by simmering the meat and water, in the same one-to-one ratio, in a covered saucepan for 40 to 50 minutes.

RECIPES FOR DRIED FOODS

Blueberry Waffles

Mock Boursin Herb Cheese Appetizer

Herb Butter Blend

Hummus with Dried Tomatoes

Eight-Bean Soup

Split-Pea Soup

Shiitake Mushroom Soup

Mushroom Barley Soup

Vegetable Rice Beef Soup

Herbed Rice Mix

Dried-Mushroom Ragout

Mexican Salad Terra Noble

Tomato Leather

Barbecued Beef Jerky

Oriental Turkey Jerky

Cranberry Bread

Apple Coffee Cake

Quiet Spirit Tea Blend

High-Calcium Tonic

Blueberry Waffles

Dried blueberries bring a bit of summer to a winter's Saturday or Sunday brunch menu. Substitute dried raspberries for a flavor change.

1¾ cups all-purpose flour

3 teaspoons baking powder

¼ teaspoon salt

2 eggs

1¼ cups milk

6 tablespoons vegetable oil

1 cup dried blueberries

1. In a medium-size bowl, combine the dry ingredients.

2. In a large mixing bowl, beat the eggs until they are light colored and foamy.

3. Add milk and oil. Mix and set aside.

4. Gradually add the mixed dry ingredients to the egg mixture. Beat just until smooth.

5. Fold in the dried blueberries.

6. Pour batter onto hot waffle iron, following manufacturer's directions for baking.

YIELD: 4 CUPS (FOUR 1-CUP SERVINGS)
NUTRITION PER SERVING

Calories	480	Total fat	26g
% from fat	48	Saturated	5g
Carbohydrates	51g	Cholesterol	102mg
Fiber	3g	Sodium	473mg

Mock Boursin Herb Cheese Appetizer

Summer's dried herbs help make this mock Boursin cheese appetizer a great gift when packed in a ceramic crock with lid. My friends Ruth and Allie Blue shared this recipe with me years ago. By freezing this, I have found it a ready solution for impromptu entertaining. Try substituting low-fat cream cheese.

2 packages (8 ounces each) cream cheese, softened

2 teaspoons garlic powder

2 tablespoons milk

1 teaspoon dried parsley

¾ teaspoon salt

½ teaspoon dried basil leaves

¼ teaspoon dried tarragon

¼ teaspoon dried chives

½ teaspoon caraway seeds

½ teaspoon dried sage

¼ teaspoon dried thyme

Freshly ground black pepper

½ cup butter or margarine, softened

1. Combine all ingredients in a food processor and blend until smooth.

2. Spoon into ceramic crocks or ramekins.

3. Store, well wrapped, in refrigerator for 1 week or freeze for up to 2 months.

YIELD: 2½ CUPS (TWENTY 1-OUNCE SERVINGS)
NUTRITION PER SERVING

Calories	122	Total fat	13g
% from fat	91	Saturated	8g
Carbohydrates	<1g	Cholesterol	37mg
Fiber	0g	Sodium	194mg

Herb Butter Blend

· · · · · · · · · · · ·

This blend makes great herb butter with an Italian accent!

¼ cup garlic powder

¼ cup dried minced garlic

¼ cup dried basil

¼ cup dried parsley

1 tablespoon paprika

1 teaspoon ground black pepper

1. Combine all ingredients and store in an airtight jar away from heat and light.

2. When ready to use, mix 2 tablespoons of herb mixture with 1 softened stick of butter or margarine for use as a bread spread.

3. Spread mixture on top of or between slices of bread and warm in oven.

TIP

· · · · · ·

If you are rushed, roll the stick of butter in the herb mixture and let guests spread it on their own bread at the table.

YIELD: 1 CUP (SIXTEEN 1-TABLESPOON SERVINGS)
NUTRITION PER SERVING

Calories	15	Total fat	<1g
% from fat	7	Saturated	0g
Carbohydrates	3g	Cholesterol	0mg
Fiber	<1g	Sodium	2mg

Hummus with Dried Tomatoes

This favorite dip, borrowed from the Middle East, brings a bit of summer heat when you use last year's sun-dried tomatoes and spicy dried red pepper flakes.

1 can (15 ounces) chickpeas, rinsed and drained

1 cup sun-dried tomatoes

2 cloves garlic, minced

½ cup mayonnaise (regular or low fat)

¼ cup freshly grated Parmesan cheese

1. Puree chickpeas in food processor.

2. Add tomatoes and process again.

3. Add garlic, mayonnaise, and cheese and process the mixture until it is smooth.

4. Serve it immediately with crackers, flat bread, or vegetable sticks.

5. To freeze: Pour into a clean freezer container. Label and freeze. When you're ready to use it, let it thaw in the refrigerator.

YIELD: 2 CUPS (EIGHT 2-OUNCE SERVINGS)
NUTRITION PER SERVING

Calories	325	Total fat	16g
% from fat	42	Saturated	3g
Carbohydrates	36g	Cholesterol	7mg
Fiber	10g	Sodium	291mg

Eight-Bean Soup

This is a great gift idea given to me by my friend Corinne. Layer the dried beans to create contrasting colors in a jar, or mix them up in a plastic bag, and include the recipe on a card.

¼ cup each: red kidney beans, green split peas, yellow split peas, lentils, black-eyed peas, navy beans, lima beans, pinto beans, rinsed and picked over

2 tablespoons fine pearl barley

1 bay leaf

1 teaspoon garlic powder

1 tablespoon chili powder

½ teaspoon dried thyme leaves

1 teaspoon dried savory

1 beef or ham bone

2 quarts water

1 can (28 ounces) tomatoes, mashed

2 tablespoons fresh or bottled lemon juice

1. Place beans in a 2-cup container and package herbs in a separate smaller container. Store in a cool, dark place away from heat and light.

2. To prepare, mix beans in a large pot or bowl and cover with water. Soak beans overnight. Pour off water.

3. In a large soup pot, combine beans with barley, spices, bone, water, and tomatoes. Simmer 2½–3 hours in a covered pot, until beans are tender.

4. Add lemon juice and cook another 15 minutes. Remove bone.

YIELD: 2 CUPS DRY, 8 CUPS PREPARED (EIGHT 1-CUP SERVINGS)

NUTRITION PER SERVING

Calories	233	Total fat	3g
% from fat	12	Saturated	<1g
Carbohydrates	38g	Cholesterol	13mg
Fiber	12g	Sodium	39mg

Split-Pea Soup

Here is an old favorite to warm your winter chills.

1 pound (about 2¼ cups) dried, green split peas, rinsed and picked over

6 cups chicken or vegetable stock

2 tablespoons butter

½ teaspoon salt

1 medium onion, chopped

1 celery stalk, chopped with leaves

1 clove garlic, minced

2 medium carrots, chopped

1 medium unpeeled potato, cubed

1 cup diced ham or turkey sausage, cooked (optional)

1. Combine all ingredients except ham in a heavy 6-quart covered saucepan.

2. Bring to a boil, then reduce heat and simmer 2½ hours. A slow-cooker may be used on low 6–8 hours. Stir occasionally.

3. Meat can be added the last 5 minutes to heat thoroughly.

YIELD: 9 CUPS (SIX 1½-CUP SERVINGS)
NUTRITION PER SERVING

Calories	539	Total fat	15g
% from fat	25	Saturated	6g
Carbohydrates	62g	Cholesterol	63mg
Fiber	21g	Sodium	3620mg

Shiitake Mushroom Soup

. . . .

Never underestimate the potency of dried shiitake mushrooms.
This richly flavored soup will be one of your most memorable.

3 ounces dried shiitake mushrooms

1 medium potato, unpeeled

1½ quarts chicken broth

2 tablespoons butter

2 bunches scallions, coarsely chopped, including tops

4 tablespoons frozen apple juice concentrate

½ teaspoon salt

⅛ teaspoon freshly ground black pepper

1 cup half-and-half

1. Reconstitute mushrooms by pouring boiling water over them to cover. Let stand 30 minutes.

2. Drain mushrooms on paper towels, reserving liquid for added flavor in other soups or sauces.

3. Wash potato and cut in ½-inch cubes.

4. Heat broth to a simmer in a 4-quart pot. Add cubed potato and cook until tender, 10 minutes.

5. Sauté mushrooms in butter along with scallions in a large skillet until scallions are soft.

6. Add mushroom mixture to simmering stock. Increase the heat to medium high and cook approximately 15 minutes.

7. Stir in juice concentrate, salt, and pepper.

8. Spoon out the solids and puree them in a blender or food processor.

9. Return puree to the pot, stir in half-and-half, and reheat slightly. Serve immediately.

. . . .

YIELD: 8 CUPS (EIGHT 1-CUP SERVINGS)
NUTRITION PER SERVING

Calories	155	Total fat	7g
% from fat	39	Saturated	4g
Carbohydrates	20g	Cholesterol	19mg
Fiber	2g	Sodium	1791mg

. . . .

Mushroom Barley Soup

· · · · · · · · · · · ·

This great recipe answers the question, "What on earth can I have for Saturday lunch?"

Air-Dried Mushrooms

· · · · · · · · · · · · · · · · · ·

Most vegetables are preserved most success-fully when blanched first, but mushrooms are the exception and require little advance preparation.

To dry the mushrooms, remove their stems and wipe (not wash) the cups with a damp cloth. String them on a strong thread, using a sewing needle. Don't choose a needle that is so large in diameter that it will split the mush-room when pierced.

Hang the strings of mushrooms in the sun several days, until dry and almost brittle. Re-member to bring them in at night to avoid exposure to the morning dew.

Another drying method is to use several thicknesses of newspaper covered with a layer of paper towels. Spread cleaned mushrooms on the paper towel. Turn occasionally and change paper if it becomes damp until all the mushrooms are uniformly dry. Once again, it may take more than one day. A good breeze helps.

Heat the dried mushrooms in a 175°F oven on a cookie sheet 15 minutes to pasteurize.

Cool on wire racks for several hours. Store in a cool, dry place in clean, covered glass jars. These mushrooms should keep 6 months to one year.

½ cup dried medium-size barley

¼ cup dried mushroom slices of your choice

2 tablespoons dried minced onions

2 tablespoons dried parsley

2 tablespoons dried thyme

2 bay leaves

2 chicken (or vegetable) bouillon cubes

1. Combine all ingredients in a clean 1-pint canning jar. Store in dark, dry place until needed.

2. Make the soup by adding the dried ingredients to 1 quart of boiling water in a 2-quart saucepan.

3. Cover and reduce heat to simmer until barley and mushrooms are tender, about 45 minutes.

· ·

YIELD: 6 CUPS (FOUR 1½-CUP SERVINGS)
NUTRITION PER SERVING

Calories	147	Total fat	1g
% from fat	6	Saturated	<1g
Carbohydrates	32g	Cholesterol	0mg
Fiber	6g	Sodium	584mg

· ·

Vegetable Rice Beef Soup

This is a great way to use those dried vegetables. The ones listed are just suggestions — use them or any combination from your stock of dried goods.

2 cups dried vegetables:
    ½ cup chopped onions
    ½ cup chopped green beans
    1 cup chopped carrots

2 cups boiling water

1 large meaty beef soup bone

6 cups water or beef broth

1½ cups tomato puree, or sauce, or whole tomatoes, chopped

1 clove garlic, minced

½ teaspoon salt

2 tablespoons dried parsley

1 bay leaf

¼ teaspoon freshly ground black pepper

¼ cup uncooked long-grained white rice

1. Rehydrate vegetables in 2 cups boiling water, 1–2 hours.

2. In a heavy soup pot cover bone with 6 cups of water or broth and simmer covered 1 hour. Remove bone and reserve.

3. Add tomatoes, garlic, seasonings, and rice to the broth. Simmer covered 20–30 minutes.

4. Cut meat from the bone, and add it to the pot.

5. Add rehydrated vegetables and simmer covered, 45–60 minutes.

YIELD: 12 CUPS (SIX 2-CUP SERVINGS)
NUTRITION PER SERVING

Calories	87	Total fat	1g
% from fat	13	Saturated	<1g
Carbohydrates	17g	Cholesterol	1mg
Fiber	3g	Sodium	1066mg

Herbed Rice Mix

. . . .

Your dried herbs keep on giving in this blend. Pour it in a handsome, reclaimed jar,
add a bow of raffia or ribbon, and plain rice becomes a festive gift.
My friend Ann Herman shared this method of cooking perfect rice with me.

1 cup long grained converted white rice, uncooked

2 beef bouillon cubes or 2 all-natural vegetable bouillon cubes

¼ teaspoon salt

½ teaspoon dried marjoram

½ teaspoon dried thyme

1 teaspoon dried chives

1. Mix all ingredients and store in an airtight container away from heat and light.

2. To cook, combine the mixture with 2 cups water in a heavy covered saucepan about 1 quart in size. Add 1 tablespoon oil or butter. Bring to a boil and cover. Turn heat to medium. Do not lift the lid. Simmer rice exactly 30 minutes.

3. Leaving the lid snugly in place, turn off heat and let rice rest 30 minutes. Uncover and fluff rice with fork. Serve immediately. Leftovers can be frozen for later use.

. . . .

YIELD: 1 CUP UNCOOKED, 2½ CUPS COOKED
   (FIVE ½-CUP SERVINGS)
NUTRITION PER SERVING

Calories	160	Total fat	3g
% from fat	15	Saturated	2g
Carbohydrates	30g	Cholesterol	6mg
Fiber	<1g	Sodium	376mg

. . . .

Dried-Mushroom Ragout

Your dried mushrooms contribute concentrated flavor year-round. This recipe will make a Sunday-night supper a real treat.

1 cup boiling water

1 cup dried mushrooms of your choice

2 tablespoons butter or margarine

2 tablespoons all-purpose flour

1 cup milk

½ teaspoon salt

⅛ teaspoon white pepper

¼ cup Parmesan cheese

1. Combine water and mushrooms in a 1-quart saucepan. Simmer, covered, 20–30 minutes or until completely reconstituted.

2. Drain, reserving liquid for other uses such as soups.

3. Preheat oven to 350°F.

4. Melt butter in a 1-quart flameproof casserole.

5. Stir in flour and gradually add milk. Stir constantly until white sauce is smooth and thick.

6. Add mushrooms and seasonings. Top with cheese.

7. Bake 25–35 minutes.

8. Serve over toast triangles.

YIELD: 2 CUPS (FOUR ½-CUP SERVINGS
NUTRITION PER SERVING

Calories	111	Total fat	3g
% from fat	23	Saturated	<1g
Carbohydrates	18g	Cholesterol	2mg
Fiber	3g	Sodium	2,003mg

Mexican Salad Terra Noble

Dried banana chips lend a tropical note to this cool, satisfying salad.

2–3 medium carrots (1½ cups), shredded

2 cups shredded red cabbage

2 cucumbers, cleaned and diced

1 tablespoon sesame seeds, toasted

1 large head shredded iceberg lettuce (4 cups)

½ cup dry-roasted, salted peanuts, chopped

1 cup dried banana chips

1 fresh pear, diced

DRESSING

⅔ cup olive oil

¼ cup lime juice, freshly squeezed (2 medium limes)

1. Combine oil and lime juice and mix until smooth.

2. In a large salad bowl, combine all salad ingredients and toss well.

3. Add dressing ¼ cup at a time until salad fixings are coated according to taste.

YIELD: 7 CUPS (SEVEN 1-CUP SERVINGS)
NUTRITION PER SERVING

Calories	491	Total fat	38g
% from fat	67	Saturated	14g
Carbohydrates	37g	Cholesterol	0mg
Fiber	8g	Sodium	106mg

Tomato Leather

This is one vegetable leather worth trying.

4–5 medium tomatoes, chopped (2 cups)

1 medium onion, chopped

½ large stalk celery, chopped (¼ cup)

½ teaspoon salt

¼ teaspoon freshly ground black pepper

1. Mix all ingredients in a 2-quart saucepan and simmer, covered, 15 minutes.

2. Cool slightly and puree in a food processor. Drape a wet cloth over the lid to prevent the hot liquid from spattering out of the bowl.

3. Return puree to pan and cook another 15 minutes until thickened, being careful not to burn the puree.

4. Spread mixture on a cookie sheet covered in plastic wrap and tilt cookie sheet until mixture is evenly distributed.

5. Dry in 120°F oven 6–8 hours, until mixture can be pulled away from the plastic wrap easily.

6. Invert on another plastic wrap sheet, remove the plastic wrap from the bottom, and dry about 6 hours more at 120°F.

7. Remove wrap and let cool to room temperature.

8. Wrap carefully in foil or plastic wrap. Roll and store in an airtight container away from heat and light for up to 1 year. Some people prefer dusting the roll with corn-starch to keep it from sticking before storing and rolling. To use, cut off portions of the roll for a nutritious snack.

YIELD: 1 ROLL, 1½ CUPS (EIGHT 1½-OUNCE SERVINGS)

NUTRITION PER SERVING

Calories	21	Total fat	<1g
% from fat	4	Saturated	0g
Carbohydrates	5g	Cholesterol	0mg
Fiber	<1g	Sodium	140mg

Barbecued Beef Jerky

* * * * * * * * * *

This is adapted from the recipe for Barbecued Beef Jerky in the Ball Blue Book. *Once you've tasted homemade jerky, you'll never want the store-bought variety again.*

3 pounds lean beef (flank or round), trimmed of all fat

1 cup ketchup

½ cup red wine vinegar

¼ cup brown sugar

2 tablespoons Worcestershire sauce

2 teaspoons dry mustard

1 teaspoon onion powder

1 teaspoon salt

¼ teaspoon cracked pepper

Dash of hot pepper sauce

1. For ease in cutting, freeze beef, uncovered, in a bowl until ice crystals form, about 1–2 hours. Cut into thin strips against the grain (an electric knife is good for this).

2. Combine remaining ingredients in a large nonporous bowl.

3. Add beef strips, cover bowl tightly, and refrigerate overnight.

4. To dry beef strips using a dehydrator, follow manufacturer's directions.

5. To use your oven for drying jerky, set temperature at 145°F.

6. Drain meat and pat dry. Lay meat strips on oven racks and prop oven door open with a wooden spoon handle to allow moisture to escape. Dry the meat 4–6 hours, then let it cool. Test one piece by bending. If it doesn't break, it's ready. (If it does, it's overcooked.) If moisture is present, dry a little longer.

7. Place in a clean freezer container and freeze 3 days.

8. Store in an airtight container in a dry, cool place for 3 weeks, or 2 months in your refrigerator, or up to 6 months in the freezer.

* * * * * * * * * * * * * * * *

YIELD: ¾ POUND (TWENTY-FOUR ½-OUNCE SERVINGS)

NUTRITION PER SERVING

Calories	143	Total fat	8g
% from fat	52	Saturated	3g
Carbohydrates	6g	Cholesterol	35mg
Fiber	<1g	Sodium	248mg

* * * * * * * * * * * * * * * *

Oriental Turkey Jerky

Low fat and delicious, this turkey jerky will spice up your next picnic.

1 pound boned, skinned turkey breast, trimmed of all fat

¼ teaspoon onion powder

¼ teaspoon garlic powder

½ cup water

¼ cup soy sauce

2 teaspoons Worcestershire sauce

2 tablespoons firmly packed brown sugar

1 teaspoon freshly ground black pepper

1. To tenderize, pound turkey breast between layers of waxed paper. For ease in slicing, freeze it until ice crystals form and then slice thinly against the grain (an electric knife is good for this).

2. Combine remaining ingredients in a nonporous bowl, stirring well. Add turkey breast slices. Refrigerate overnight, tightly covered.

3. To dry using a dehydrator, follow manufacturer's directions.

4. To use oven, preheat temperature control to 150°F.

5. Place drained, patted-dry meat strips on oven racks. Prop oven door open with a wooden spoon handle to allow moisture to escape, and dry meat 18–24 hours. Let cool. Test one piece by bending. If it doesn't break, it's ready. (If it does, it's overcooked.) If moisture is present, dry a little longer.

6. Place in clean freezer container and freeze 3 days.

7. Store in an airtight container in a dry, cool place for 3 weeks, or 2 months in the refrigerator, or up to 6 months in the freezer.

YIELD: ½ POUND (SIXTEEN ½-OUNCE SERVINGS)
NUTRITION PER SERVING

Calories	50	Total fat	2g
% from fat	33	Saturated	<1g
Carbohydrates	2g	Cholesterol	17mg
Fiber	<1g	Sodium	279mg

Cranberry Bread

* * * * * * * * * *

Dried cranberries are good additions to muffins, waffles, and cookies as well.

1 cup dried cranberries with sweetener added

¾ cup orange juice, heated in 2-cup saucepan just to boiling

1 cup whole-wheat flour

1 cup all-purpose flour

½ cup wheat germ

¼ teaspoon salt

2 teaspoons baking powder

½ teaspoon baking soda

Rind of 1 orange, grated

¾ cup honey

1 egg

2 tablespoons oil

1. Combine cranberries with orange juice to reconstitute them. Let sit 30 minutes.

2. Grease a loaf pan and line it with waxed paper; grease the waxed paper.

3. Combine dry ingredients in a separate 4-cup bowl.

4. Preheat oven to 350°F. Mix together orange rind, honey, egg, oil, and reconstituted cranberries with any remaining juices.

5. Add dry ingredients to cranberry mixture, stirring after each addition. Stir until smooth but do not overmix.

6. Pour batter into a prepared loaf pan and bake 50 minutes, or until a toothpick inserted in the center tests clean.

7. Cool 15 minutes in the pan, then turn out on a cake rack to cool completely.

* * * * * * * * * * * * * * * * * * *

YIELD: 1 LOAF (TWELVE SERVINGS)
NUTRITION PER SERVING

Calories	191	Total fat	3g
% from fat	15	Saturated	<1g
Carbohydrates	38g	Cholesterol	15mg
Fiber	3g	Sodium	164mg

* * * * * * * * * * * * * * * * * * *

Apple Coffee Cake

*Dried apples make this a great winter treat. Double this recipe if you wish,
and eat one warm out of the oven and save the other one! These may be frozen.*

2 cups dried apples

1 teaspoon lemon juice

½ cup butter or margarine

¼ cup sugar

2 eggs

1½ cups all-purpose flour

½ teaspoon salt

2 teaspoons baking powder

½ cup milk

1 teaspoon pure vanilla extract

SUGAR TOPPING

½ cup sugar

2 teaspoons ground cinnamon

1. In a nonreactive saucepan, combine apples, lemon juice, and enough boiling water to cover. Cook until completely reconstituted. Drain.

2. Cream butter and sugar. Add eggs one at a time, beating well after each addition.

3. Sift dry ingredients. Add dry ingredients alternately with milk to the cream mixture.

4. Add vanilla; beat well.

5. Grease and flour a 9-inch-square pan or glass casserole.

6. Pour batter into pan and top with rehydrated apple slices.

7. Mix together sugar and cinnamon and sprinkle on top.

8. Bake at 325°F for 30–45 minutes.

YIELD: 1 9-INCH-SQUARE CAKE
(NINE 3½-OUNCE SERVINGS)
NUTRITION PER SERVING

Calories	302	Total fat	12g
% from fat	32	Saturated	7g
Carbohydrates	52g	Cholesterol	70mg
Fiber	3g	Sodium	338mg

Quiet Spirit Tea Blend

Delicious hot or cold, this blend of dried herbs and cloves has a wonderfully calming effect on nerves and the digestive tract.

½ cup dried rosemary leaves

½ cup dried lavender flowers

½ cup dried mint leaves

¼ cup dried chamomile

¼ cup dried cloves

1. Combine all ingredients and store in an airtight container away from the heat and light.

2. Use 1 teaspoon of mix to 6 ounces boiling water, using a tea ball or teapot and strainer. Let steep 5–8 minutes.

**YIELD: 2 CUPS TEA MIX
(NINETY-SIX 1-TEASPOON SERVINGS)**

High-Calcium Tonic

A great morning ritual or afternoon tea break, this concoction has more calcium than other herb teas thanks to the chamomile and oatstraw.

2 ounces (3 tablespoons) dried oatstraw (available at health food stores)

2 ounces (4 tablespoons) dried chamomile flowers

1 ounce (3 tablespoons) dried alfalfa

1 ounce (3 tablespoons) dried red raspberry leaves

2 ounces (3 tablespoons) dried mint leaves

1. Mix all ingredients and store in an airtight container in a cool, dark place.

2. To brew, use 1 teaspoon per 6 ounces boiling water. Infuse 10 minutes. Use a tea ball or strain from the pot.

YIELD: 1½ CUPS TEA MIX (SEVENTY-TWO 1-TEASPOON SERVINGS)

CHAPTER 4

Freezing

SINCE THE ADVENT of electricity, food preservation has changed dramatically. The freezer equipment available today is far superior in ability and efficiency to that from even a decade ago. Although freezing does not stop the clock, cold temperatures considerably slow the deterioration of foodstuffs and postpone spoilage by temporarily stopping the growth of organisms. While an initial investment in a good freezer can be expensive, along with the ongoing electrical bills for operating it, freezing food is superior to other preserving methods. More nutrients are preserved by freezing, and the texture, color, and flavor of frozen foodstuffs are better than in food preserved by other methods.

CONTAINERS AND WRAPPERS

Air (oxygen) and moisture loss are the main enemies of frozen products. For that reason it's important to use airtight packaging. Moisture loss occurs when ice crystals evaporate from the surface of frozen food, and the result is freezer burn. Though freezer burn is not harmful, it dries out and toughens the food and can cause off flavors. Using moisture- and vapor-proof wrapping prevents this. Warped and cracked plastic containers or storage containers designed for the refrigerator should never be used for freezing. Clean glass jars can be recycled for use in the freezer as long as you leave plenty of headspace for expansion when you fill the jars. You'll want to make your freezer containers as uniform in size and shape as possible to

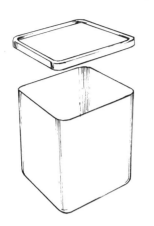

This plastic container is appropriate for freezer storage.

· · · · · ·

Always squeeze out any air in the freezer bag before you seal it.

maximize the freezer's interior space and avoid empty gaps on freezer shelves. Keeping air at freezing temperatures takes more energy than than keeping food at freezing temperatures, since frozen food retains cold much better than air can. However, you need to allow for a some air circulation within the freezer. Paper freezer boxes in handy 1- and 2-cup sizes do solve the uniform space problem, but I don't recommend them because they are not completely airtight and can't be recycled.

The wrapping used to package meat and poultry in the supermarket allows air to penetrate and moisture to evaporate and is not adequate for long-term storage in the freezer. In addition to freezer burn, any fat on meat will turn rancid within a few weeks if not properly packaged. You can repackage these foods in moisture- and vapor-proof containers or wrapping or you can overwrap the entire unopened package.

My favorite container is a zip-seal bag of thick plastic especially designed for the freezer. These bags can be reused if they are of good quality and have not been damaged or permeated by strong odors of previously frozen contents.

Square milk cartons are good for freezing some items. I especially like to freeze fish, shrimp, and other seafoods in them (fins and tails can puncture a plastic bag). Put loosely packed seafood in the clean carton, then add water to 1 inch from the top, allowing for expansion. Flatten the carton top by pushing it down. Seal it with sturdy freezer tape. Don't forget to label your package.

Freezing in Zip-Seal Bags
· ·

Never place plastic storage bags full of semiliquid foodstuffs directly on a freezer shelf. They will bulge around the shelf rungs, freezing to the shelf. Even if you can get the bag off the shelf when frozen, you will still have the problem of uneven packaging, which wastes interior freezer space. Instead, lay the filled freezer bags side by side on a tray that fits on the freezer shelf, allowing the packaged food to take on the flat, square shape of the freezer bag. When the bags are frozen solid, simply remove them from the tray, label them, and stack them right on the freezer shelf.

Selecting a Freezer

Freezers come in a wide variety of sizes and styles. In chosing one, consider the space you have available for it, how much food you plan to store, its energy efficiency, and how accessible you need the freezer to be. The more often you intend to go to the freezer, the more convenient it should be. Don't put your freezer in the basement if you have trouble going up and down stairs. Spend some time comparing models that fit your requirements to find the best brand.

Freezers must be kept at 0°F to prevent spoilage. Separate, freestanding freezers require less energy to do this than combination refrigerator-freezers, although combination models with separate doors are much better than single-door combination models. Larger freezers use more energy than smaller ones, so don't buy a freezer that's larger than you need. Since it takes more energy to cool air than it does solid matter, a half-full freezer uses more electricity than a full one. Buying the right size for your needs can save you money.

A self-defrosting freezer costs more to operate than manual models — as much as 60 percent more — so determine whether you are willing to pay for the convenience. If you chose a manual-defrosting freezer, defrost it once the frost is ¼ inch thick to keep it running efficiently.

To further cut energy costs, choose a well-insulated freezer, place it away from heat sources, and freeze food in small batches. No more than 3 pounds of food should be added at one time to prevent an increase in energy.

Maintain your freezer by cleaning the motor housing and the condenser coils every three or four months, following the manufacturer's guidelines. Also check the tightness of the rubber gaskets that seal the door by placing a sheet of paper between them to see if it will stay there.

Allow enough space between the freezer and the wall for ventilation. For a longer-lasting piece of equipment, keep its coils and grill free of dust and dirt.

TIP
• • • • • •

When adding a batch of food to be frozen, set your freezer's control to sustain -10°F and the freezer will remain below 0°, ensuring proper temperature storage for the foods already there. A large batch of room-temperature food added to a freezer will raise the air temperature and possibly affect the foods that are already frozen.

· · · · · ·

Keep your freezer well
stocked. A full freezer
actually costs less in
electricity bills to maintain
than one that is half full.

LABELING, INVENTORY, AND STORAGE

Do you have mystery meat frozen in trapezoid-shaped lumps? Do you have huge jars of chicken stock that are longing to be soup? All of this recycling is economical and creative, as long as you don't lose track of what you have and how long it's been in the freezer. If you don't use the food you've preserved, your planning and effort will be wasted.

Clearly label each package with its contents and date, using a marker designed for freezer use. Every cook has defrosted what was supposed to be soup only to discover, to her horror, defrosted turkey gravy. Labels can fall off in the freezer, so write on the package of frozen food itself.

Start an inventory list and make a habit of adding and subtracting items from your list *every time* you open the freezer door. Train your family to do the same. I once cleaned out a sick neighbor's freezer at her request. In 1989 that freezer had two roasts from 1962 and a casserole from 1978! I post my inventory list on the freezer door or inside a nearby cupboard door. The list is organized by shelf. I keep a pencil on a string next to the list so it will be easy for everyone to strike through an item when it is removed, or add a note when food is added.

What to Do if the Freezer Stops Working

· ·

If the electricity is cut off, or if your freezer just stops working, don't open the door. You have approximately two days before a fairly full freezer begins to heat up, especially if it contains lots of meat rather than produce and bread, which are less dense. You can prolong the survival time by wrapping the whole exterior of the freezer in insulation material or even, in a pinch, several quilts or multiple layers of newspaper.

Never refreeze completely defrosted, low-acid foods such as vegetables, shellfish, or prepared casseroles that have reached room temperature. Very high-acid fruits can be refrozen if they're still cold. When in doubt, throw it out! Most foods that still have ice crystals and are cold can be cooked and refrozen or eaten immediately. There will, however, be a loss in taste, texture, and food quality.

Be sure to re-mark refrozen foods accordingly and use them quickly after refreezing. Refrozen foods do not have the shelf life of one-time frozen foods.

Thawing Frozen Foods

Freezing stops or slows down the deterioration clock for food, but some microorganisms remain, although they may be inactive or at least slowed down considerably. Bacteria are not destroyed by freezing, and once food is thawed, the bacteria will begin to multiply again. That's why the best way to thaw food is to do it slowly at cold temperatures. Thawing at room temperature or in hot water will not only cause bacteria to grow again, but heat will cause them to grow faster. Because of that hazard, thaw frozen foods at the lower temperatures in your refrigerator — certainly not on your kitchen counter at room temperature, where warmth can stimulate the breeding of microorganisms.

Freezing also slows the growth of the enzymes that are present in plants and animals, though it doesn't stop it altogether. Enzymes speed up the growth and ripening process of live foods and continue to cause these chemical reactions even after harvested. The changes in color, texture, and flavor of food that occur as food ages and moves toward spoiling is caused by these enzyme reactions. To halt enzyme activity altogether, two methods — blanching and adding chemical compounds such as ascorbic acid — are used to treat food before freezing.

Pretreating Vegetables for Freezing

Vegetables that are blanched and then frozen turn out better than those that are frozen raw. While blanching is a must in order to retain color, taste, and texture in vegetables, blanching is optional for fruits. Not only do blanched vegetables win on taste, color, and texture, but blanching also helps them retain nutrients. Blanching helps prevent loss of vitamins A and C and the B vitamins.

TIP

Freeze water in clean milk cartons to make large blocks of ice to use in water for cooling food rapidly. They last longer than ice cubes.

Steam blanching is the most effective method for retaining taste, texture, and nutrients.

There are several ways to blanch food. For both steam and boil blanching, heat 1 minute longer than the time given if you live 5,000 feet or more above sea level.

Steam blanching. This method produces the very best taste after freezing, as well as providing the most protection against vitamin loss. You may use a steamer pot especially designed for steaming or a steamer basket inserted into a pot with lid. Bring 4 or 5 inches of water to a boil under the steamer basket. Place the vegetables in the basket in a thin layer. Begin timing when you put the lid on the steamer. (See chart at right for timing different vegetables.)

Boil blanching. This is an easy method, but the outcome is not as good as with steam blanching because the high temperature and immersion in water tend to diminish flavor. Bring 4 quarts of water to a rapid boil and then add 1 pound of clean, pared vegetables. Allow the water to return to a boil and begin timing for the specified amount of time. (See chart at right for timing different vegetables.)

Microwave blanching. Follow the manufacturer's directions. Although this method seems attractive, experts disagree in their recommendations, and only one plastic pint- or quart-size bag of produce can be processed at a time.

The final step. Regardless of which blanching method you use, stop the cooking by plunging vegetables into ice-cold water.

Equipment for Freezing

• • • • • • • • • • • • • • • • • • •

8–10 quart pot

Wire mesh basket, preferably with handles that fit in the top of the pot

Large strainer

Clean, dry tea towels

Blocks of ice made in recycled milk cartons, or two zip-seal plastic bags filled with ice cubes, or a clean dishpan of ice water. Station this part in your sink to avoid messy cleanups.

Freezing Vegetables

With the exception of pumpkin, which stores only about 2–3 months, these vegetables will keep for 1 year at 0°F if properly prepared and packaged.

Item	Harvest	Preparation	Blanch Time in Minutes	
			Boil	Steam
Artichokes	Small is best	Cut tops and thorns; trim stems; wash.	8	8–10
Asparagus	Young, very green	Cut even-size pieces; wash.	4	3
Beans (green)	Young, tender	Wash; cut desired lengths; remove stem end.	3	4
Beans (yellow)	Small beans inside pods	Wash; cut desired lengths; remove stem end.	3	4
Beans (lima)	Bright green, slightly filled-out pods	Wash, blanch, and shell.	2	4
Broccoli/Brussels sprouts	No yellow heads or pithy stalks	Wash; trim into uniform sizes. Check for worms. Soak in cold salt water 10–15 minutes.	2–4	3–6
Cabbage	Tender green heads	Wash. Shred or wedge.	1½–2	2–3
Cauliflower	Well-formed heads; no brown spots	Wash, cut into florets. Check for worms. Soak in cold salt water 10–15 minutes.	3	5
Corn	Young, ripe, small ears*	Husk, remove silk, wash. Blanch 3 ears/batch, cool, then cut from cob.	4	6
Eggplant	Small and tender skinned	Wash, peel, slice, or cube. Blanch using 1 T. lemon juice to 1 qt. water.	4	6
Okra	Tender, small pods	Wash, cut stem, and slice if desired.	2–3	5
Peas (green)	Filled-out, green, and tender*	Shell but do not wash.	2	3
Peas (snow or sugar)	Green, not filled out	Wash.	2	3
Peppers, bell (sweet)	Shining skin, deep color	Wash and halve, remove seeds. Does not require blanching, but blanched is easier to pack.	2	2
Pumpkins and Squash	Deep color, hard shell; best frozen in cooked form	Wash; cut in uniform pieces. Bake in 350°F oven until soft; remove skins from cooked mixture.		
Summer Squash	Tender skins; small	Wash and shred, slice, or cube.	3–4	3–4
Tomatoes	Deep color, firm	See page 124.		
Zucchini	Deep green, tender skins, small	Wash and shred, slice, or cube.	2–3	2–3

*Work quickly so that sugar does not turn to starch.

Freezing Fresh Vegetables

1. I like to organize my equipment and supplies the night before. This saves valuable time the next morning, when time is of the essence. Line your equipment up in the order needed.

When you come in from the garden or farmer's market, you'll be ready to begin. Remember that you'll want to work quickly and carefully, using only small batches of food if at all possible.

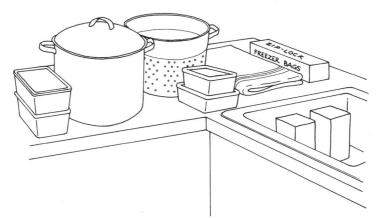

2. As always, choose fresh and tender produce. Freezing can never improve inferior-quality food. Early in the day harvest or buy slightly underripe vegetables, avoiding those with blemishes or bruises.

3. Wash the vegetables and cut them into uniform-size pieces where practicable.

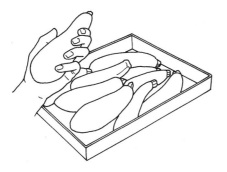

4. To steam blanch the vegetables, fill the wire mesh basket of the steamer with 1 pound of prepared produce. Set it over 1 or 2 inches of boiling water and cover the pot. Begin timing. See chart on page 121 for exact times.

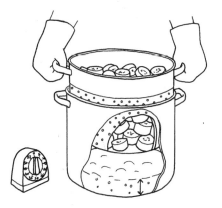

5. To cool the vegetables quickly, plunge them into ice water, basket and all. Set the basket on blocks of ice and cover it with ice cubes, or place the basket on prepared zip-seal bags filled with ice and cover the top of the

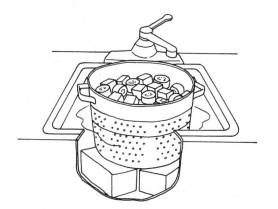

vegetables with a second prepared bag. (This method keeps extra water to a minimum.)

6. Pour the cooled vegetables from the basket onto a clean tea towel. Gently roll up the towel to remove excess moisture, but don't squeeze.

7. Pack in freezer containers at once, seal, label, and freeze. Vegetables that pack with air spaces around each piece (such as broccoli, asparagus, and artichokes) need no expansion (head) space.

FREEZING TOMATOES

Tomatoes can easily be frozen in a variety of ways — stewed or cooked down in the oven, slow-cooker, or saucepan; frozen whole, peeled or unpeeled. (Add other clean, blemish- free vegetable scraps from other freezing projects and you've got a hearty soup in the making.)

It is a remarkable convenience, late in the season when the harvest is rolling in, to freeze tomatoes whole, even though it takes extra space in the freezer. My favorite way to freeze tomatoes is to wash 12 to 24 firm ones of uniform size, then core and place them on a cookie sheet in the freezer. When they're solid, I place them in a plastic freezer bag to use as needed. Skins will slide off as they thaw. To thaw, spray a little shower of warm water over the frozen tomatoes to speed up the process.

It is possible to skin fresh tomatoes by first plunging them into boiling water for 30 seconds to 1 minute. Then lift off the skins before freezing them whole on trays; or remove skins from the pot as the tomatoes simmer.

For sauces or stewed tomatoes wash, core, and quarter the tomatoes. Simmer covered in a heavy saucepan until soft, then remove the lid. For stewed tomatoes, cook another 15 to 30 minutes. Cook sauces several hours, being careful not to burn them. Using a slow-cooker or your oven makes burning less likely than cooking on the stove top. Cook four to six hours, checking every half hour to prevent sticking.

FREEZING FRUITS

Fruits are the ultimate food for freezing. Freezing them involves less labor overall because no blanching is needed. Fruits retain a good portion of their nutrients while frozen, and their color, texture, and flavor are superior to what they are after canning. They do, however, suffer some softening in the process of being frozen. Freezing converts the water contained in any food from a liquid to a solid. Because water expands when it freezes, the structure of the cells is altered, breaking down the cell walls. Consequently, all food will be softer once it has thawed. The more water in a food, the greater this change will be, and that's why some fruits and vegetables don't fare as well as others after freezing.

Fruit can be frozen two ways, using the dry-pack method or the wet-pack method. As always, use mature, ripe, fresh fruits free of blemishes.

Dry Pack

The dry-pack method is the easiest way to freeze fruit. It involves freezing fruit without added liquids or other ingredients. All that's required to dry pack is washing the fruit and drying it on clean towels. Handle the fruit carefully to avoid bruising, and quickly to prevent it from darkening from exposure to air.

Spread the clean, dry fruit in single layers on cookie sheets and place in the freezer. When the fruit is solid, package it loosely in clean containers. While this way of dry packing fruit is extremely convenient and helps to maintain the shape of the fruit, it may cause more texture, flavor, and color loss than freezing it in sealed containers. To prevent any loss of flavor or color, pack the fruit directly in a carton or other container, bypassing the cookie-sheet step. The dry-pack method results in fewer calories than the wet-pack method and is wonderful for those with health issues that relate to sugar consumption. Allow ½ inch headspace in your packages.

Wet Pack

As the name implies, freezing food using the wet-pack method involves adding a liquid to the fruit before freezing. The liquid can be syrup, juice, or water.

Sugar syrup pack. To pack fruit in a sugar syrup, add ⅓ to ½ cup of the cold sugar syrup of your choice (see chart) to 2-cup containers packed with clean fruit. Mix

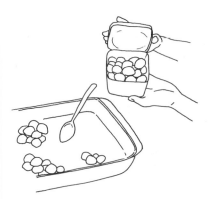

TIP
● ● ● ● ● ●

Because of cellular changes, frozen fruits to be eaten raw are at their best texture and taste when they still contain ice crystals and have not completely defrosted.

Packing the fruit before freezing is one method of dry packing.

Freezing the fruit before packing is also dry packing.

them gently, label, and freeze. Allow ½ inch headspace for pints and 1 inch headspace for quarts.

The day before freezing the fruit, make a syrup using the recipe below. Bring it to a boil to dissolve the sugar and then chill it.

SYRUPS FOR FREEZING FRUIT

CONSISTENCY	AMOUNT OF SUGAR	AMOUNT OF WATER	FINISHED AMOUNT
Thin	2 cups	4 cups	5 cups
Medium	3 cups	4 cups	5½ cups
Heavy	8¾ cups	4 cups	8⅔ cups

Juice pack or water pack. To pack fruit in juice or water, use the same proportions as with syrup. If you can't use sugar and wish to use an artificial sweetener, add it when you serve the fruit. Allow ½ inch headspace for pint jars and 1 inch headspace for quarts.

Sugar pack. Packing frozen fruit with sugar requires the sprinkling of sugar to taste over fresh fruit. Mix the fruit and sugar carefully or mash the mixture slightly to allow the juices to be drawn from the fruit. Stir to dissolve all sugar. Pack the sweetened fruit into clean containers, label, and freeze. Allow ½ inch headspace for pints and 1 inch headspace for quarts.

Honey pack. The easiest, lightest method of packing fruit, honey pack also has the fewest calories without resorting to articificial sweeteners. To substitute honey for sugar syrup, use exactly half the amount as called for in the sugar recipe. Working with honey is easiest when it is at room temperature. Add ½ cup Honey Syrup Blend (see recipe at left) of the consistency of your choice to 1-pint containers of fruit, and 1 cup Honey Syrup Blend to 1-quart containers. Allow ½ inch headspace for pints and 1 inch headspace for quarts.

Honey Syrup Blend

. . . .

Thin honey:
   1 cup mild honey
   4 cups water

Medium honey:
   2 cups mild honey
   3 cups water

Heat water to warm, and stir in honey to blend. Cool to room temperature.

FREEZING FRUITS

Fruit	Harvest	Preparation
Apples	Firm, crisp, but ripe	Wash, peel, core, and slice. Pretreat fruit to prevent darkening or use wet pack of your choice. Cook as for puree (page 88) and then freeze.
Apricots	Soft and ripe, but firm	Dip in boiling water 15–30 seconds then in cold water. Slip off skins, halve, remove pit. Wet pack with nondarkening agent.
Avocados	Soft but not overly ripe	Peel, pit, and puree. Add nondarkening agent, best frozen unflavored for versatility's sake when thawed.
Bananas	Ripe but not overly ripe	Peel, cut in chunks.* Or peel, freeze, mash when thawed for banana bread. Use nondarkening agent dip.
Berries: blue, elder, huckle	Fresh, firm, sweet, but soft	Wash, dry pack loosely in cartons. Or mash, puree, or wet pack.
Cherries: sour and sweet	Soft, fresh; plump with glossy skin	Wash, halve, pit. Dry pack with nondarkening agent dip.
Cranberries	Soft, ripe, but firm; plump with glossy skin	Wash, pit. Dry pack. Or crush fruit, simmer 1 cup water with 1 pint (2 cups) fruit until skins burst, then wet pack.
Figs	Soft, ripe, but firm	Wash, cut off stems. Dry pack or wet pack with liquid of your choice. Use nondarkening agent with both methods.
Grapes: seedless	Soft, sweet, firm, but ripe	Wash, stem, and dry pack.*
Kiwi	Soft, but firm and ripe	Peel and slice. Wet pack only.
Melon	Sweet, ripe	Cube, slice, or ball melon flesh. Dry pack.*
Nectarines	Ripe, unblemished, soft but firm	Wash, peel, and pit. Slice or halve. Wet pack with nondarkening agent.
Peaches	Ripe, unblemished, soft but firm	Wash, peel, and pit. Slice or halve. Wet pack with nondarkening agent.
Pineapple	Ripe, sweet, but firm**	Peel, core, slice, or cube. Wet pack.
Plums	Ripe, sweet, but firm	Wash, halve, and pit. Wet pack with nondarkening agent.
Raspberries	Firm, sweet, and ripe	Gently wash and pick over. Dry pack. Or wet pack with very light syrup.
Rhubarb	Firm, tender red stalks	Wash and cut in small pieces. Remove tough stalks. Blanch 1½ minutes in steam or boiling water; dry pack. Or wet pack with syrup without blanching.
Strawberries	Ripe, soft, unblemished	Gently wash, slice, halve, or freeze whole for dry pack. Or wet pack in light syrup.

*Half thawed, makes a delicious snack.
**Pineapple is ripe if a spiky leaf is easily pulled.

Pretreating the Fruit before Freezing

Some fruits will darken after being pared for freezing. Apples, apricots, peaches, and nectarines all have this tendency. To prevent darkening, dip the cut-up fruit in ascorbic acid, citric acid, lemon juice, or concentrated fruit juice before freezing. Be aware that fruit juice, citric acid, or lemon juice may change the flavor of the fruit, sometimes for the better. Steam blanching for three to five minutes eliminates the darkening without altering the taste.

Concentrated frozen fruit juice such as cranberry or orange can be thawed and used as a dip for fruits. A 12-ounce can should be enough for several quarts of fruit. Fold the fruit very gently in the concentrate, coating well. Use a mesh basket to drain excess juice.

Citric acid in crystalline (powder) or bulk (chunked) form is available from drugstores or health food stores. Use 3 tablespoons of water for dissolving the required amount. Follow package directions.

Lemon juice contains citric and ascorbic acid. While it may impart its flavor to the fruit, it is easy to use. Add 1 or 2 tablespoons of lemon juice to the freezing liquid of your choice — honey or sugar syrup, juice, or water.

Ascorbic acid in tablet or crystalline form is more commonly known as vitamin C. It can be found in drug- or health food stores. Use ½ teaspoon of the crushed tablets or crystalline powder dissolved in 1 quart of water as a dip for the fruit before you pack it in containers.

Freezing Herbs

Drying herbs may seem the easiest method, but freezing wins the taste test by far for some herbs.

Choose herbs that are still in season and the peak of their essence. Harvest them before the hot sun wilts the plants, cutting them in 3- to 6-inch stalks. Holding the cut herbs by their stalks, swish them in water to get rid of all grit.

Freezing Herbs

* * * * * * * * * * * *

The herbs listed below freeze particularly well.

Basil
Chives
Comfrey
Chervil
Cilantro (coriander)
Dill
Sweet fennel
Lovage
Mint (most kinds)
Parsley
Savory
Thymes (a few kinds)

1. To blanch the herbs, fill your pot with water and bring to a boil. Dip stalks in boiling water until the color brightens. This will take only a few seconds per stalk. Because herbs are so tender, there's no need to blanch for long periods of time. If necessary, hold the herbs with tongs while you dip them in the boiling water.

2. Place the blanched stalks on layers of paper towels to blot dry and cool.

3. Here you have choices: Remove the stem and leave the leaves whole or chop them, or leave the herbs whole on the stem. I like to leave mine whole on the stalk for versatility and ease of handling later. Place the prepared herbs in single layers on waxed paper. Make a flattened "roll" about 4 inches wide. Store the roll in an airtight plastic zip-seal freezer bag; press gently to remove all air from the bag.

4. Label and freeze your herbs for enjoyment all winter long. Use them as needed or thaw the entire roll (which will keep five to seven days in the refrigerator).

Blanch herbs by dipping them in boiling water.

Herbs can also be frozen in clean ice cube trays. Wash and chop fresh herbs and place a portion in each cube compartment. Add sufficient boiling water to cover the herbs and freeze. No need to blanch, as the boiling water takes care of that. When the cubes are solid, pop them out of the trays, then bag and label accordingly. Herb cubes are a great item to toss into sauces or soups. Another great way to freeze fresh herbs is in a prepared butter or paste.

Freeze fresh chopped herbs in ice cube trays filled with water.

Grape Leaves
• • • • • • • • • • • •

Grape leaves fare well when frozen by the method above. (Spring leaves are the most tender.) Note that they require a two-minute blanching and that their color will then darken rather than lighten. Plunge several leaves into cold water at one time. Place them on layers of paper towels and gently blot dry. Place in single layers on waxed paper. Make a flattened "roll" about 4 inches wide. Store the roll in a zip-seal freezer bag. Use for stuffed grape leaves later on.

Freezing Meats and Poultry

Fresh meats and poultry freeze very successfully and, when properly packaged, can be stored for many months. The same is not true of cured meats. Meats with a high salt content, such as bacon and cured ham, will keep for only a month or two in the freezer. That's because salt increases the rate at which rancidity develops in fat, and freezing does not prevent fat from becoming rancid. Added spices or seasonings limit the freezer life of ground meats and sausages, and hot dogs and luncheon meats are not suitable for freezing at all.

Freshly butchered meats such as beef, lamb, and veal can chill for up to 48 hours in the refrigerator at 40°F before freezing without loss of flavor. (This also takes a big load off your freezer if, for instance, you have a whole lamb to process because the meat is prechilled before freezing.) Chilling first allows the natural enzymes to age the meat as well as tenderize it. Fresh-killed poultry can prechill at 40°F for no longer than 12 hours before it starts to lose flavor. Meats and poultry purchased at a supermarket, however, should be rewrapped and frozen immediately after purchase.

Packaging Meat and Poultry

The meat and poultry inside will be only as good as the wrap on the outside. Using regular plastic wrap, aluminum foil, or waxed paper is a false economy. Don't do it. Freezer wrap should be strong and pliable, moisture-proof, and impervious to air (oxygen). Heavy-duty plastic, aluminum foil, and freezer paper are recommended. For longer storage times, it's a good idea to prewrap meat and poultry in heavy plastic and then again in one of the recommended wraps or freezer bags. To prevent freezer burn, make sure all the air pockets are squeezed out of the final packaging, paying special attention to irregular shapes and sizes.

Freeze meat and poultry in the quantity that you intend to use it, and trim excess fat, which will become rancid over time and give food an "off" odor. If you plan to remove bones before you cook the food, remove them before you freeze it. They take up space in your freezer. When freezing cut pieces of poultry, put freezer paper between them to help you separate them as they thaw. Package giblets separately; they don't keep in the freezer as long as the rest of the bird.

Label well, giving exact contents, weight, and date. Then freeze. When you're freezing large quantities of anything, it's a good idea to turn your freezer temperature control down to the coldest position. A large batch of room-temperature food added to a freezer will raise the air temperature and possibly affect the foods that are already frozen. Remember to reset your temperature control back to 0°F after 24 to 48 hours.

Caution
. . . .

Never stuff poultry before freezing! You may run the risk of creating the ideal environment for bacteria to grow as it thaws.

THAWING POULTRY IN THE REFRIGERATOR

Chickens	4 pounds and over	1–1½ days
Ducks	3–7 pounds	1–1½ days
Geese	6–12 pounds	1–2 days
Turkeys	4–12 pounds	1–2 days
	12–20 pounds	2–3 days
	20–24 pounds	3–4 days
	Pieces of large turkey (half, quarter, half breast)	1–2 days
	Cut-up pieces	3–9 hours
	Boneless roasts	12–18 hours

Courtesy of the University of Missouri Extension Publications Library

FREEZING FISH

Freeze fish immediately after catching or purchasing. To improve the quality, fish should be treated before freezing. Fish containing fat — salmon, tuna, mackerel, mullet, and trout, for instance — can become rancid and should be dipped for 20 seconds in an ascorbic acid solution made from 2 teaspoons of crystalline ascorbic acid to 1 quart of cold water. Flounder, cod, whiting, redfish, snapper, grouper, and other lean fish should be dipped for 20 seconds in a brine of ¼ cup salt to 1 quart of cold water.

PACKAGING FISH

Wrap fish in heavy plastic wrap, aluminum foil, freezer paper, or other moisture- and vapor-proof wrapping. Place freezer paper between pieces for ease of separation during thawing, then freeze.

Another method involves placing the fish in a shallow pan, covering with water, and freezing. Remove the ice block from the container and wrap with moisture- and vapor-proof wrapping.

Glazing is another method that preserves the flavor of fresh fish. Place the unwrapped fish in the freezer. As soon as it freezes, remove it and dip in ice water. Again place the fish in the freezer to harden the glaze. Repeat until the fish is covered in ice, then wrap in moisture- and vapor-proof wrapping or place in a freezer bag.

Freezing Dairy Products

Most dairy products can be frozen if the proper procedure is followed. Dairy products that have been frozen should be thawed in the refrigerator and consumed within a few days.

Whole eggs. Stir to mix whites with yolks, but don't whip in air. To each cup of whole eggs, add 1½ teaspoons sugar (for use in sweet foods) or ½ teaspoon salt (for use in salty foods or for scrambling) to prevent gumminess. Pour into container, allowing for headspace, seal, label, and freeze.

Egg yolks. Separate eggs, and stir the yolks together. To each cup of egg yolks, add 2 teaspoons sugar (for use in sweet foods) or 1 teaspoon salt (for use in salty foods). Pour into container, allowing for headspace, seal, label, and freeze.

Egg whites. Separate eggs, and strain egg whites through a sieve. Do not stir or add sugar or salt. Pour into container, allowing for headspace, seal, label, and freeze.

Butter and cheeses. Wrapped in vapor- and moisture-proof wrapping, butter and cheeses freeze well. Like most foods, they should be thawed in the refrigerator. The texture of cheese that has been frozen changes slightly and it crumbles more easily, but when used cooking, there is no discernible difference. Freeze in small blocks or portions, 1 pound or less and no more than 1 inch thick.

Cream. Pasteurized cream that is at least 40 percent butterfat may be frozen whipped or unwhipped, although unwhipped cream that has been frozen and thawed will not whip well. To freeze liquid cream, heat it to 170°F for 10 to 15 minutes. For each quart, add ⅓ cup sugar, pour into containers, allowing for headspace, seal, label, and freeze.

TIP
• • • • • •

Don't freeze eggs in their shells. The shells will break because of expansion. Instead, break the eggs into a bowl and freeze in the quantities you will use. An alternative is to suspend whole egg yolks in water and then freeze. An ice cube tray may be used.

TIP
• • • • • •

Do not freeze whipped butter, buttermilk, cream cheese, cottage cheese, or sour cream, all of which either separate or become mushy when thawed.

SHELF LIFE OF HOME-FROZEN FOODS

Food	Storage Period at 0°F
Butter	6–9 months
Margarine	12 months
Cheese	
natural	6–8 weeks
processed	4 months
Cream (all kinds)	2 months
whipped	1 month
Eggs (whole, white, yolks)	9–12 months
Fish	
fatty (perch, salmon, mackerel)	2–3 months
lean (cod, flounder, haddock, sole)	3–6 months
Fruit and fruit juice	
(except citrus)	8–12 months
citrus fruit and juice	4–6 months
Ice cream or sherbet	2 months
Meat	
bacon	1 month
frankfurters and luncheon meat	not recommended
ham	1 month
ground beef, lamb, veal	2–3 months
ground pork	1–2 months
Roasts	
beef	6–12 months
lamb, veal	6–9 months
pork	3–6 months

Food	Storage Period at 0°F
Steaks, chops	
beef	6–12 months
lamb, veal	1–2 months
lamb, veal	3–6 months
Milk, fresh fluid	1 month
Poultry (chicken, turkey, duck)	
Whole: chicken or turkey	12 months
duck or goose	6 months
Cut up: chicken	9 months
turkey	6 months
Giblets	3 months
Home-prepared foods	
bread	3 months
cake	3 months
casseroles (meat, fish, poultry)	3 months
cookies (baked and unbaked)	3 months
pies (unbaked fruit)	8 months
Vegetables	
home frozen	10 months
purchased	8 months
Yogurt	
plain	1 month
flavored	5 months

Courtesy of the University of Missouri Extension Publications Library

RECIPES FOR FREEZING

Croustade Appetizer Cups

Spiced Pear Butter

Eggplant Caviar

Pungent Eggplant Chutney

Pâté of Chicken Livers

Picnic Chicken Roll

Rosemary Paste for Angel-Hair Pasta

Pesto with Green Bell Peppers

Garden Tomato Sauce

Apple Beet Puree

Tomato Salsa

Gazpacho

Tomato-Basil Soup

Winter Onion Soup

Butternut Squash Soup Base

Pumpkin Soup

Black Bean Soup

Lentil and Sausage Soup

Vegetarian Chili

Ratatouille

Oriental Pork Roll

Marinated Italian Pork

Broiled Flank Steaks Oriental

Baked Beans

Green and Gold Squash Casserole

Mashed Winter Squash

Sweet Potatoes and Carrots

Caramel Onions

Fresh Tomato Pudding

Colorful Freezer Slaw

Mushroom Stacks

Mediterranean Artichokes

Avocado Frozen Yogurt with Candied
Lime Zest Garnish

Laura's Banana Bread

Pineapple Sherbet

Frozen Fruit Salad

Apple Crumb Pie

Nectarine Cobbler with Pecan Crunch Topping

Herbed Water Tonic

Croustade Appetizer Cups

With very little labor you can make these little bread cups and produce them from the freezer as an elegant appetizer whenever company stops in to visit. Once you see how easy they are you'll make sure to keep your freezer stocked.

2 tablespoons butter or margarine

24 slices fresh white bread, sliced thinly

1. Preheat oven to 400°F.

2. Use your clean fingers or a paper towel to coat the inside of minimuffin tins of 12 cups each with butter.

3. Cut each bread slice in a 3-inch round; reserve outside crusts for another use (I make toast points for serving appetizer spreads).

4. Push bread rounds into muffin tins similar to pie crust in a pie plate.

5. Toast croustades in preheated oven about 10 minutes, or until browned.

6. Cool, pack into a plastic freezer bag, label, and freeze.

YIELD: 24 MUSHROOM CROUSTADES (ONE FILLED CROUSTADE PER SERVING)

NUTRITION PER SERVING

Calories	79	Total fat	3g
% from fat	37	Saturated	2g
Carbohydrates	10g	Cholesterol	7mg
Fiber	<1g	Sodium	167mg

FILLING FOR CROUSTADES: MUSHROOM
Yield: 2 cups filling (about thirty-two 1-tablespoon servings)

½ pound fresh mushrooms, finely chopped

3 tablespoons chopped green onions, with tops

4 tablespoons butter or margarine

2 tablespoons flour

1 cup whole milk

½ teaspoon salt

⅛ teaspoon cayenne pepper

1 tablespoon finely chopped fresh parsley

½ teaspoon lemon juice (bottled may be used)

2 tablespoons grated Parmesan cheese

1. Sauté the mushrooms and green onions in the butter in a heavy skillet. Do not let them brown, but make sure all moisture from the mushrooms has evaporated.

2. Sprinkle the flour over the mushrooms and stir constantly to mix. Remove from heat and add the milk and salt. Mix well.

3. Return to heat and cook, stirring constantly, until sauce thickens. Season with pepper, parsley, and lemon juice. Cool.

4. Mushroom filling may be frozen at this point or refrigerated, covered, until ready to use, up to 4 days later.

FILLING FOR CROUSTADES: QUICK WHITE SAUCE
Yield: 2 cups filling (about thirty-two 1-tablespoon servings)

6 tablespoons butter or margarine

8 tablespoons flour

2 cups whole milk

2 tablespoons grated Parmesan cheese

1. Melt butter in heavy 1-quart saucepan. Add flour and stir evenly and carefully.

2. Remove from heat, and add the milk, stirring constantly.

3. Return to heat. Stir carefully to keep from burning and continue until mixture is thickened.

TO ASSEMBLE

Preheat oven to 350°F. Remove croustades from the freezer and insert back into the muffin tins. Let them thaw slightly. Fill each bread cup with filling and top with Parmesan cheese.

Bake about 10 minutes, until filling is hot and cheese is golden brown. Serve immediately.

Filling Suggestions

Croustades are a great invention — as long as the filling is a thick, cream-type sauce. Custards or thin sauces will make your croustades soggy. Vary the Quick White Sauce with these options and enjoy!

Shrimp and cheese. Add 1 cup finely chopped shrimp and Swiss cheese to taste.

Cheese and ham. Add cayenne pepper, 1/2 cup ham bits, and 1/2 cup Swiss cheese.

Bacon and cheese. Add 4 slices sautéed bacon, finely chopped, and 1/4 cup Swiss cheese.

Spinach and bacon. Add sautéed bacon bits and chopped, cooked, squeezed, and drained frozen spinach to taste.

Note: Add a teaspoon of garlic or your favorite prepared mustard for added zip to any of the sauce suggestions.

YIELD: 24 CROUSTADES WITH QUICK WHITE SAUCE (ONE FILLED CROUSTADE PER SERVING)
NUTRITION PER SERVING

Calories	93	Total fat	4g
% from fat	40	Saturated	2g
Carbohydrates	12	Cholesterol	10mg
Fiber	1g	Sodium	143mg

Spiced Pear Butter

Biscuits, waffles, pancakes, and English muffins will never be the same again after you've tasted them spread with this Pear Butter.

5 ripe pears, peeled, cored, and chopped

2 tablespoons lemon juice

2 tablespoons honey

1 tablespoon cider vinegar

¼ teaspoon ground allspice

½ teaspoon ground cinnamon

1 tablespoon finely minced fresh gingerroot

¼ teaspoon ground nutmeg

1. Combine the pears, lemon juice, honey, vinegar, allspice, cinnamon, ginger, and nutmeg in a heavy 2-quart saucepan.

2. Cook over low heat, uncovered, 30 minutes, or until mixture is very soft and relatively thick. Stir occasionally and mash with a spoon.

3. Ladle into two clean, 1-cup freezer containers. Cool in refrigerator.

4. Label and freeze one; keep the other for immediate use.

5. To use frozen pear butter, thaw it in the refrigerator. Refrigerated, it will keep 10 days–2 weeks.

YIELD: 2 CUPS (SIXTEEN 1-OUNCE SERVINGS)
NUTRITION PER SERVING

Calories	37	Total fat	<1g
% from fat	4	Saturated	0g
Carbohydrates	10g	Cholesterol	0mg
Fiber	1g	Sodium	0mg

Eggplant Caviar

This flavorful recipe is perfect for entertaining. Serve it on toast points or melba toast.

1 large eggplant, halved lengthwise

1 tablespoon olive oil

1 medium red bell pepper, seeded and finely diced

1 small onion, minced

3 cloves garlic, minced

1 large tomato, diced

3 tablespoons fresh lemon juice

2 tablespoons minced chives

1 tablespoon fresh basil, minced

1. Preheat oven to 350°F.

2. Brush the eggplant well with 1 teaspoon of olive oil and bake the halves on a cookie sheet lightly coated with a vegetable cooking spray, cut side down, about 1 hour or until tender.

3. Cool and scoop out the meat, discarding the skin. Chop.

4. Heat 2 teaspoons of olive oil in a heavy skillet, and sauté the red pepper, onion, and garlic until they are soft, about 5 minutes.

5. Stir in the eggplant, tomato, lemon juice, chives, and basil. Cook another minute to heat the mixture through and to dry up some of the tomato juices.

6. Put in 1-quart container, label, and freeze up to 1 month. This recipe may also be refrigerated and consumed the next day.

7. To use frozen eggplant caviar, thaw in the refrigerator and serve at room temperature.

YIELD: 4 CUPS (SIXTEEN 2-OUNCE SERVINGS)

NUTRITION PER SERVING

Calories	22	Total fat	1g
% from fat	36	Saturated	<1g
Carbohydrates	3g	Cholesterol	0mg
Fiber	1g	Sodium	2mg

Pungent Eggplant Chutney

This rich and elegant appetizer is perfect for a summer buffet or picnic.

¾ cup olive oil

2 medium eggplant, peeled and cubed

1 clove elephant garlic, chopped

1¼ cups finely chopped celery

2 medium onions, finely chopped

½ cup finely chopped green olives (with or without pimiento)

1 can (8 ounces) Italian tomato sauce (or 1 cup homemade)

¼ cup capers, drained

¼ cup white wine vinegar

1 tablespoon red wine vinegar

1 tablespoon sugar

Freshly ground black pepper

1. Heat the oil in a skillet. Add the eggplant cubes and garlic and cook over moderately high heat 8–10 minutes, until lightly browned. Stir often.

2. Using a slotted spoon, remove the eggplant from the oil and set aside.

3. Add the celery, onions, and olives to the oil, cooking until tender. Add the tomato sauce and simmer the mixture 5 minutes.

4. Add the capers, vinegars, sugar, and pepper. Return the eggplant to the pan; cook over low heat 5 more minutes.

5. Cool, ladle into freezer containers, and freeze.

6. To serve, defrost and serve cold or at room temperature with toast or crackers.

YIELD: 4 CUPS (SIXTEEN ¼-CUP SERVINGS)
NUTRITION PER SERVING

Calories	124	Total fat	11g
% from fat	75	Saturated	2g
Carbohydrates	7g	Cholesterol	0mg
Fiber	2g	Sodium	225mg

Pâté of Chicken Livers

This American version of Strasbourg pâté de foie gras is made with chicken liver and is a very successful appetizer for freezing.

1 medium onion, finely chopped (about ½ cup)

1 garlic clove, chopped

1 small tart apple, peeled, cored, and chopped

6 tablespoons butter

1 pound chicken livers

4 tablespoons cream or whole milk

1 stick (8 tablespoons) butter, softened

1½ teaspoons salt

1 teaspoon fresh lemon juice

¼ teaspoon black pepper

1. In a heavy 2-quart skillet, sauté the onion, garlic, and apple in 3 tablespoons butter until soft but not browned. Remove from skillet and reserve.

2. Sauté the chicken livers in 3 tablespoons butter about 10 minutes over medium heat. Livers can be pink in the center.

3. Pour the livers and butter from the skillet into a blender or food processor. Add cream and puree.

4. In a large mixing bowl, combine the two mixtures and let cool until barely warm.

5. Beat in the remaining butter and salt, juice, and pepper.

6. Pour the smooth mixture into three 8-ounce ceramic crocks.

7. Wrap, label, and freeze.

8. To use, thaw overnight in the refrigerator. Serve at room temperature with toast points or melba toast.

YIELD: 3 CUPS (TWENTY-FOUR ⅛-CUP SERVINGS)

NUTRITION PER SERVING

Calories	64	Total fat	5g
% from fat	65	Saturated	3g
Carbohydrates	2g	Cholesterol	94mg
Fiber	<1g	Sodium	183mg

Picnic Chicken Roll

· · · · · · · · · · · ·

Lean and delicious, try this American version of a French pâté at your next picnic.

2 pounds boned, skinned chicken breast, cubed

1½ teaspoons salt

1 tablespoon firmly packed brown sugar

2 tablespoons grated Parmesan cheese

3 tablespoons dried onion flakes

2 teaspoons dried oregano

2 teapoons dried basil

2 teaspoons dried marjoram

1. Finely grind chicken in a food processor or meat grinder.

2. Add the seasonings to the chicken and mix well.

3. Preheat oven to 225°F.

4. Divide the meat mixture in half on two 12- by 18-inch sheets of heavy aluminum foil. Shape chicken mixture into two logs, each about 8 inches long. Roll them up in the foil and secure the ends tightly. Prick foil logs with a fork several evenly spaced times to allow steam and juices to escape when cooking.

5. Bake in a 9-inch-square pan 3 hours or until logs are firm when pressed.

6. Peel off foil while meat is still warm and gently roll on several layers of paper towels to drain fat.

7. Wrap logs in freezer wrap and chill in refrigerator.

8. Label and freeze up to 3–4 weeks.

9. To use, thaw overnight in refrigerator. Slice very thin and serve cold.

· ·

YIELD: TWO 12-OUNCE LOGS (EIGHT 3-OUNCE SERVINGS)
NUTRITION PER SERVING

Calories	156	Total fat	4g
% from fat	21	Saturated	1g
Carbohydrates	4g	Cholesterol	70mg
Fiber	<1g	Sodium	491mg

· ·

Rosemary Paste for Angel-Hair Pasta

*My friend Silvano, who lives in Tuscany, has a rosemary hedge 4 feet wide by
15 feet long. Imagine what could be done with all that rosemary!
This sauce is also wonderful over a grilled, butterflied leg of lamb.*

2 cloves garlic, peeled

1 tablespoon grated orange rind

2 tablespoons fresh rosemary leaves

2 tablespoons fresh oregano leaves

¼ cup chopped fresh parsley

1 cup chopped scallions, with green tops

¼ cup olive oil

2 teaspoons lemon juice

1. Combine the garlic, orange rind, and herbs in the bowl of a food processor. Pulse the machine to coarsely chop mixture. Scrape down the sides of the bowl and add the scallions, pulsing again to chop.

2. With the motor running add the oil in droplets until the mixture has formed a paste.

3. Add the lemon juice and mix well, scraping the bowl.

4. Pour into a ½-cup freezer container, leaving ½ inch headspace. Label and freeze.

5. To serve, thaw the paste in the refrigerator, bring to room temperature, and pour it over ½ pound cooked angel-hair pasta. Do not heat the paste, as it might cause the oil to separate. The heated, cooked pasta is just right for combining with the room-temperature paste.

YIELD: 1½ CUPS (SIX ¼-CUP SERVINGS)

NUTRITION PER SERVING

Calories	90	Total fat	9g
% from fat	88	Saturated	1g
Carbohydrates	2g	Cholesterol	0mg
Fiber	<1g	Sodium	4mg

Pesto with Green Bell Peppers

. . . .

The garnish for this recipe can be prepared and frozen separately,
or you can simply add the garnish when you serve.

2 green bell peppers, seeded and coarsely chopped

1 cup fresh basil

4 cloves garlic, chopped

½ cup grated Parmesan cheese

¼ cup olive oil

⅔ cup salted and roasted pumpkin seeds

1. Steam blanch the green peppers over boiling water 3 minutes. Drain, then transfer to the bowl of a food processor.

2. Add the basil, garlic, cheese, and oil and process until smooth.

3. Freeze in two portions of 3–4 servings each for ease of use.

4. To use, thaw overnight in refrigerator.

5. Spoon pesto over hot, cooked pasta and top each serving with pumpkin seeds.

. . . .

YIELD: 2 CUPS (EIGHT ¼-CUP SERVINGS)

NUTRITION PER SERVING

Calories	119	Total fat	10g
% from fat	72	Saturated	2g
Carbohydrates	5g	Cholesterol	5mg
Fiber	3g	Sodium	119mg

. . . .

Garden Tomato Sauce

· · · · · · · · · · · ·

Try this as an alternative to canning those abundant tomatoes. Serve with pasta, chicken, or veal.

2 dozen Italian tomatoes, or 12 cups chopped

1 tablespoon olive oil

1 medium onion, chopped

2 cloves garlic, crushed

2 tablespoons chopped green bell pepper

2 tablespoons chopped carrot

2 tablespoons chopped celery

2 tablespoons chopped fresh parsley

1 teaspoon chopped fresh oregano

1. Wash, core, and coarsely chop the tomatoes.

2. Puree in the bowl of a food processor.

3. Heat the olive oil in a heavy saucepan or an ovenproof, flameproof casserole and sauté the onions until they are soft, about 5 minutes.

4. Add the garlic, pepper, carrot, celery, and herbs.

5. Add the tomato puree to the mixture and simmer it, uncovered, about 2 hours. Be careful not to let it burn. Stir the sauce occasionally as it thickens. (This process can also be completed in an ovenproof, flameproof casserole at 350°F uncovered.)

6. Cool slightly and pour the sauce into 1-cup freezer containers, leaving ½ inch headspace. Label them, and freeze.

7. To use, thaw in the refrigerator.

· ·

YIELD: 4½ PINTS (EIGHTEEN ½-CUP SERVINGS)

NUTRITION PER SERVING

Calories	14	Total fat	1g
% from fat	48	Saturated	<1g
Carbohydrates	2g	Cholesterol	0mg
Fiber	<1g	Sodium	3mg

· ·

Apple Beet Puree

*The best of autumn combined in one dish — and it tastes great
as a side dish with pork.*

5 medium beets, scrubbed, with tops removed

2 tablespoons plus ½ teaspoon salt

2 onions, minced

1 stick (8 tablespoons) butter

4 tart apples, peeled, cored, and sliced

1 tablespoon sugar

¼ cup red wine vinegar

1. In a saucepan, add the beets and 2 tablespoons salt, and cover with water. Cover with lid and simmer 30–40 minutes, or until they are fork-tender.

2. Drain and cool the beets, then remove their skins and roots. Set aside.

3. Sauté the onions in butter over low heat in a covered saucepan about 20 minutes, or until they are soft.

4. Add the apples to the pan and toss them in the butter mixture. Add the sugar, ½ teaspoon salt, and vinegar.

5. Uncover and continue to cook on medium heat for 15 minutes, until the onions and apples are very tender.

6. Let cool slightly and transfer the apple mixture and beets to the bowl of a food processor. Process until smooth.

7. Cool, chill, and freeze the puree in a 1-quart freezer container.

8. To serve, thaw overnight in the refrigerator. Serve chilled.

YIELD: 3 CUPS (SIX ½-CUP SERVINGS)
NUTRITION PER SERVING

Calories	122	Total fat	2g
% from fat	15	Saturated	1g
Carbohydrates	25g	Cholesterol	5mg
Fiber	5g	Sodium	2,397mg

Tomato Salsa

*This salsa is not just for chips; try it over scrambled eggs. Lovers of spicy salsa should
add a dash of bottled hot sauce when serving.*

2 tablespoons olive oil

1 medium onion, finely chopped

1½ stalks celery, minced

2 tablespoons serrano peppers, seeded
and chopped (wear rubber gloves)

1 clove garlic

4 medium tomatoes, seeded and
quartered

2 tablespoons lime juice

1 teaspoon mild honey

1 teaspoon chopped fresh basil
(½ teaspoon dried)

3 tablespoons chopped cilantro

¼ teaspoon ground cumin

¼ teaspoon chili powder

1. Heat the oil in a heavy skillet. Add the onions, celery, peppers, and garlic.

2. Sauté about 5 minutes or until soft. Add the tomatoes, lime juice, honey, basil, cilantro, cumin, and chili powder. Bring mixture to a boil, cover, and reduce heat. Simmer 15 minutes. (Fish out the tomato skins as mixture cools.)

3. Ladle into two 1-cup freezer containers, and let cool. Cover and chill overnight in the refrigerator. Label the containers, and freeze.

4. To use, thaw in the refrigerator. The sauce will be thin but delicious.

YIELD: 2 CUPS (FOUR ½-CUP SERVINGS)
NUTRITION PER SERVING

Calories	119	Total fat	7g
% from fat	51	Saturated	1g
Carbohydrates	14g	Cholesterol	0mg
Fiber	3g	Sodium	30mg

Gazpacho

Guests always ask for this recipe and can't believe it came from the freezer.
Serve it in teacups with saucer as a buffet selection or in mugs
on the patio if bowls aren't available.

6 medium tomatoes, peeled, cored, and chopped

2 medium cucumbers, peeled, seeded, and chopped

1 large onion, chopped

5 cups vegetable juice, or 40 ounces canned

1 large green bell pepper, seeded and chopped

1 stalk celery, chopped

1 tablespoon fresh dill, chopped

1 clove garlic, minced

1 teaspoon salt

¼ teaspoon coarsely ground black pepper

½ teaspoon hot pepper sauce

⅓ cup red wine vinegar

2 tablespoons olive oil

1. Combine all ingredients and toss together until vegetables are evenly coated with oil, vinegar, and herbs.

2. Pour into two 1½-quart freezer containers. Seal, label well, and freeze.

3. To serve, thaw in the refrigerator overnight and store chilled. It will keep 3 days thawed in the refrigerator.

YIELD: 2½ QUARTS (TEN 1-CUP SERVINGS)
NUTRITION PER SERVING

Calories	93	Total fat	3g
% from fat	27	Saturated	<1g
Carbohydrates	16g	Cholesterol	0mg
Fiber	3g	Sodium	668mg

Tomato-Basil Soup

· · · · · · · · · · · ·

*Tomatoes and basil are natural companions in the kitchen. Fresh from the garden,
they make this soup more than an introduction to a meal.*

1 stick (8 tablespoons) butter

6 medium onions, thinly sliced (about
3 cups)

2 cloves garlic, minced

2 quarts (8 cups) chicken stock

3 pounds plum tomatoes, chopped

1 tablespoon lime juice

Pinch of sugar

1 small orange, zest only

¾ cup chopped fresh basil leaves

1. In a heavy saucepan, melt the butter over low heat. Add the onions, cover, and cook until soft, about 15 minutes. Add garlic and cook another 2–3 minutes.

2. Add stock, tomatoes, lime juice, and sugar. Bring to a boil, reduce heat, and simmer, covered, 15 minutes.

3. Add orange zest and basil.

4. Transfer the soup to the bowl of a food processor and puree.

5. Cool. Ladle into two 10-cup freezer containers. Allow 1 inch headspace.

6. Chill in the refrigerator, label, and freeze.

7. To use, thaw in the refrigerator overnight. Serve cold or hot.

· ·

YIELD: 5 QUARTS (TWENTY 1-CUP SERVINGS)
NUTRITION PER SERVING

Calories	46	Total fat	1g
% from fat	19	Saturated	<1g
Carbohydrates	8g	Cholesterol	2mg
Fiber	2g	Sodium	872 mg

· ·

Winter Onion Soup

A plain yellow onion develops a deep, rich flavor in the long and slow cooking. After initial organization, the soup pot can simmer away almost unattended.

3 tablespoons butter

1 tablespoon vegetable oil

1½ pounds (about 5 cups) yellow onions, peeled and sliced thinly

¼ teaspoon sugar

1 teaspoon salt

3 tablespoons flour

2 quarts beef broth

1 bay leaf

Salt and freshly ground black pepper

1½ cups prepared garlic croutons

2 cups grated Swiss cheese

1. Melt butter with oil in a heavy 4-quart saucepan.

2. Add the onions, cover, and cook slowly over low heat until onions are soft.

3. Raise the heat to medium high, uncover, and stir in the sugar and salt. This step requires some watching to avoid burning the contents. Continue cooking 20–40 minutes, stirring frequently. The onions will caramelize, turning a deep, rich brown, thanks to the sugar. They will also develop a rich, nutty flavor, thanks to the slow cooking.

4. Sprinkle the flour over the onion mixture and stir 2–3 minutes, then remove it from the heat.

5. Pour and stir in the broth and bay leaf. Partially cover and simmer 45 minutes. Season to taste.

6. Allow to cool, then pour the soup into an 8-cup freezer container, allowing ½ inch headspace.

7. Chill, label, and freeze.

8. To use, thaw in the refrigerator and then heat in microwave until piping hot.

9. Prepare six soup bowls, each with ¼ cup croutons and ⅓ cup Swiss cheese.

10. Gently pour hot soup over cheese and croutons and serve.

YIELD: 6 CUPS (SIX 1-CUP SERVINGS)

NUTRITION PER SERVING

Calories	366	Total fat	24g
% from fat	59	Saturated	12g
Carbohydrates	22g	Cholesterol	54mg
Fiber	3g	Sodium	2,725mg

Butternut Squash Soup Base

This soup works well with apple juice or milk. Either way, it will make an October brunch very special.

2 large butternut squash (about 2 pounds each)

2 tablespoons olive oil

2 large carrots, peeled and sliced

2 medium onions, chopped

1 clove garlic, chopped

1 tablespoon minced fresh ginger

2 teaspoons curry powder

¼ teaspoon ground cinnamon

⅛ teaspoon ground nutmeg

3 cups apple juice or 3 cups milk

1. Preheat oven to 350°F. Bake the whole squash on a baking sheet about 45 minutes. Remove from oven and cool.

2. Open the squash and discard the seeds. Spoon out the meat and place it in the bowl of a food processor. (You can speed up this process by cubing and seeding the raw squash; boiling it 15 minutes; and then slipping off the skins before placing it in the food processor.)

3. Heat the oil in a heavy saucepan. Sauté the carrots, onions, and garlic until they are soft, about 5 minutes. Add the ginger, curry, cinnamon, and nutmeg and continue cooking until spices are evenly distributed.

4. Add this mixture to the squash in the food processor. Add 1 cup of apple juice or milk and process until smooth.

5. Ladle the soup into two 2-pint containers. Cool, chill, and freeze.

6. To use, thaw the soup overnight in the refrigerator, then add 1 cup apple juice or milk to each container.

YIELD: 4 PINTS (EIGHT 1-CUP SERVINGS)
NUTRITION PER SERVING

Calories	162	Total fat	4g
% from fat	20	Saturated	<1g
Carbohydrates	33g	Cholesterol	0mg
Fiber	4g	Sodium	16mg

Pumpkin Soup

This recipe is so thick and creamy that guests will think it is high in calories, but instead of rich, fat cream, the creamy texture is achieved by adding pureed pumpkin.

2 pounds pumpkin, cut into chunks

3 large baking potatoes, cut into chunks

1 large onion, coarsely chopped

3 cups chicken stock

2 cups water

½ teaspoon dried rosemary

¼ teaspoon ground white pepper

¼ teaspoon ground nutmeg

½ teaspoon salt

½ cup grated Parmesan cheese

1. In a heavy, 2-quart saucepan combine the pumpkin, potatoes, onion, stock, water, and rosemary. Cover and simmer about 30 minutes or until pumpkin is tender.

2. When cooled, peel skin away from pumpkin pieces. Return pumpkin to broth. Puree mixture in batches in a blender or food processor. Add remaining spices and cheese. Adjust the seasonings.

3. Ladle into a 10-cup freezer container, label, and freeze up to 2 months.

4. To serve, thaw in the refrigerator. Heat and serve with additional Parmesan cheese, if desired.

YIELD: 10 CUPS (TEN 1-CUP SERVINGS)
NUTRITION PER SERVING

Calories	79	Total fat	2g
% from fat	20	Saturated	1g
Carbohydrates	12g	Cholesterol	4mg
Fiber	2g	Sodium	849mg

Black Bean Soup

Serve it with a salad and bread, and this rich bean soup
becomes a complete, hearty meal.

1 cup dried black beans, rinsed and picked over

4 cups water

3 bay leaves

2 cloves garlic, minced

2 large onions, chopped

1 large green bell pepper, seeded and chopped

⅛ cup red wine vinegar

⅛ cup olive oil

1. Soak dried beans overnight in large pot of water.

2. Discard soaking water and cover beans with fresh water. Add bay leaves, garlic, onions, and pepper, and cook until beans are tender, about 1–1½ hours.

3. Remove 1 cup of beans and broth and puree in a blender or food processer. Return to pot to thicken liquid.

4. Cool, chill, and freeze in a 6-cup freezer container.

5. To serve, thaw in the refrigerator overnight.

6. Add vinegar and olive oil; mix well. Heat until bubbly. Garnish with dollop of low-fat sour cream and serve.

YIELD: 5 CUPS (FIVE 1-CUP SERVINGS)
NUTRITION PER SERVING

Calories	212	Total fat	6g
% from fat	25	Saturated	<1g
Carbohydrates	32g	Cholesterol	0mg
Fiber	7g	Sodium	10mg

Lentil and Sausage Soup

My friend Lane, who is an excellent cook, gave this recipe to me.
It has been a family favorite ever since. I use green lentils for this recipe.
If you use brown lentils, reduce the cooking time as noted.

2 cups lentils, rinsed, and picked over

7 cups water

1½ teaspoons fresh thyme, minced

½ teaspoon salt

½ teaspoon freshly ground black pepper

1 bay leaf

⅛ teaspoon dried rosemary

⅛ teaspoon dried tarragon

1 pound bulk sausage

1 pound hot Italian sausage, removed from casings

2 carrots, sliced

2 stalks celery, sliced

2 medium onions, sliced

Chopped fresh plum tomatoes, about 2 cups

1 package (1.8 ounces) oxtail soup mix, or 4 tablespoons beef bouillon granules

½ cup dried angel-hair pasta, broken in 2-inch pieces

1. In a 3-quart kettle cover lentils with water, add seasonings, and simmer 30–40 minutes. If you are using brown lentils, simmer 20 minutes.

2. Sauté sausage in a large skillet. Remove from skillet with a slotted spoon and drain on a paper towel.

3. Sauté carrots, celery, and onions in sausage skillet.

4. Add tomatoes, sautéed vegetables, and sausage to lentil mixture.

5. Add soup mix and simmer 1 hour, stirring frequently. Add pasta the last 10 minutes.

6. Cool. Ladle into one 10-cup freezer container, or into individual serving-size freezer containers according to your family's needs.

7. Label and freeze up to 2 months.

YIELD: 10 CUPS (EIGHT 1¼-CUP SERVINGS)
NUTRITION PER SERVING

Calories	676	Total fat	42g
% from fat	56	Saturated	15g
Carbohydrates	44g	Cholesterol	83mg
Fiber	17g	Sodium	1,343mg

Vegetarian Chili

Serve this hearty soup with or without rice for a filling, satisfying meal.

1 cup dried brown lentils, rinsed and picked over

6 cups water

2 medium onions, chopped

2 tablespoons vegetable oil

2 inches fresh gingerroot, peeled and minced

1 serrano chile pepper, seeded and chopped (wear rubber gloves)

1 tablespoon coriander

1 tablespoon curry powder

1 teaspoon chili powder

1. Simmer the lentils and water in a heavy saucepan until they're tender, about 20 minutes.

2. Sauté the onions in oil until soft, about 10 minutes.

3. Add ginger, chile pepper, and seasonings to onions and cook 5 minutes, stirring to mix flavors.

4. Add onions to lentils. Cook, covered, about 15 minutes.

5. Cool. Ladle chili into freezer containers. Chill, label, and freeze.

6. To serve, thaw in the refrigerator overnight. Heat in microwave or on stove top.

YIELD: 8 CUPS (FOUR 2-CUP SERVINGS)
NUTRITION PER SERVING

Calories	264	Total fat	8g
% from fat	25	Saturated	<1g
Carbohydrates	36g	Cholesterol	0mg
Fiber	17g	Sodium	26mg

Ratatouille

An old favorite adapts to the freezer. Serve this with eggs, over pasta, or with lamb or beef. Whatever the time of year, your kitchen will be perfumed with the essence of the summer's garden.

2 yellow onions, sliced

4 small zucchini, sliced

3 cloves garlic, minced

2 green bell peppers, seeded and chopped

6 tablespoons olive oil

3 medium tomatoes, peeled, seeded, and chopped

3 small eggplant, cubed

½ teaspoon salt

1 tablespoon chopped fresh basil

2 tablespoons chopped fresh parsley

1 teaspoon dried oregano

1. In a heavy 2-quart skillet, sauté the onions, zucchini, garlic, and peppers in 4 tablespoons oil until soft. Add the tomatoes and heat thoroughly to help evaporate liquid.

2. Meanwhile "sweat" the eggplant by tossing the eggplant cubes with the salt in a large bowl. Let rest 30 minutes. Drain the eggplant well.

3. Sauté the eggplant in remaining 2 tablespoons oil.

4. Add eggplant to the onion mixture and stir well.

5. Add fresh herbs and stir to distribute evenly. Cool.

6. Pour into a 3-quart casserole or divide into two portions and store in plastic freezer bag. Chill, label, and freeze.

YIELD: 7½ CUPS (FIFTEEN ½-CUP SERVINGS)

NUTRITION PER SERVING

Calories	87	Total fat	6g
% from fat	55	Saturated	<1g
Carbohydrates	9g	Cholesterol	0mg
Fiber	3g	Sodium	78mg

Oriental Pork Roll

· · · · · · · · · · · ·

*Rich in flavor, but low in calories, this homemade sausage roll will be a
winner at your next party or picnic.*

2 pounds pork tenderloin, trimmed
and cubed

½ teaspoon salt

4 teaspoons firmly packed brown sugar

1 tablespoon soy sauce

2 teaspoons crushed, dried, hot chile
peppers

1½ teaspoons ground ginger

½ teaspoon garlic powder

1. Preheat oven to 225°F.

2. Finely grind meat in a food processor.

3. Add remaining ingredients to processor
bowl and mix well.

4. Divide meat mixture in two and place
each on its own 12- by 18-inch sheet of
heavy-duty aluminum foil.

5. Roll each meat mixture into a log
about 8 inches long. Wrap each tightly
in its foil blanket, securing the ends.
Use a fork to prick the foil, which will
allow steam and juices to escape as the
pork roll cooks.

6. Bake in a 9-inch-square pan 3 hours
or until logs seem firm when pressed.

7. When the logs are done but still warm,
peel off the foil and blot the meat on
several layers of paper towels to degrease.
Wrap logs in freezer wrap and chill.

8. Label and then freeze them up to
3–4 weeks.

9. To serve, thaw overnight in the
refrigerator. Slice very thin and serve cold
on crackers or melba toast. Add a dollop of
spicy mustard to each cracker.

· ·
**YIELD: TWO 16-OUNCE LOGS (THIRTY-TWO
1-OUNCE SERVINGS)**
NUTRITION PER SERVING

Calories	37	Total fat	1g
% from fat	25	Saturated	<1g
Carbohydrates	<1g	Cholesterol	18mg
Fiber	0g	Sodium	80mg

· ·

Marinated Italian Pork

· · · · · · · · · · ·

This dish is easy, delicious, and a perfectly presentable leftover.

1 medium onion, sliced

2 cloves garlic, chopped

¼ cup cider vinegar

3 tablespoons fresh rosemary
(1½ tablespoons dried)

2 tablespoons minced fresh sage leaves
(1 tablespoon dried)

1 tablespoon chopped fresh parsley

⅔ cup balsamic vinegar

Juice of ½ lemon

1 tablespoon whole peppercorns

½ cup plus 2 tablespoons olive oil

1½ pounds boneless pork tenderloin

½ teaspoon salt

½ teaspoon freshly ground black pepper

⅓ cup unsweetened apple juice

½ cup water

1. To prepare the marinade, simmer the onion, garlic, and cider vinegar 5 minutes in a heavy, nonreactive saucepan. Add the rosemary, sage, parsley, balsamic vinegar, lemon juice, peppercorns, and ½ cup olive oil. Stir and set aside to cool.

2. Preheat oven to 375°F. Pat the meat dry, rub it with 1 tablespoon of olive oil, and sprinkle with salt and pepper.

3. Brown meat in the remaining tablespoon of oil over medium-high heat in an ovenproof skillet. Turn the meat to be sure it browns on all sides.

4. Add the apple juice and water, then place the skillet in preheated oven for 25 minutes or until the meat is cooked internally to 160°F (check with a meat thermometer).

5. When cool, transfer the meat to a heavy-duty freezer bag, then pour in the marinade. Chill in the refrigerator 12 hours. At this point, it's ready to be served sliced and chilled, or at room temperature. Or label and freeze.

6. To serve, thaw overnight in the refrigerator, slice thinly, and serve chilled or at room temperature as a main course.

· ·

YIELD: 24 OUNCES (FOUR 6-OUNCE SERVINGS)
NUTRITION PER SERVING

Calories	542	Total fat	40g
% from fat	65	Saturated	7g
Carbohydrates	11g	Cholesterol	111mg
Fiber	<1g	Sodium	356mg

· ·

Broiled Flank Steaks Oriental

Wow your dinner guests with this easy, lean version of steak. Leftovers are wonderful for sandwiches or added to a stir fry.

2 pounds flank steak, scored with a knife

2 tablespoons vegetable oil

1½ teaspoons soy sauce

1 tablespoon red wine vinegar

1½ teaspoons Worcestershire sauce

2 tablespoons lemon juice

2 tablespoons water

⅛ teaspoon ground ginger

Sprinkle of garlic powder to taste

1. Tenderize the meat and put in a heavy-duty zip-seal plastic freezer bag.

2. Combine the remaining ingredients and pour over meat in bag.

3. Label, chill, and then freeze 3–4 weeks.

4. To serve, thaw in the refrigerator overnight. Remove the steak from the marinade and grill or broil 3 minutes on each side for rare. Slice on the diagonal and serve.

Tenderizing Meat

Meat mallets, used to tenderize meat, are usually made of hardwood and have one flat end and one textured end. Pounding the meat with a mallet breaks up meat's tough fibers. It also flattens and compacts the meat, making it easier to roll around stuffings.

Generally, use the textured side of the mallet on tougher cuts of beef, and the flat side on chicken and other tender cuts of meat. Lightly flour the mallet or spray it lightly with cooking spray to prevent sticking.

If your meat needs tenderizing and you do not have a mallet, try pounding the meat with the edge of a heavy saucer or even a large, heavy serving spoon. If you are pounding on a wooden surface, a heavy unopened can will also work.

YIELD: 32 OUNCES (EIGHT DINNER SERVINGS, 4 OUNCES EACH)

NUTRITION PER SERVING

Calories	263	Total fat	15g
% from fat	53	Saturated	5g
Carbohydrates	<1g	Cholesterol	58mg
Fiber	0g	Sodium	153mg

Baked Beans

• • • • • • • • • • • •

Adults and children love these beans.

3 pounds dried navy beans, rinsed and picked over

3 teaspoons dry mustard

2¼ cups dark molasses

3 tablespoons frozen orange juice concentrate

3 medium onions

16 whole cloves

1. In a large pot, cover dried beans with water and soak overnight.

2. Drain beans and cover with new water. Simmer, covered, in a 6-quart pot, until tender, 2–3 hours. (A 4-quart slow-cooker may be used 6–8 hours for this purpose.)

3. Preheat oven to 300°F.

4. For storing and serving convenience, divide the precooked beans into two 2-quart bean pots or slow-cookers.

5. Mix together the mustard, molasses, and orange juice. Add, in equal amounts, to each pot.

6. Cut each onion in half and stud each half with cloves. Include 3 onion halves in each pot.

7. Cover and bake 5–6 hours in pre-heated oven, being careful not to let beans dry out. Add water if necessary.

8. Cool bean pots. Chill, wrap the entire bean pots in freezer paper, label, and freeze, or pour baked beans into freezer bags to save space.

9. To use, thaw overnight in the refrigerator.

10. Heat in saucepan 20–30 minutes until hot, or, if stored in bean pots, bake in 350°F oven until heated throughout.

Note: In a pinch, canned, rinsed beans can be seasoned in this manner. Omit the freezing step.

• •

YIELD: 4 QUARTS TOTAL; 2 QUARTS EACH POT OR PLASTIC BAG (SIXTEEN 1-CUP SERVINGS)

NUTRITION PER SERVING

Calories	445	Total fat	3g
% from fat	5	Saturated	<1g
Carbohydrates	91g	Cholesterol	0mg
Fiber	24g	Sodium	72mg

• •

Green and Gold Squash Casserole

Capture the harvest in late summer when the zucchini and yellow squash are at their peak. I usually double this recipe to make one for dinner and one for the freezer. It disappears fast.

1 medium onion, chopped

2 tablespoons olive oil

2 medium zucchini (about 1 pound), coarsely grated

2 medium yellow summer squash (about 1 pound), coarsely grated

2 tablespoons fresh parsley, chopped

1½ teaspoons fresh oregano, chopped (or ½ teaspoon dried)

1¼ teaspoons ground black pepper

½ teaspoon salt

3 eggs, beaten (egg substitute may be used)

1 cup Saltine crumbs

1 cup grated cheddar cheese (use Swiss for a different flavor)

1. In a large skillet, sauté the onion in oil until soft.

2. Add the squash to the onion and sauté until much of the moisture disappears, about 15 minutes.

3. Remove from heat and stir in seasonings, eggs, and cracker crumbs. Blend well and place in a greased 9-inch casserole.

4. To prepare immediately, preheat oven to 325°F.

5. Top squash with grated cheese and bake in preheated oven 45 minutes.

6. To save for future use, omit the cheese, pour into a foil-lined 9-inch casserole, chill, then freeze. When squash is frozen solid, remove it from the dish, wrap, label, and store it in the freezer.

7. For use, remove wrap and thaw in a casserole dish. Top with cheese, and bake at 325°F for 30 minutes. Test for doneness with baking straw or toothpick, as you would a cake.

YIELD: 6 CUPS (SIX 1-CUP SERVINGS)
NUTRITION PER SERVING

Calories	344	Total fat	18g
% from fat	46	Saturated	6g
Carbohydrates	34g	Cholesterol	111mg
Fiber	3g	Sodium	838mg

Mashed Winter Squash

This dish will warm you all winter long.

2 medium winter squash (about 3–4 pounds each), scrubbed, or about 6 cups cooked pureed squash

FOR EACH CUP OF PUREE, ADD

1 tablespoon butter

1 teaspoon firmly packed brown sugar

¼ teaspoon salt

⅛ teaspoon ground ginger

Orange juice

1. Preheat oven to 375°F.

2. Oil and prick the squash skins and bake on a cookie sheet about 1 hour. Remove squash from oven when soft, split in half, and remove seeds.

3. Spoon out pulp into a large mixing bowl and mash.

4. Add the butter, brown sugar, salt, and ginger. Mix well, adding a little orange juice to thin the pulp if necessary to make the consistency of a thick puree.

5. Spoon squash into a freezer container, packing the pulp according to your family's needs.

6. To serve, thaw in the refrigerator overnight. Heat in oven or on top of stove and serve.

YIELD: 6 CUPS (SIX 1-CUP SERVINGS)
NUTRITION PER SERVING

Calories	129	Total fat	11g
% from fat	77	Saturated	7g
Carbohydrates	7g	Cholesterol	31mg
Fiber	<1g	Sodium	652mg

Sweet Potatoes and Carrots

Two fall vegetables team up to make a remarkable combination. Double this recipe so you can freeze one and have the other right away.

4 large sweet potatoes

1 pound carrots, peeled and sliced in ½-inch slices

2½ cups water

1 tablespoon sugar

4 tablespoons unsalted butter

½ cup no-fat sour cream

½ teaspoon ground nutmeg

1 tablespoon frozen orange juice concentrate

½ teaspoon orange rind, finely grated

Salt and freshly ground black pepper

1. Preheat oven to 350°F.

2. Scrub sweet potatoes and bake until done, about 1 hour. The sweet potatoes can be cooked the day before and refrigerated until ready to use.

3. In a large saucepan, add carrots, water, sugar, and 2 tablespoons butter. Cover and simmer until they're soft. Remove cover and boil until the water has evaporated. Check after 15 minutes. Shake the pan to move the sizzling carrots around in the butter.

4. Spoon out the sweet potato flesh and combine with the carrots in the bowl of a food processor.

5. Add sour cream, nutmeg, orange juice concentrate, orange rind, and remaining butter to food processor bowl and process until smooth. Adjust seasonings. Pour into a foil-lined casserole dish and freeze it solid.

6. Remove frozen vegetables from the dish, wrap, label, and replace in freezer.

7. When you're ready to use, remove the foil, return the sweet potato–carrot mixture to the original dish, and thaw the preparation in the refrigerator overnight.

8. Bake at 350°F until very hot (about 30 minutes).

YIELD: 6 CUPS (SIX 1-CUP SERVINGS)
NUTRITION PER SERVING

Calories	187	Total fat	9g
% from fat	41	Saturated	5g
Carbohydrates	26g	Cholesterol	23mg
Fiber	4g	Sodium	41mg

Caramel Onions

This exceptional way to prepare onions will complement almost all meat dishes.

1 cup balsamic vinegar

½ cup olive oil

5 teaspoons sugar

6 large mild onions, peeled

1. Preheat oven to 425°F, and grease a covered casserole dish.

2. Mix together the vinegar, olive oil, and sugar.

3. Drizzle the mixture over the onions in the casserole dish. Cover and bake 1 hour.

4. Remove the cover and move the casserole to the bottom rack of the oven to bake 45 minutes longer. Check the oven often to make sure sauce does not burn. The sauce will thicken as it turns a rich brown. Roll the onions in the thickening sauce to coat them well.

5. After cooking, cool the onions in the refrigerator, then place them in a clean freezer container, label, and freeze. Easy!

6. To use, thaw overnight in the refrigerator. Transfer onions and sauce to an uncovered casserole dish and bake in 350°F oven 20 minutes or until heated through.

YIELD: 6 ONIONS (SIX SERVINGS)
NUTRITION PER SERVING

Calories	235	Total fat	18g
% from fat	67	Saturated	3g
Carbohydrates	19g	Cholesterol	0mg
Fiber	3g	Sodium	5mg

Fresh Tomato Pudding

This freezes extremely well — so well that it goes into my freezer in August for Thanksgiving dinner. A great vegetable side dish, Tomato Pudding goes well with poultry or pork as well as turkey. This version is adapted from The Joy of Cooking.

14 very ripe medium tomatoes

1 cup fresh white bread crumbs

¼ teaspoon salt

5 tablespoons firmly packed light brown sugar

2 teaspoons chopped fresh basil

1 teaspoon chopped fresh chives

1 teaspoon chopped fresh parsley

¼ cup melted butter or margarine

1. Blanch tomatoes by dropping them in boiling water for 1 minute. Remove skins and seeds, and puree using a blender or food processor.

2. Make bread crumbs in a blender or food processor and pour the crumbs into a foil-lined 9-inch baking dish prepared with vegetable cooking spray.

3. In a heavy, nonreactive saucepan, heat the tomato puree until it boils. Add salt, sugar, and herbs, and mix well. Boil gently 3 minutes.

4. Pour melted butter over crumbs in foil-lined baking dish.

5. Pour tomato mixture over all and mix well.

6. Cool. Cover. Chill and freeze.

7. When pudding is frozen, remove it from the dish; wrap, label, and return to freezer.

8. When ready to thaw, return the casserole to its dish, removing foil.

9. Place the dish on a cookie sheet on the bottom oven rack, cover loosely with foil, and bake 2½–3 hours in a 325°F oven until it cooks down to pudding consistency. Uncover during the last hour of cooking.

YIELD: 5 CUPS (TEN ½-CUP SERVINGS)
NUTRITION PER SERVING

Calories	150	Total fat	6g
% from fat	33	Saturated	3g
Carbohydrates	24g	Cholesterol	12mg
Fiber	3g	Sodium	213mg

Colorful Freezer Slaw

This recipe swells when shredded and then shrinks when dressed. Unique and delicious, it can be enriched by adding 3 tablespoons of olive oil.

1 pound red cabbage, shredded

1 pound green cabbage, shredded

1 large green bell pepper, seeded and grated

3 large carrots, washed and grated

1 medium onion, chopped

1 teaspoon salt

1 cup sugar (or less if desired)

1 teaspoon dry mustard

½ cup water

1 cup cider vinegar

1 teaspoon celery seed

1. Combine vegetables in a crockery bowl and sprinkle salt over them. Let stand about 1 hour, then drain off the liquid that forms.

2. Combine the remaining ingredients in a heavy nonreactive saucepan and boil 3 minutes. Let the dressing cool before you pour it over the cabbage.

3. Let the prepared slaw stand 5 minutes. Ladle it into freezer containers.

4. Seal and label. Chill. Freeze.

5. To use, thaw in the refrigerator overnight. Serve chilled.

YIELD: 5 PINTS (TWENTY ½-CUP SERVINGS)
NUTRITION PER SERVING

Calories	57	Total fat	<1g
% from fat	2	Saturated	0g
Carbohydrates	14g	Cholesterol	0mg
Fiber	1g	Sodium	116mg

Mushroom Stacks

Use this scrumptious concoction for an elegant first course or a complimentary side dish for a buffet with beef or veal.

2 tablespoons olive oil

6 portobello mushrooms, cleaned and stems removed

1 small eggplant, sliced 1 inch thick (6 slices)

12 tablespoons tomato sauce, for pasta

2 tablespoons basil pesto

6 slices roasted red bell pepper

⅛ teaspoon garlic powder

¼ cup grated Parmesan cheese

1. Heat 1 tablespoon olive oil in a skillet. Sauté the mushrooms until they are soft and all moisture is dried up.

2. In a large skillet, sauté 6 eggplant "circles" in 1 tablespoon olive oil until soft. Drain on paper towels.

3. On a lightly greased baking sheet, construct 6 stacks of vegetables, layering eggplant, 2 tablespoons tomato sauce, mushrooms, pesto, and red pepper slices.

4. Sprinkle each stack with garlic powder and then cheese.

5. Freeze uncovered on a tray until solid, about 4 hours.

6. When frozen, wrap in freezer wrap, label, and return to freezer. Stacks will keep in the freezer up to 6 weeks.

7. To use, thaw overnight in the refrigerator. Transfer stacks to a greased baking sheet and heat in a 400°F oven 20 minutes until hot and cheese has melted.

Fresh Frozen Shiitake Mushrooms

Trim, stem, and wipe fresh mushrooms clean with a damp cloth — slice in half. Place slices on a baking sheet and place uncovered in the freezer. When frozen solid, store in an airtight freezer bag. Use within 2 months as you would fresh mushrooms in sauces and soups.

Buy mushrooms in spring and fall when plentiful and enjoy a fresh-tasting supply months later.

YIELD: 3 CUPS, 6 STACKS (SIX ½-CUP SERVINGS)
NUTRITION PER SERVING

Calories	128	Total fat	8g
% from fat	56	Saturated	2g
Carbohydrates	11g	Cholesterol	5mg
Fiber	3g	Sodium	301mg

Mediterranean Artichokes

* * * * * * * * * * * *

This presentation of intense flavors makes a savory low-calorie luncheon or side dish.

4 large artichokes, thorns, choke, and pith stem removed

1 lemon, sliced, with seeds removed

4 tablespoons plus 1 teaspoon olive oil

2 cups eggplant, peeled and cubed

1 cup chopped zucchini squash

1 cup chopped onion

2 cloves garlic, chopped

1 cup chopped tomatoes

6 mushrooms, cleaned and chopped

½ teaspoon chopped fresh thyme

½ teaspoon chopped fresh basil

2 tablespoons chopped fresh parsley

½ teaspoon salt

Freshly ground black pepper

1 tablespoon capers

4 black olives, sliced

½ cup crumbled feta cheese

1. In a 4-quart pot, cover the artichokes with water. Add lemon, cover, and boil 20–30 minutes or until tender. This can be done up to 2 days ahead.

2. In 4 tablespoons oil, sauté the eggplant, squash, onion, and garlic in a heavy skillet until tender, about 4–5 minutes. Add the tomatoes and continue to heat 2–3 minutes. Add the mushrooms and cook until vegetable moisture disappears. The mixture will be thick. You can prepare the recipe to this point 1–2 days ahead and refrigerate or freeze in clean containers until you're ready to continue.

3. If you freeze the mixture, thaw it in the refrigerator. Reheat the artichokes by wrapping them in plastic wrap and reheating in the microwave oven at medium. Check at 30-second intervals until hot but not overcooked.

4. Add all other ingredients except the feta cheese to the mushroom mixture.

5. Fill the warm artichokes by gently spreading the leaves apart and spooning in vegetable mixture. Pour remaining filling over the top of each artichoke.

6. Top each with cheese. Heat in a 325°F oven 10–15 minutes, or until they are warmed throughout.

* *

YIELD: 4 STUFFED ARTICHOKES (FOUR SERVINGS)
NUTRITION PER SERVING

Calories	288	Total fat	19g
% from fat	53	Saturated	4g
Carbohydrates	29g	Cholesterol	13mg
Fiber	10g	Sodium	614mg

* *

Avocado Frozen Yogurt
with Candied Lime Zest Garnish

- - - - - - - - - - - -

*Light and refreshing, this recipe may make your guests wonder
what this surprising flavor actually is.*

2 ripe avocados

⅔ cup lime juice

½ cup sugar

1 quart nonfat vanilla frozen yogurt

1. Remove skin and pit from each avocado.

2. Blend the flesh of the avocado, the lime juice, and sugar in a blender or food processor.

3. In a medium mixing bowl, add the avocado and the yogurt and blend.

4. Pour into an 8-inch-square pan. Cover, chill, and freeze.

5. To serve, remove the pan from freezer and use an ice cream scoop to fill bowls. Garnish with Candied Lime Zest Garnish.

CANDIED LIME ZEST GARNISH

¼ cup thinly sliced lime rind strips

¼ cup water

¼ cup sugar

1. In a small, heavy saucepan, cook lime strips in boiling water 5 minutes. Drain well.

2. Make a syrup of sugar and water, boiling over medium heat. Add lime strips and simmer 2 minutes. Cool, drain, then chill candied lime strips.

YIELD: 48 OUNCES (SIX 8-OUNCE SERVINGS)
NUTRITION PER SERVING

Calories	339	Total fat	13g
% from fat	33	Saturated	5g
Carbohydrates	55g	Cholesterol	2mg
Fiber	2g	Sodium	90mg

Laura's Banana Bread

The best banana bread ever, this recipe freezes beautifully.

2 cups sugar

1 cup softened butter, margarine, or shortening

1 teaspoon vanilla

4 eggs

6 ripe bananas, mashed

2½ cups flour

½ teaspoon salt

2 teaspoons baking powder

½ teaspoon baking soda

1. Cream together sugar, butter, and vanilla until fluffy.

2. Add eggs one at a time and beat well after each addition.

3. Stir in bananas gradually.

4. Sift together dry ingredients. Add to banana mixture, carefully folding in. Do not overmix.

5. Preheat oven to 350°F.

6. Lightly grease two loaf pans.

7. Pour batter into pans and bake in preheated oven for 45–60 minutes.

8. Let cool 10 minutes, then remove from pans to cooling rack.

9. When cool, wrap, label, and freeze.

Note: Overripe bananas can be peeled, wrapped in a freezer bag, and frozen until needed to make this bread. When thawed they will be soft and ready for the batter without much mashing at all. Don't be put off because they have turned dark. They will work beautifully for this bread. This is a good way to save that last banana in the bunch that is so ripe no one wants to eat it.

YIELD: 2 LOAVES (TWENTY-FOUR SERVINGS)
NUTRITION PER SERVING

Calories	207	Total fat	9g
% from fat	36	Saturated	5g
Carbohydrates	31g	Cholesterol	51mg
Fiber	<1g	Sodium	188mg

Pineapple Sherbet

This is an old-fashioned favorite my mother-in-law taught me. Both children and adults love it.

1 quart buttermilk

1 cup sugar, or ½ cup honey

½ medium, ripe, cored pineapple (about 1½ cups), chopped, with juice

1. Mix all the ingredients in a clean, 6-cup freezer container, stirring until sugar is dissolved.

2. Chill, label, and freeze.

3. Thaw slightly before serving. Delicious!

YIELD: 6 CUPS (TWELVE ½-CUP SERVINGS)
NUTRITION PER SERVING

Calories	114	Total fat	<1g
% from fat	7	Saturated	<1g
Carbohydrates	25g	Cholesterol	3mg
Fiber	<1g	Sodium	86mg

Frozen Fruit Salad

This is a variation of Pineapple Sherbet.

1 quart buttermilk

1 cup sugar, or ½ cup honey

½ medium, ripe, cored pineapple (about 1½ cups), chopped, with juice

1 cup white (or red) seedless grapes, halved

2 medium ripe peaches, peeled, pitted, and sliced

½ teaspoon mint flavoring

1. Combine all the ingredients in a clean, 8-cup freezer container. Stir well to dissolve the sugar.

2. Chill, label, and freeze.

3. When ready to serve, remove from freezer and thaw slightly.

Note: One serving method is to make the salad in two 4-cup loaf pans, then freeze it so it can be sliced for serving.

YIELD: 8 CUPS (SIXTEEN ½-CUP SERVINGS)
NUTRITION PER SERVING

Calories	95	Total fat	<1g
% from fat	6	Saturated	<1g
Carbohydrates	21g	Cholesterol	2mg
Fiber	<1g	Sodium	66mg

Apple Crumb Pie

· · · · · · · · · · · ·

An easy, delicious alternative to pie with a crust, this recipe can be made by substituting an equal quantity of peaches or a combination of peaches and blackberries for the apples.

FILLING

- 4 large tart apples, peeled and sliced thickly
- ½ cup sugar
- 1 teaspoon cinnamon

CRUMB TOPPING

- ½ cup sugar
- ¾ cup all-purpose flour
- ⅓ cup butter

1. Toss apples, sugar, and cinnamon until apples are well coated.

2. Mix the topping ingredients in the bowl of a food processor.

3. Line a 9-inch pie plate with foil.

4. Add the apple filling, and top it with crumb topping.

5. To use immediately, bake in 400°F oven 40–50 minutes, until crust has browned.

6. To store, freeze the unbaked pie. When it's solid, remove the pie from the plate, wrap and label it, and return it to the freezer.

7. When it is time to cook the frozen pie, remove the wrapping and put it back into the pie plate.

8. Bake on a cookie sheet in the middle third of the oven 45–60 minutes, or until the crumb mixture is brown and crusty.

· ·

YIELD: ONE 9-INCH PIE (EIGHT SERVINGS)
NUTRITION PER SERVING

Calories	238	Total fat	8g
% from fat	29	Saturated	5g
Carbohydrates	42g	Cholesterol	20mg
Fiber	2g	Sodium	79mg

· ·

Nectarine Cobbler
with Pecan Crunch Topping

This is so good that I usually double the recipe.

8 medium (about 2 pounds) ripe unpeeled nectarines, pitted and sliced

¼ cup sugar

1 tablespoon all-purpose flour

1 tablespoon lemon juice

TOPPING

1 cup all-purpose flour

¾ cup firmly packed light brown sugar

1 teaspoon ground cinnamon

½ cup unsalted butter, cut into small pieces

½ cup coarsely chopped pecans, very lightly toasted

1. If baking immediately, preheat oven to 375°F and use center rack.

2. In a large mixing bowl, combine fruit, sugar, flour, and lemon juice, folding gently so as not to hurt the fruit slices.

3. Pour batter into an 8- by 8-inch baking pan.

4. Combine the topping ingredients in food processor until crumbly. Sprinkle crumb topping over the fruit mixture.

5. If making two cobblers, freeze one at this point, wrapping well and labeling. It will keep in the freezer 6 months.

6. To bake immediately, place on a cookie sheet and bake 45–50 minutes until browned.

7. To bake frozen cobbler, place in oven on a cookie sheet 50–60 minutes until browned.

YIELD: 1 COBBLER (EIGHT SERVINGS)
NUTRITION PER SERVING

Calories	355	Total fat	15g
% from fat	37	Saturated	8g
Carbohydrates	55g	Cholesterol	33mg
Fiber	3g	Sodium	10mg

Herbed Water Tonic

* * * * * * * * * * * *

When hot weather makes your herbs begin to flower, pinch off the buds and enjoy this refreshing idea all winter long. Quantities can vary according to availability of herbs and your tastes.

Fresh thyme flowers

Fresh sage flowers

Fresh rosemary flowers

Fresh lavender flowers

Fresh chamomile flowers

Fresh basil flowers

Fresh lemon balm flowers

Garnish with fresh lemon slice

1. Thoroughly wash all the flowers and divide them evenly in an ice cube tray. Cover with water and freeze.

2. When frozen, transfer the herb cubes to a plastic bag. Label and store in freezer.

3. Use 1 cube per glass. Cover with chilled sparkling water and garnish with fresh lemon slice.

CHAPTER 5

AT MY HOME IN NORTH CAROLINA it would not seem like August if I weren't making jams from the bounty of seasonal fruit that bursts into and overflows from the farmer's markets. The trick is to "transform" and "transfix" the booty into beautiful rows of preserved concoctions that wait patiently to be taken from the shelf in the leaner times of winter. The comforting pleasure of a cup of an herbal-blend tea accompanied by toast with homemade apple butter is an underrated joy of life. (The toast is merely the vehicle for getting as much jam as possible to the palate.)

The perfume of simmering raspberries wafting through the house is another memory maker. Part of the seasonal ritual can include berry picking with the children. Go to a pick-your-own orchard, or pick wild blackberries. (I once had to throw away the clothes my children wore for blackberry picking because they were so stained. But years later, nobody remembers that part — only the fun we had together!)

The art and science of preserving fresh fruits into tempting fruit spreads is a satisfying experience. Frequently young berry pickers like to help make the jam as well. It's never too early to learn creative, economical, environmental, and conservation-minded habits. Besides, preserving can turn your kitchen, pantry shelf, or freezer into a virtual rescue mission for the distressed cook. A ½-pint jar of apple jelly can serve not only for breakfast bread but also as a basting sauce for a pork roast or a grilled

Jams & Jellies

Fresh fruit may be frozen for future jam or jelly making.

chicken. A supply of orange marmalade can be added by the tablespoonful to gravy or sauces for duck, pork, or Cornish hens. Let your culinary imagination run wild.

Making homemade fruit spreads is easy. The main ingredients are sugar, fruit (which contains acid), additional fruit acid (for nonacidic fruits), and pectin. The ratio of these ingredients creates the gel and preserves the flavor of a homemade fruit spread.

Sugar. This acts as a preserving agent in the large quantities called for in fruit spread recipes.

Fruit. The distinctive flavor comes from the fruit. Also, depending on the fruit and its ripeness, natural fruit acids contribute to the gel quality. If the fruit is not naturally acidic enough, the recipe will call for added acid, usually lemon juice.

Pectin. Along with the fruit acid and sugar, pectin makes the proper consistancy for a fruit spread.

Fruit spreads are easy to make and a good project for beginning canners. However, be sure to follow the recipe without changing the ratio of sugar, fruit, and pectin; nor should you change the order in which they are added in a recipe. Your Cooperative Extension agent can help if complicated changes need to be made.

INGREDIENTS

The basic ingredients for fruit spreads never vary: sugar, fruit, fruit acid when needed, and pectin. While each spread is slightly different, you will, as always, want to start with the best fresh produce. I steer away from supermarket produce unless I am sure of its origin. However, you can freeze just-picked fruit for using later to make fruit spreads without a significant loss of flavor.

There's no need to thaw frozen fruit before cooking; just combine it in the kettle with the other ingredients in your recipe. For jams, mash the fruit and add a little fruit juice, if necessary — ¼ cup for each 1 quart of fruit.

Freezing Fruit for Jams and Jellies

In my hometown, my friend Nancy is noted for her preserves and jellies. She recommends the following simple method for making fruit spreads.

Dry-packed fruits (clean, dry fruit frozen without any liquid or sweetening; see page 125) can be frozen premeasured and ready for making into your favorite fruit spreads. Label them with the quantity, the kind of unsweetened dry-packed fruit, and the date. Later, the frozen fruit may be pureed in a food processor for immediate jam making.

Preserves can be made from the frozen fruit placed in a nonreactive saucepan, heated slightly, and mashed with a little fruit juice (¼ cup juice per 1 quart of fruit).

PECTIN

Pectin is a gelling agent found naturally in all fruits. Fruit that is underripe contains much more pectin than ripened fruit. Including some underripe fruit in the fruit portion called for in a recipe can help the final product to gel. You can buy pectin in either powdered or liquid form in most supermarkets. Commercial pectins are usually made from the white material under the skin of citrus fruits, although some kinds are made from apples. Recipes that call for purchased pectins will benefit in flavor and consistency from using ripe fruit.

The fruit's ripeness, its natural pectin content, its natural acid content, and the amount of sugar added all influence the quality of the gel of the finished product. In recipes that do not call for commercial pectin, the sugar acts as a preservative and gel agent, along with the natural pectin found in the fruit.

Fruit spreads are slow cooked or fast cooked, depending on whether the pectin is added or is only derived from the fruit used. In the slow-cook method (see page 185), no pectin is added, and the ¾-to-¼ ratio of fully ripe to slightly

TIP

Work with frozen fruit to keep the fruit from browning as it thaws.

TIP

Stick with the original recipe. Don't change the proportions or the ratio of sugar to fruit or the ingredient order — you may end up with syrup or glue instead! Don't double a recipe, either. It is better to make one batch at a time.

Don't substitute powdered pectin for liquid pectin in a recipe. Changing this ingredient can influence the gelling results. Always follow the directions on the package and in the recipe for combining the pectin into the fruit mixture.

ripe fruit is used to produce the gel. This slow-cooked, no-added-pectin method requires a lot of guesswork, however, and can be chancy for the less experienced cook, who might not be able to judge the fruits' ripeness accurately.

The faster-cooking method, in which purchased pectin is added, can reduce guesswork (see page 184). The recipe will instruct you in the exact quantity of pectin and the exact cooking time. Never cook a recipe for more than 20 minutes when pectin is added, because after that the pectin will begin to break down. Less fruit, of course, is required for recipes with added pectin.

Making Your Own Pectin

Underripe apples are all you need to make your own pectin. In mid-August in my area, small, immature green (underripe) apples begin appearing before the regular crop of apples starts rolling in. These little apples are loaded with natural fruit pectin and acid and can be used to contribute pectin for preserving. You can get the jump on the

Pectin and Acid in Fruit

The amount of naturally occurring pectin and acid varies from fruit to fruit and depends on the fruit's ripeness. The fruits in the lists below are given from highest pectin and acid content to lowest.

Fruits with High Natural Pectin and Acid Content	Fruits with Low Natural Pectin and Acid Content	Fruits with Very Low Natural Pectin and Acid Content
Sour apples	Apples, ripe	Apricots
Plums (Damson)	Blackberries, ripe	Peaches
Blackberries	Sour cherries	Grapes (Western Concord)
Crab apples	Grapefruit	Guavas
Cranberries	Oranges	Figs
Grapes (Eastern Concord)	Grape juice (Concord, from commercial concentrate)	Prunes
Quince		Pears
Currants		Raspberries
Lemons		Strawberries

apple crop by using these small apples, but if you want crystal-clear jelly, you'd be better off waiting for the mature apples to appear.

Our trees are Golden Delicious, and we don't spray them. I have found that these young apples, even with insect holes and bruises and bumps, can be used successfully for making pectin by merely cutting away the damage. No need to peel the apples, as the pectin is mostly found in or near the peelings. Do wash them carefully, however, and slice them rather thinly.

TIP

. . . . . .

Make your own pectin the day before you make your fruit spread. Store it in the refrigerator overnight. This will save considerable time on jelly-making day.

Making Pectin
. . . .

To make the pectin, follow these simple instructions:

1. Combine in a large stockpot 1 pint of water for each 1 pound of apple slices. Boil for about 15 minutes, stirring occasionally.
2. Line a strainer with one thickness of cheesecloth. Pour the apple pulp and juices through the strainer into a large pot that comfortably fits the strainer. Pour juices into a 4-cup-capacity measuring cup.
3. Pour the pulp back into the stockpot and add the same amount of water as before, depending on the number of pounds of apples you used in the beginning. Cook the mixture over medium heat this second time for about 15 minutes.
4. Remove from the heat and let stand another 10 minutes. Strain this second time through another single thickness of cheesecloth lining your strainer. Add this second round of juice to the 4-cup measuring cup.
5. When cool enough to handle, gather up the cheesecloth containing the pulp into a bag shape. Squeeze the bag to extract all the remaining juices. (Caution: Never squeeze the cheesecloth bag or jelly bag unless the recipe specifically directs you to do this, as I do here. Squeezing the pulp bag can sometimes cloud your finished fruit spread.) Add this last juice to the 4-cup measurer. You should have 1 quart of cooked juice for every pound of apples. This "stock" will serve as your pectin. Some folks refer to this as "jelly stock." Four cups of jelly stock equals a half bottle or 3 ounces of commercial liquid pectin.
6. I prefer to freeze my jelly stock for future use. Pour it into clean 4-cup freezer containers and allow at least 1 inch headspace for freezing expansion.

TIP

If you're not using purchased pectin in a recipe, use 1 part barely ripe fruit to 3 parts very ripe fruit.

LOW-METHYL PECTIN

Low-methyl pectin is a natural product used for gelling derived from citrus peel, which requires the addition of dicalcium phosphate, a calcium salt. It can be purchased in most health food stores and has the advantage of needing no sweetener (except for taste) in order to gel. Follow package directions to combine the low-methyl pectin and the dicalcium phosphate. Recipes that call for low-methyl pectin cook much more quickly and thus result in a fruit spread with a fresher flavor.

What's the Difference?

Although people use the word "preserves" to refer to all forms of sweetened jarred fruit, there are many different varieties.

Butter. This fruit spread is made from pureed fruits with sugar and sometimes spices added. The mixture is cooked down and naturally thickened, and is very easy to make. Apples and pears are the favorite fruits for making butter. When cooking, be careful not to scorch it.

Conserve. At their height in popularity in Victorian England, conserves were whole or sliced fruits preserved in a syrup base. They were eaten for dessert and were much richer and more syrupy than conventional jams and jellies. Today they are often made with two or more chopped fruits, may contain nuts or raisins, and have the ingredients and consistency of jam.

Curd. A type of preserve that contains, in addition to the fruit, eggs and butter. Very smooth and rich, curds are most often made with citrus, lemon being the most common. Because they contain dairy products, curds should always be refrigerated and should not be stored for longer than three months.

Jam. This is the least labor-intensive way to process spreadable fruit. It consists of washed, crushed fruit, sugar, and possibly pectin (depending on the recipe). Jams can be cooked or freezer preserved with sugar or sugar substitute. Jams may even be made by an uncooked method (see page 192).

Jelly. Made from strained fresh fruit juices or purchased frozen fruit juices, plus sugar, with or without pectin, jelly is clear with no fruit pieces.

Marmalade. More like jelly than jam, marmalade has small pieces of suspended fruit or peel added to the gel.

Preserves. Similar to jams, preserves have bits of one or more fruits and are made with or without pectin.

The disadvantage is that recipes made with low-methyl pectin sometimes "weep." Liquid will puddle around a spoonful of the jam on a plate, or the whole jar will have a puddled liquid. This is a natural occurrence and is caused by the calcium. Simply blot the liquid with paper towels or spoon it or drain it out of the jar. Another disadvantage to low-methyl pectin is that the absence of sugar (which is a natural preservative) means you can't store the fruit spread as long after it is opened. You must use it within two to three weeks of opening the jar and, of course, refrigerate it. Low-methyl pectin recipes are processed in a boiling-water-bath canner for 5 minutes for jellies using ½-pints and for 10 minutes for jams using ½-pints. Follow your recipe instructions carefully.

Spreads made with low-methyl pectin sometimes "weep."

SWEETENERS

Sweeteners for fruit spreads vary greatly. Following is a list of choices both natural and artificial. Artificial sweeteners cannot be used in fruit spreads that require cooking, as the sweetener breaks down under heat. Sugar's purpose goes beyond making the fruit sweet; it is used as a preservative and gelling agent in large quantities when making fruit spreads. Never change the ratio of sugar, fruit and pectin in your recipes.

Sugar. Besides adding flavor to fruit spreads, sugar is a key ingredient in the gelling. (A large amount of sugar does, however, add calories.) Granulated sugar made from cane or beets or light brown sugar, which has maltose added, is appropriate for making fruit spreads.

Honey. Light and mild honey can be used instead of sugar. Because it has double the sweetening power of sugar, it adds fewer calories. Choose a recipe that specifies the use of honey. Don't switch from sugar to honey on your own. Honey will cause more foam on top of the cooked fruit mixture.

Perils of Paraffin

Those of us who remember Granny's pantry shelves lined with sparkling jars of preserves and jellies remember the thick layer of paraffin that covered the contents. There were always sticky fingers in the house when the children tried to push it in and pry it out. While we remember those days with fondness, we must not return to that method of preserving fruit spreads. Paraffin allows mold to grow, and some forms of mold can be dangerous. Rather than paraffin, use new rubber-lined lids and clean screw-rings in the recommended boiling-water-bath canner.

Equipment for Fruit Spreads

• • • • • • • • • • •

Most of the equipment you'll need for jams and jellies is already in your kitchen if you've done some canning, but a few items are needed especially for fruit spreads.

Heavy, large, stainless steel or enamel pot (not aluminum or iron)
Regulation jars and lids (see page 24)
Cooling rack
Measuring cups and spoons
Jelly bag, or cheesecloth and kitchen twine
Potato ricer, Victorio brand strainer, or other masher
Long-handled wooden spoon
Pierced long-handled metal spoon
Clean tea towels
Candy thermometer
Colander
Soft vegetable brush
Knife
Timer
Spatula
Ladle
Widemouthed funnel
Jar lifter
Boiling-water-bath canner
Kitchen scales

Artificial sweeteners. Saccharin, aspartame, and other artificial sweeteners cannot be used in cooked products, as they break down when heated. Use artificial sweetener only in uncooked fruit spread recipes for the freezer or refrigerator. For a cooked and processed recipe, add artificial sweetener when you open the individual jar for use.

EQUIPMENT FOR MAKING FRUIT SPREADS

The method for preserving jams, jellies, conserves, preserves, and other fruit spreads is boiling-water-bath canning, the same method used for fruits and other high-acid foods. If you have canned fruits or other foods, you probably have most of the equipment you need, since the same equipment is used and the same process is followed. For a more detailed explanation of the boiling-water-bath method, refer to chapter 2 (page 27).

The Victorio food mill is useful for separating the raw fruit pulp from the seeds and skins. Another brand of food mill is Squeezo. You may also use a potato "ricer," which forces the raw fruit pulp through small holes, but smaller seeds can slip through.

A candy or cooking thermometer is essential for the beginning cook. It allows a foolproof method of gelling. Treat your thermometer kindly when it's not in use and avoid mistreatment such as dropping or bumping it.

A timer is a valuable tool for anyone who wants to master the art and science of canning. "Precision" is the order of the day for fruit spread making, as well as for other forms of canning.

JELLY BAGS AND JUICING

A jelly bag is used to strain juice from the fruit pulp. It is a simple cloth bag that can be purchased or made from several layers of muslin or cheesecloth, filled with fruit pulp, and tied into a pouch with kitchen twine. Be sure to dampen it first in water to prevent juice from being wicked into the fabric instead of dripping into the bowl. The bag is then suspended by the string over a clean glass or enamel bowl. The weight of the fruit pulp allows the juice to drip into the bowl below, a process that usually takes 8 to 10 hours. I like to use an 8-cup glass mixing/measuring bowl with a handle.

TIP

· · · · · ·

Begin straining the juice in the evening the night before and have your bowl of juice ready for jelly making early in the morning. You can also freeze fresh juice for jelly making later on.

You may have to be creative to find an effective setup for the jelly bag.

TIP

· · · · · ·

For a less labor-intensive procedure, use frozen commercial juice concentrate and add commercial pectin.

PREPARATION OF FRUITS FOR JUICING

As always, start with ripe, blemish-free fruit. Wash the fruit well to remove all grit. Crush the fruit before adding to the wet jelly bag. You don't need to remove seeds or skins since straining through the jelly bag will take care of that.

FRUIT	AMOUNT	PREPARATION	WATER	COOK TIME (MINUTES)	CONSISTENCY	FINISHED AMOUNT
Apples, crab apples, guavas	1 lb.	wash, cut up coarsely	1 cup	15–20	soft	2 cups
Grapes, cherries, currants, peaches	3 lbs.	wash, pit, cut up	½ cup	5–10	translucent	5½ cups
Plums	3 lbs.	wash, cut up, pit, mash	little or none	15	soft	5½ cups
Berries	2½ qts.	wash, crush in kettle	none	5–10	soft	5½ cups

Unless your recipe specifies it, don't squeeze the bag and force more juice out, as this may make the final product cloudy. Add a little water to the pulp and continue the straining if you come up short.

Be sure to wash the bag thoroughly after use. The pulp makes a great addition to your compost pile!

The Process of Preserving Fruit Spreads

Making fruit spreads is relatively simple, although sometimes experience is needed to achieve the perfect taste and texture. The challenge is to combine the fruit, the sugar, and in some cases the pectin, depending on the fruit and method used, in the correct ratio and for the right amount of time to create the desired gel consistency when the fruit is cooked and then canned. The recipes included in the second part of this chapter will take the guesswork out of the process.

Cooking the Fruit and Juices for Canning

The goal of cooking the fruit is to acquire the proper gel for the final fruit spread product. Follow the recipe instructions exactly; add ingredients in the order given.

There are two ways to cook the fruit and juices for fruit spreads: the fast way, which uses added pectin, and the slow way, which relies on the pectin found naturally in the fruit being processed.

The Fast Way — Adding Pectin

Bring the mixture to a full boil that you cannot stop by stirring and maintain it for the exact amount of time called for in your recipe. If pectin is overcooked, it may break down, resulting in runny jam. Always add the liquid or powdered pectin exactly how and when the recipe indicates. Never substitute liquid pectin for powdered, or vice versa.

The Slow Way — Without Adding Pectin

The less exact way, the slow or "cook-down" method of preserving fruits for spreads, worked great for Granny and it still works today as well. This method relies on the pectin found in fruit to make the spread congeal. Use fruits that have a high pectin content, such as sour apples, crab apples, blackberries, Concord grapes, lemons, oranges, Damson plums, quince, and raspberries. Place the fruit or fruit acid and the sugar in an uncovered pot and cook for the proper time to create the gel. Because the amount of pectin in fruit will vary, depending on ripeness as well as variety, there is some guesswork involved. The recipe will indicate approximate cooking times to achieve the gel, but there are other ways to determine whether the fruit mixture is ready to pour into the jars.

Some recipes may not indicate a specific cooking time but may say instead, "Cook until done," or "Cook until it reaches 220°F." In such cases, you'll need to use your candy thermometer or cooking thermometer for making jelly or marmalade. When it reaches 220°F, your jelly is ready. For jams and preserves, you know it is ready when a spoonful holds its shape or "mounds up" on a cold spoon or plate. At high altitudes, take away 2 degrees for each 1,000 feet of height over sea level.

Preserves and conserves. When a spoonful of fruit mixture holds its shape or mounds up on a cold spoon or plate, it's ready for canning. Remove the fruit mixture from the heat and stir it for about five minutes before you fill the jars. This prevents the fruit from floating after canning.

Jams. When a spoonful of fruit dropped in a cold bowl holds its shape, it is ready for the canning jar and boiling-water-bath canner.

Butters. This is a slow cook-down process that can work quite well in your oven at 300° to 325°F. The mixture will become a thick brown mash. Using the oven takes four or five hours and helps prevent burning and the labor intensity of a watched pot.

Use a thermometer to determine when jelly or marmalade is ready.

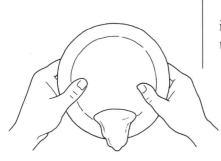

One alternative to using a thermometer to test for doneness is the sheeting method.

Jelly or marmalade. If you don't have a candy or cooking thermometer, try one of the old-fashioned methods of testing doneness that follow:

- *The sheeting method.* Put a tablespoon or so of the hot fruit mixture on a cold plate or spoon, then turn the plate or spoon on its side over the sink. If the fruit mixture falls off or "sheets off" in one large drop, the jelly is done.
- *The freezer method.* Put a tablespoon of the hot fruit mixture on a cold plate and place it in the freezer for two to three minutes. Remove and shake the plate. If the fruit mixture quivers, it is done.
- *The metal bowl method.* Take a metal bowl from the freezer and drop a teaspoon of hot fruit mixture in the bowl. Wait one minute. Run your finger through it; if it stays in two parts and doesn't run back together, the mixture is ready for processing.

Prewashing and Sterilizing Jars and Lids

The jars you use for jellies and jams must fit the same standards as those you use for other canning methods. They must be free of cracks and chips and otherwise in good condition. Jars made for commercial use should never be used; they are not of the same sturdy quality as jars made specifically for canning and may not be able to withstand the lengthy exposure to the high temperatures of the boiling-water bath. Commercial jars can shatter, destroying your food and possibly causing injury to you or others.

Most recipes for fruit spreads call for ½-pint jars. Each jar must have a two-piece lid that consists of a new metal vacuum lid and a new or used metal screw-ring. The Mason jars and lids made by Ball and Kerr fill this requirement.

The screw-ring holds the vacuum lid in place, and unlike the vacuum lid, it can be used year after year. Twenty-four hours after the canning process, when the jars have thoroughly cooled, remove the metal screw-rings from the jars before storing your canned goods in the pantry. Metal screw-rings that are left on jars may rust. If a screw-ring is stuck or stubborn, don't force it and risk breaking a seal, but rather leave the ring in place. *Under no circumstances should you tighten the screw-ring after processing.* This action could break the seal and leave the fruit spread vulnerable to spoilage.

The USDA says it is not necessary to sterilize jars for fruit, tomatoes, or pickled foods that will be processed *more than 10 minutes* in a boiling-water bath. Instead, before each use, wash your empty jars and rings in the dishwasher or submerge them in hot soapy water. Rinse the jars and rings from the dishwasher or dishpan thoroughly, being careful to remove all traces of soap. Keep the lids and rings hot in gently boiling water until you are ready to use them.

For boiling water bath processing times of under 10 minutes, it is necessary to sterilize them by submerging the clean, prewashed jars in a boiling water bath. To do this, fill jars with hot tap water and lower the water-filled jars into a canner of hot (not boiling) water, making sure the water level rises to 1 inch above the jar tops. Boil the jars for 10 minutes at sea level. At higher elevations, boil one additional minute for each 1,000 feet.

After the proper number of minutes have passed, use a jar lifter to remove one sterilized jar at a time and fill immediately with prepared fruit spread. Be sure to leave appropriate head-space. Repeat until every jar is filled. Be sure to wipe any spillage from the jar rims with a clean cloth. Add the metal lid and rings by the method below, one jar at a time. (Save the boiling water for the canning process.)

TIP
● ● ● ● ● ●

Use the dishwasher to pre-wash jars for canning fruit spreads as long as the process canning time will be longer than 10 minutes. If the processing time is less than 10 minutes, you must wash and then sterilize the jars.

FILLING AND SEALING CONTAINERS

Begin filling the jars one at a time. This is where the wide-mouthed funnel and ladle are invaluable.

Be careful to avoid drips when you remove the funnel from the filled jar. Not only can drips burn the cook, but they can also spoil the canning seal if they are allowed to remain on the lid or the mouth of the jar. I like to use a very clean, thin, wet dish towel pulled over my index finger to rub around the rim of the jar to get the smallest drip of food or liquid. This allows you to feel the slightest chip on the rim as well. A wet paper towel works for this cleaning job, also.

Do not overfill or leave too much headspace in the jars. Be sure to fill the fruit spread according to the headspace requirements and in the exact size of jar specified in the recipe. Precision is important here. Too little headspace may cause the food to be forced out of the jar during processing when the heat causes the contents of the jar to expand. In addition to being messy, the leakage prevents the proper seal from forming. Too much headspace leaves too much air to be forced out during processing, also preventing a seal from forming.

If bubbles appear in the liquid, tap the side of the jar with a knife handle. If your fruit spread has pieces of fruit in it, run a clean, plastic spatula along the sides of the jar to help remove bubbles between the pieces of fruit. Don't stir. That would create more bubbles.

In a saucepan, prepare the metal self-sealing lids by submerging them in boiling water for 10 minutes. Place the clean metal lids on the mouth of the jars and secure with the metal ring.

The canning lids will best be kept clean and hot in the boiling-water bath mentioned above. After filling the first hot, sterile jar with fruit spread, place the hot metal lid on the first jar and secure with the metal ring. Then proceed with the next jar until all the jars are filled with fruit spread and ready to be processed.

TIP
• • • • • •

Jar and metal rings may be re-used if they're in good condition, but never recycle the self-sealing metal lids.

Boiling-Water-Bath Method for Fruit Spreads

Follow these steps for successful boiling-water-bath canning of jellies, jams, preserves, marmalades, and conserves:

1. Fill the canner halfway with water.

2. Preheat the water to 180°F for hot-pack fruit spreads.

3. Load filled jars, fitted with lids, one at a time into the canner rack and use the handles to lower the rack into the hot water; or fill the canner one jar at a time with a jar lifter.

4. Add boiling water, if needed, so the water level is at least 1 to 2 inches above the jar tops.

5. Turn the heat to its highest position until the water boils vigorously.

6. Set a timer for the minutes required for processing the fruit spread.

7. Cover with the canner lid and lower the heat setting to maintain a gentle boil throughout the process stated in your fruit spread recipe. Be sure to allow for altitude.

8. Add more boiling water, if needed, to keep the water level above the jars.

9. When jars have boiled for the recommended time, turn off the heat and remove the canner lid.

10. Using a jar lifter, remove the jars and place them on a clean towel, leaving at least 1 inch of space between the jars as they cool.

TIP

The paraffin wax method is no longer acceptable for sealing fruit spread in jars. It is still being done throughout the world but is definitely not recommended.

CHECK SEALS

After the filled and finished jars of fruit spread have cooled, in 12 to 24 hours, use your thumbs to test the seal of the metal lids. Press hard on the center of one. If the lid does not move downward or "give," your jar is complete. If one or two aren't sealed, you can store those faulty jars in the refrigerator to enjoy, though you must use them quickly.

Another method to ensure that your jar is properly sealed is to remove the screw-ring and try lifting your newly canned jar by its lid using the weight of the jar to test the strength or weakness of the seal. (Protect yourself and the jar by doing this over the sink prepared with a towel to pad the possible fall.)

A List of Questions to Ask Yourself

1. Did I properly use the processing method called for in the recipe?
2. Did I fill the canner with the correct amount of water to cover jars properly?
3. Did I correctly figure the altitude adjustment and headspace?
4. Did I verify that the jar rims were free of cracks and chips and use new lids?
5. Did I fill the jar to the proper density and cap it in the prescribed method?
6. Did the jars cool naturally at room temperature and in a reasonable amount of time, about 12 to 24 hours?
7. Were the metal screw-rings left intact after the canning process or were they tightened before putting on the pantry shelves or being readied to be opened for eating? Remove easily removable screw-rings, but leave them in place if they are stubborn. Under no circumstances should you tighten them down after canning, as this could spoil the seal.

LABELING AND STORAGE

Always label fruit spreads with the contents, the processing method, and the date. You can purchase decorative glue-on labels, which are wonderful to use when you plan to make a gift of your fruit spread. You can make your own labels on the computer, as well.

Home-canned fruits require no expensive storage equipment — just a cool shelf in a dark, dry place. No matter how you label your fruit spreads and where you store them, make sure they are in a place where they won't be knocked off a shelf or exposed to high temperatures or sunlight. The many attributes of home canning, including the pleasure of enjoying and sharing quality, chemical-free food all winter long, are lost when jars fall and break the seal or your food spoils.

Homemade jams, jellies, and preserves always make wonderful hostess gifts, and are a great way to say "thank you" to a neighbor who was kind enough to collect your mail while you were away for the weekend. But they can serve as the focal point of more elaborate gifts, too. Refer to chapter 9 (page 317) for gift ideas.

Refer to chapter 9 (page 317) for gift ideas.

EVALUATING YOUR JAMS AND JELLIES

Evaluating your jams and jellies can teach you as well as, if not better than, any instructions. Here are the questions to ask after preserving fruits:

1. *Did I examine each jar carefully before storing them away?* This gives you a good chance to admire your work as well as time to spot problems.

2. *Are my jars sealed properly?* If the top inch of a jar of fruit spread turns dark later on, it can indicate improper seals or storage in a place that's too warm. Mold is the most common indicator of spoilage from improper seals,

TIP

● ● ● ● ● ●

The best storage temperature for fruit spreads is between 50° and 70°F.

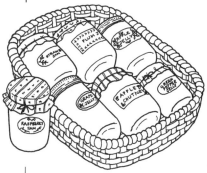

A basket of homemade jams and jellies makes a wonderful gift.

but if the fruit spread is discolored, doesn't look the same as other jars, or has an unpleasant, "off" odor, don't take chances; throw it away. (Also, see box on page 48.) However, if you used honey instead of sugar, your spread will be darker in color. If the seal is good and no other signs of spoilage are present, the fruit spread is probably okay. Bright fruits, like strawberries, darken naturally after processing.

3. *Has the fruit in my preserves floated to the surface?* Stirring off the heat for five minutes after kettle cooking and before bottling can eliminate this problem.

4. *Is the fruit spread too soft?* When the jar is tilted sideways does the fruit mixture move more like a liquid? If the consistency is too liquid and you used pectin, it may mean you boiled the mixture too long. Or that you doubled the recipe, used liquid instead of powdered pectin, or used honey instead of sugar. If pectin wasn't used, it could mean you didn't cook the mixture long enough.

5. *Was the finished fruit spread too thick?* This can be caused by the pectin-fruit-sugar ratio being off. Also, overcooking a no-pectin spread can make the finished product stiff.

No-Cook Freezer and Refrigerator Fruit Spreads

Today's busy world doesn't always allow time to stock a pantry the old-fashioned way. Throughout this book are recipes designed to let your refrigerator be your "pantry."

To make no-cook jelly, use fresh, uncooked fruit and juice or frozen juice concentrate. (Do not use canned commercial sweetened juices with the no-cook method. This would defeat the fresh flavor advantage.) If you dry packed fruit and froze it earlier in the season (see page 125), this is an ideal use for it. Combine sugar, fruit juice, and pectin according to the pectin directions. Use sterilized containers for storage and allow 1 inch headspace for expansion during freezing. Because there is no cooking and, therefore, no sterilizing, no-cook jams keep only up to three weeks in the refrigerator and up to six months in the freezer.

6. *Is the finished product weeping?* Too-warm storage or the use of low-methyl pectin can cause weeping. Also, honey recipes tend to weep more than sugar ones because sugar is a natural preservative. If there are no signs of spoilage, the spread is probably still safe to eat. Before using, drain off the liquid or blot it out with paper towels.

Low-Sugar, No-Cook Freezer Fruit Spreads

For those on special diets or who enjoy the sometimes-tart taste of the fresh fruit, try this unconventional way of making fruit spreads.

Agar is a gelling, stabilizing agent that is used to solidify the no- or low-sugar, no-cook fruit spreads. This plant product, sometimes called Asian gelatin or agar-agar, is derived from ocean algae and is available in natural food stores and Asian markets.

Common household gelatin, the animal product, also can be used as a solidifying agent for low- or no-sugar cooked fruit spreads for refrigerator or freezer.

Agar strands and flakes are used to solidify fruit spreads.

Strawberry Jelly with Liquid Pectin

1. Using a wooden spoon, crush 2½ quarts of washed, hulled, ripe strawberries. Strain the pulp through a jelly bag.

2. Put pulp into a damp jelly bag or cheesecloth and allow juice to drip through. This will vary from a few hours to overnight, depending on the juiciness of the fruit. To avoid cloudy jelly, don't squeeze. Combine the juices, sugar, and liquid pectin.

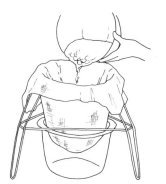

3. Measure 3¾ cups juice into a large saucepan. Add ¼ cup lemon juice and 7½ cups sugar. Place over high heat and bring to a boil, stirring constantly. Stir in liquid pectin, bring to a full rolling boil, and boil hard for one minute, stirring constantly. Skim off the foam with a metal spoon.

4. Remove from heat and skim off all foam with a metal spoon.

5. Pour quickly into hot, sterilized glasses, leaving ¼ inch headspace. Wipe rims clean.

6. Adjust lids and process in a boiling-water bath for five minutes to ensure a good seal. Be sure to allow for altitude. Set upright to cool.

Equipment

• • • • • • • • • •

The equipment you need for the recipes in this chapter is the same in each. You'll need a boiling-water-bath canner and jars of the appropriate size. For a complete list of supplies for making fruit spreads, see page 182.

RECIPES FOR JAMS, JELLIES, PRESERVES, CONSERVES, MARMALADES, AND BUTTERS

Agar Berry Jam

Fresh Strawberry Preserves

Spiced Strawberry Jam Using Fruit Pectin

Baked Low-Sugar Strawberry Jam

Strawberry Rhubarb Jelly

Strawberry and Blackberry Jam

Blackberry Preserves

Blackberry, Cranberry, and
Pink Grapefruit Preserves

Red Raspberry Preserves

Lime Marmalade

Lemon Jelly

Lemon-Pineapple Preserves

Old-Fashioned Peach Preserves

Spiced Peach Jam

Grape Jelly

Spiced Grape Jelly for Freezer

Blueberry Marmalade

Blueberry and Cherry Preserves

Apple Ginger Marmalade

Marion's Apple Butter

Apple-Plum Butter

Apple-Zucchini Butter

Basil-Apple Jelly

Coriander and Honey Jelly

Nutmeg-Scented Geranium Jelly

Mint Jelly

Ginger Jam

Carrot and Orange Marmalade

Summer Squash Conserve

Horseradish Jelly

Quick Chile Pepper Jelly

Five-Pepper Jelly

Tomato Marmalade

Tomato Jam

Yellow Tomato Jam

Ginger Shallot Marmalade

Garlic Jelly

Preserved Lemons

Cranberry-Lime Curd

Pear Butter

Agar Berry Jam

This no-process, low-sugar fruit jam is wonderful with strawberries, raspberries, black-berries, or blueberries. Experiment with combinations.

1 tablespoon lemon juice

3 cups washed, hulled, and finely chopped berries, at room temperature (about 1 quart whole)

1 cup cold water

2 tablespoons agar flakes

¼ cup mild-flavored honey, such as clover

1. In a mixing bowl, stir the lemon juice into the fruit. Set aside.

2. Place the water in a small saucepan and stir in the agar flakes. Wait 1 minute and then, without further stirring, bring the agar to a simmer over medium-low heat. Once it's simmering, stir 2–5 minutes, or until the agar is completely dissolved.

3. Stir in the honey into the agar. Use a heatproof rubber spatula to scrape the sides and bottom of the pot.

4. Pouring with one hand and stirring with the other, add the agar mixture to the fruit (do not add the fruit to the agar). Continue stirring until it's completely mixed. Taste at this time and add more honey if desired, up to 3 tablespoons more.

5. Pour the jam into hot, scalded ½-pint jars, leaving ½ inch headspace.

6. Cap and seal. Allow them to cool in the refrigerator 10–12 hours before freezing. Label and freeze.

7. When ready to use, thaw the jam in the refrigerator. It will keep about 3 weeks in the refrigerator, 6 months in the freezer.

YIELD: 4 ½-PINTS (THIRTY-TWO 1-OUNCE SERVINGS)
NUTRITION PER SERVING

Calories	12	Total fat	<1g
% from fat	3	Saturated	0g
Carbohydrates	3g	Cholesterol	0mg
Fiber	<1g	Sodium	1mg

Fresh Strawberry Preserves

Freezer no-sugar, no-cook jam using gelatin adapted from Stocking Up, *Rodale Food Center.*

1 cup water

1 envelope unflavored gelatin

2 teaspoons lemon juice

2 cups coarsely chopped strawberries (about 1 quart whole berries), hulls and stems removed

2 tablespoons honey

4 packets (.035 ounce each) aspartame

1. Pour the water into a saucepan and sprinkle gelatin over it. Let it stand 5 minutes.

2. Heat the mixture over medium heat 1 minute, stirring constantly to dissolve gelatin.

3. Remove the mixture from heat and add the lemon juice, fruit, and honey. Stir well and cool slightly.

4. Add the aspartame and stir well.

5. Pour the mixture into hot, scalded containers, leaving ½ inch headspace.

6. Cap and seal. Allow them to cool in the refrigerator 10–12 hours before freezing.

7. Label and freeze.

8. When ready to use, thaw preserves in the refrigerator. These will keep about 3 weeks in the refrigerator, 6 months in the freezer.

YIELD: 3 ½-PINTS (TWENTY-FOUR 1-OUNCE SERVINGS)

NUTRITION PER SERVING

Calories	16	Total fat	<1g
% from fat	2	Saturated	0g
Carbohydrates	3g	Cholesterol	0mg
Fiber	<1g	Sodium	2mg

Spiced Strawberry Jam Using Fruit Pectin

*Easy to prepare and spicier than most, this jam will
delight children and adults alike.*

5 cups crushed strawberries (about
2 quarts cleaned and stemmed)

½ teaspoon ground allspice

½ teaspoon ground cinnamon

¼ teaspoon ground cloves

1 box (1¾ ounces) powdered fruit
pectin

½ teaspoon butter or margarine

7 cups sugar

1. In an 8-quart saucepan combine strawberries and spices. Add pectin and butter to saucepan.

2. Bring to full boil on high heat, stirring constantly.

3. Stir in exactly 7 cups of sugar and mix well.

4. Bring back to full boil and boil 1 minute exactly, stirring constantly.

5. Remove saucepan from the heat and skim off any foam using a metal spoon.

6. Ladle into sterilized jars, leaving ¼ inch headspace.

7. Cap, seal, and process 5 minutes in a boiling-water-bath canner.

YIELD: 5 ½-PINTS (FORTY 1-OUNCE SERVINGS)
NUTRITION PER SERVING

Calories	145	Total fat	<1g
% from fat	<1	Saturated	0g
Carbohydrates	37g	Cholesterol	0mg
Fiber	1g	Sodium	4mg

Baked Low-Sugar Strawberry Jam

Try substituting raspberries or blackberries for the strawberries.

8 cups strawberries, washed, drained, and patted dry, halved

3 tablespoons lemon juice

1 cup sugar

1. Preheat oven to 375°F.

2. Combine all ingredients in a 2-quart casserole dish.

3. Bake in preheated oven about 15 minutes, uncovered.

4. Reduce heat to 325°F. Stir often. Bake 1– 1½ hours. Let a spoonful of jam cool and test for gelling capabilities (see pages 185–186).

5. If it is too runny return to oven at 325°F another 45 minutes or less and test again for thickening.

6. Place in clean freezer cartons. Refrigerate up to 2 weeks or freeze up to 6 months.

YIELD: 3 ½-PINTS (TWENTY-FOUR 1-OUNCE SERVINGS)

NUTRITION PER SERVING

Calories	47	Total fat	<1g
% from fat	3	Saturated	0g
Carbohydrates	12g	Cholesterol	0mg
Fiber	1g	Sodium	1mg

Strawberry Rhubarb Jelly

A southern tradition, this jelly recipe has been adapted from the USDA.

1½ pounds red rhubarb stalks, washed and cut into 1-inch pieces

1½ quarts strawberries, washed, hulled, and crushed

6 cups sugar

6 ounces liquid fruit pectin

1. Puree rhubarb by pulverizing in a blender or food processor.

2. Prepare your jelly bag by pouring boiling water through it. Squeeze out excess moisture. Line bag with a double layer of cheesecloth.

3. Place both fruits in bag, let drain, and squeeze gently to remove excess juice.

4. Measure 3½ cups strained juice in a 3-quart saucepan. Add sugar, mix thoroughly, and boil to dissolve sugar.

5. Remove from heat and stir in pectin.

6. Return to heat and bring to a full boil. Boil exactly 1 minute. Remove from heat and skim off any foam with a metal spoon.

7. Ladle into sterile ½-pint jars, leaving ¼ inch headspace.

8. Seal and process 5 minutes in a boiling-water-bath canner.

YIELD: 7 ½-PINTS (FIFTY-SIX 1-OUNCE SERVINGS)
NUTRITION PER SERVING

Calories	99	Total fat	<1g
% from fat	<1	Saturated	0g
Carbohydrates	26g	Cholesterol	0mg
Fiber	<1g	Sodium	7mg

Strawberry and Blackberry Jam

This old favorite is adapted from the Ball Blue Book.

2 cups strawberries, rinsed, hulled, halved, and crushed

1 cup blackberries, firmly packed

3 tablespoons lemon juice

1 package (1¾ ounces) powdered pectin

½ cup light corn syrup

3½ cups sugar

1. Combine the berries and lemon juice in a large bowl; stir well.

2. Slowly add the pectin, stirring constantly for 2 minutes.

3. Let the mixture stand 30 minutes, stirring occasionally.

4. Add the light corn syrup and stir well.

5. Gradually stir in the sugar, beating well. The jam is ready when the sugar has completely dissolved.

6. Pour the jam into canning or freezer jars, leaving ½ inch headspace.

7. Cap, seal, and cool in refrigerator. Let stand until set, up to 24 hours.

8. Label and freeze.

YIELD: 6 ½-PINTS (FORTY-EIGHT 1-OUNCE SERVINGS)

NUTRITION PER SERVING

Calories	73	Total fat	<1g
% from fat	<1	Saturated	0g
Carbohydrates	19g	Cholesterol	0mg
Fiber	<1g	Sodium	5mg

Freezer Tip

Precool the filled containers of no-process fruit spread in the refrigerator overnight before freezing them: It saves strain on your freezer.

Blackberry Preserves

James R. Coffee shared this recipe with me after he read my Preserving Fruits *and* Vegetables *book (Storey Publishing). His recipe won the 1996 Ball Canning award in his local Pennsylvania fair.*

3 quarts blackberries*

6 cups sugar

*Note: Blackberries can be frozen, then made up later as needed. Do not wash them before freezing. Just put them in containers and freeze. When you're ready to use the berries, put them in a colander and rinse them thoroughly. This washes them and starts the thawing process. Place the washed berries in a bowl and cover it with plastic wrap. Store them in the refrigerator overnight, then proceed with the recipe instructions.

1. In a 4-quart saucepan, heat the berries slowly until the juice is extracted, then add the sugar. Boil the mixture, uncovered, 20 minutes.

2. Skim off the foam. Pour the preserves into sterilized jars, leaving ½ inch headspace.

3. Wipe each sealing edge clean. Prepare canning lids and seal jars as directed by the manufacturer.

4. Process in a boiling-water-bath canner 10 minutes.

YIELD: 4 PINTS (SIXTY-FOUR 1-OUNCE SERVINGS)
NUTRITION PER SERVING

Calories	86	Total fat	<1g
% from fat	1	Saturated	0g
Carbohydrates	22g	Cholesterol	0mg
Fiber	1g	Sodium	0mg

Blackberry, Cranberry, and Pink Grapefruit Preserves

Present this tart but sweet spread to a neighbor and have a friend for life.

1 bag (12 ounces) fresh cranberries

2 pink or ruby red grapefruit, juiced (about 1 cup)

1½ cups sugar

6 cups frozen blackberries, thawed, with their juice

1. Pick over the cranberries to remove any stems or bad berries.

2. Mix the grapefruit juice in a heavy nonreactive saucepan with the sugar, 4 cups of the blackberries, and all the cranberries.

3. Bring to a boil over medium to high heat until the mixture sheets on the end of a spoon (page 186), about 25 minutes. Stir frequently and be careful not to burn.

4. As the mixture cooks, add the remaining 2 cups of thawed blackberries and juice into the hot mixture and bring it to a boil again.

5. Ladle the hot mixture into clean jars, leaving ¼ inch headspace. Cap and seal. Process in a boiling-water-bath canner 15 minutes.

YIELD: 4 PINTS (SIXTY-FOUR 1-OUNCE SERVINGS)
NUTRITION PER SERVING

Calories	31	Total fat	<1g
% from fat	2	Saturated	0g
Carbohydrates	8g	Cholesterol	0mg
Fiber	<1g	Sodium	0mg

Red Raspberry Preserves

A classic — not only a favorite, but also easy to prepare.

4 cups raspberries, washed, picked over, and drained

3 cups sugar

¼ cup fresh lemon juice, strained

1. Combine all ingredients in a ceramic 2-quart bowl, stirring occasionally to let all sugar dissolve, about 2 hours.

2. Pour mixture into a heavy 3-quart saucepan.

3. Bring to a boil, reduce heat, and simmer, stirring frequently, until a cooking thermometer reaches 220°F or until it passes a jelly test on page 186. (Allow about 5 minutes, depending on how juicy the berries are.)

4. Remove from heat and skim off any foam that may have formed with a metal spoon.

5. Ladle into three ½-pint jars that are sterile, allowing ¼ inch headspace. Cap and seal.

6. Process 10 minutes in a boiling-water-bath canner.

YIELD: 3 ½-PINTS (TWENTY-FOUR 1-OUNCE SERVINGS)

NUTRITION PER SERVING

Calories	107	Total fat	<1g
% from fat	<1	Saturated	0g
Carbohydrates	28g	Cholesterol	0mg
Fiber	<1g	Sodium	0mg

Lime Marmalade

· · · · · · · · · · ·

A trip to England produced this recipe. Try it instead of the more familiar orange marmalade.

3 pounds (about 18) large Persian limes, peels cut into thin strips 2 inches long

9 cups water

6 pounds sugar (13 cups)

Note: My British exchange student's family advised that citrus softens in a microwave for 10 seconds per fruit, making it easier to peel or juice.

1. Cut the limes in halves and squeeze the juice. Set juice aside.

2. Scrape the pulp and seeds from the lime halves.

3. Combine the pulp and seeds in a cheesecloth bag.

4. Place the cheesecloth bag, the peels, the juice, and the water in a 6-quart saucepan and soak overnight or about 8 hours, covered.

5. Bring water mixture to a boil and cook about 2 hours, until peels are soft.

6. Remove the cheesecloth bag.

7. Add sugar to pan and stir to dissolve.

8. Boil, stirring often, until cooking thermometer reaches 220°F.

9. Ladle into clean jars, leaving ¼ inch headspace. Cap and seal.

10. Process 5 minutes in a boiling-water-bath canner.

· ·

YIELD: 10 PINTS (ONE HUNDRED-SIXTY 1-OUNCE SERVINGS)

NUTRITION PER SERVING

Calories	68	Total fat	0g
% from fat	0	Saturated	0g
Carbohydrates	18g	Cholesterol	0mg
Fiber	<1g	Sodium	1mg

· ·

Lemon Jelly

Not only good with tea and toast, this jelly is also great on an angel food cake with fresh strawberries for a no-fat dessert.

3 pounds lemons (about 15 lemons)

9 cups water

3 pounds sugar (6¾ cups)

1. Peel the lemons and cut peelings into 2-inch strips.

2. Halve the lemons. Squeeze juice into large bowl. Set aside.

3. Scrape pulp out of lemon halves. Set aside. Save the seeds.

4. Combine 2½ cups water with the seeds and peelings and boil 30 minutes in a 2-quart saucepan. Cover and let cool.

5. Place lemon pulp and juice in a 4-quart saucepan with remaining 6½ cups water. Strain in the seed/peeling water and simmer 40 minutes, uncovered.

6. Pour pulp mixture through a wet jelly bag and let drain over 6-quart saucepan overnight. Do not squeeze the bag.

7. Measure juice. Combine juice and 2 cups sugar for each 2½ cups juice in a saucepan.

8. Stir over low heat to dissolve sugar.

9. Bring to a boil, stirring frequently, and boil until mixture reaches 220°F on your cooking thermometer, about 10 minutes.

10. Ladle into clean jars, leaving ¼ inch headspace. Cap and seal.

11. Process 5 minutes in a boiling-water-bath canner.

YIELD: 5 PINTS (EIGHTY 1-OUNCE SERVINGS)
NUTRITION PER SERVING

Calories	69	Total fat	0
% from fat	0	Saturated	0g
Carbohydrates	19g	Cholesterol	0mg
Fiber	<1g	Sodium	1mg

Lemon-Pineapple Preserves

This is delicious on banana bread or toast at breakfast, or on a muffin at teatime.

3 large lemons, squeezed of all juice, strained

3 pounds fresh pineapple, cleaned, cored, and chopped (about 2 whole)

2½ cups water

3 pounds sugar (6¾ cups)

1. In a cheesecloth bag combine the lemon shells and seeds from strained juice.

2. Combine the lemon juice, pineapple, and cheesecloth bag in a 4-quart saucepan with the water. Bring to a boil and simmer until pineapple is tender, about 15–20 minutes.

3. Remove cheesecloth bag and add sugar to the pan, stirring to dissolve.

4. Bring to a boil and simmer, stirring frequently, until thermometer reaches 220°F or about 12–15 minutes.

5. Ladle into clean jars, leaving ¼ inch headspace. Cap and seal.

6. Process 20 minutes in a boiling-water-bath canner.

YIELD: 6 PINTS (NINETY-SIX 1-OUNCE SERVINGS)
NUTRITION PER SERVING

Calories	59	Total fat	0g
% from fat	0	Saturated	0g
Carbohydrates	15g	Cholesterol	0mg
Fiber	<1g	Sodium	0mg

Old-Fashioned Peach Preserves

What can be said about such a classic?

½ teaspoon ascorbic acid (crystals, powder, or crushed tablets)

3½ pounds peaches, peeled, pitted, and chopped (about 7 large)

5 cups sugar

¼ cup lemon juice

¾ teaspoon almond extract

1. Prepare an acid bath by adding the ascorbic acid to 1 quart water.

2. Dip the peaches in the acid bath and then drain well. Combine fruit, sugar, and lemon juice in a heavy 6–8 quart saucepan, stirring over medium heat to dissolve sugar.

3. Boil slowly, stirring constantly, until mixture thickens and fruit is translucent and reaches 220°F on a cooking thermometer.

4. Stir in almond extract.

5. Remove from heat and skim foam, if there is any, with a metal spoon. Ladle into sterile jars, allowing ¼ inch headspace. Cap and seal.

6. Process 10 minutes in a boiling-water-bath canner.

YIELD: **7 PINTS** (ONE HUNDRED TWELVE 1-OUNCE SERVINGS)

NUTRITION PER SERVING

Calories	39	Total fat	0g
% from fat	0	Saturated	0g
Carbohydrates	10g	Cholesterol	0mg
Fiber	<1g	Sodium	0mg

Spiced Peach Jam

This is an old standby enjoyed by all who try it.

4 pounds peaches, peeled, pitted, and chopped (about 8 large)

2 tablespoons lemon juice

5 cups sugar

½ teaspoon ground nutmeg

⅛ teaspoon ground cinnamon

1. Place all ingredients in a heavy 8-quart saucepan. Cook over medium heat to dissolve sugar, stirring constantly.

2. Bring to a boil, stirring constantly, and boil until mixture reaches 220°F on a cooking thermometer. (Or use one of the methods to test for doneness found on pages 185–186.)

3. Ladle into sterile jars, allowing ¼ inch headspace. Cap and seal.

4. Process 10 minutes in a boiling-water-bath canner.

YIELD: 5 ½-PINTS (FORTY 1-OUNCE SERVINGS)

NUTRITION PER SERVING

Calories	112	Total fat	0g
% from fat	0	Saturated	0g
Carbohydrates	29g	Cholesterol	0mg
Fiber	<1g	Sodium	0mg

Grape Jelly

* * * * * * * * * * * *

Using green grapes gives a finished product that is surprisingly pink!

3 pounds green grapes, washed, stemmed, picked over, and chopped

2 lemons, juiced

2⅓ cups water

2¼ cups sugar

1. Bring grapes, juice, and water to a boil in an 8-quart saucepan and simmer about 30 minutes, until fruit is very soft.

2. Meanwhile, scald your jelly bag by pouring boiling water through it. Squeeze out excess water. Hang the bag in a convenient but out-of-the-way place with a large drip pot positioned underneath. (I use a dowel threaded through cabinet hardware for the bag, with the drip pot on the counter below.)

3. Pour juice into wet jelly bag. Let drip 24 hours or less. (Do not squeeze the pulp in the bag.)

4. Measure the strained juice. Add the juice and 2¼ cups sugar for each 2⅓ cups juice to a heavy 3-quart saucepan.

5. Stir mixture over medium heat until sugar has dissolved.

6. Boil grape mixture 10–12 minutes or until a cooking thermometer reaches 220°F. Read about other methods of testing on page 186.

7. Skim off any foam with a metal spoon. Ladle into sterile jars, leaving ¼ inch headspace. Cap and seal.

8. Process 5 minutes in a boiling-water-bath canner.

* *

YIELD: 4 ½-PINTS (THIRTY-TWO 1-OUNCE SERVINGS)

NUTRITION PER SERVING

Calories	81	Total fat	<1g
% from fat	2	Saturated	0g
Carbohydrates	21g	Cholesterol	0mg
Fiber	<1g	Sodium	2mg

* *

Spiced Grape Jelly for Freezer

Just a touch of cinnamon and nutmeg makes this jelly a whole new flavor sensation.

1 package (1¾ ounces) powdered pectin

2 cups lukewarm water

6 ounces frozen grape juice concentrate

3½ cups sugar

⅛ teaspoon ground cinnamon

⅛ teaspoon ground nutmeg

1. Carefully combine the pectin and the lukewarm water in a 4-quart bowl, stirring constantly. Let it stand 45 minutes.

2. Thaw the grape juice concentrate and pour it into a 2-quart bowl.

3. Add 1¾ cups sugar to the juice bowl, stirring to dissolve it completely.

4. Add the remaining 1¾ cups sugar to the pectin mixture, again stirring well to dissolve the sugar completely.

5. Add the juice mixture to the pectin mixture, then add the spices.

6. Ladle the jelly into freezer containers. Leave ½ inch headspace. Cap containers.

7. Let the containers stand until the mixture is set.

8. Label and freeze.

YIELD: 4 ½-PINTS (THIRTY-TWO 1-OUNCE SERVINGS)

NUTRITION PER SERVING

Calories	99	Total fat	0g
% from fat	0	Saturated	0g
Carbohydrates	26g	Cholesterol	0mg
Fiber	0g	Sodium	4mg

Blueberry Marmalade

· · · · · · · · · · ·

This is a new combination of flavors that is certain to please.

1 lemon

1 medium orange

¾ cup water

⅛ teaspoon baking soda

4 cups blueberries, rinsed, picked over, and crushed

5 cups sugar

6 ounces liquid fruit pectin

1. Peel the lemon and orange, and chop rinds.

2. Remove all white membranes from citrus and chop pulp. Set aside.

3. Combine chopped rinds, water, and soda in small saucepan. Bring to a boil, reduce heat, and simmer about 10 minutes, stirring occasionally. Drain well and reserve the rinds.

4. Combine blueberries, citrus pulp, and sugar in an 8-quart saucepan and bring to a boil. Reduce the heat and simmer 5 minutes.

5. Remove from heat. Let cool 5 minutes. Add drained rinds.

6. Add liquid pectin and return to a boil. Boil 1 minute, exactly, stirring constantly.

7. Skim off foam with a metal spoon.

8. Ladle into sterile jars, leaving ¼ inch headspace. Cap and seal.

9. Process in a boiling-water-bath canner 10 minutes.

YIELD: 6 ½-PINTS (FORTY-EIGHT 1-OUNCE SERVINGS)
NUTRITION PER SERVING

Calories	100	Total fat	<1g
% from fat	1	Saturated	<1g
Carbohydrates	26g	Cholesterol	0mg
Fiber	<1g	Sodium	11mg

Blueberry and Cherry Preserves

Two great taste sensations team up to make a mellow spiced spread.

3 cups cherries, washed, pitted, and crushed

3 cups blueberries, rinsed, picked over, and crushed

1 tablespoon lemon rind, thinly sliced

4½ cups sugar

½ teaspoon ground nutmeg

1. Combine all ingredients in a heavy 4-quart saucepan. Stir over medium heat to dissolve sugar.

2. Boil over high heat, being careful not to burn, until mixture reaches 220°F on a cooking thermometer (or use one of the methods found on pages 185–186).

3. Ladle into sterile jars, allowing ¼ inch headspace. Cap and seal.

4. Process 10 minutes in a boiling-water-bath canner.

YIELD: 5 ½-PINTS (FORTY 1-OUNCE SERVINGS)
NUTRITION PER SERVING

Calories	102	Total fat	<1g
% from fat	1	Saturated	<1g
Carbohydrates	26g	Cholesterol	0mg
Fiber	<1g	Sodium	1mg

Apple Ginger Marmalade

*A particular favorite of adults, this has just the right blend of flavors
to delight the palate.*

3 lemons

2½ cups water

3 pounds apples (9–10 apples), peeled, cored, and sliced, about 7½ cups (reserve peelings)

4 ounces preserved ginger, finely chopped

2¼ teaspoons ground ginger

8 cups sugar

1. Grate zest from lemons and reserve. Cut lemons in half and squeeze, reserving juice.

2. Make a "stock" with the water and apple peelings. Boil, covered, in an 8-quart saucepan about 15 minutes.

3. Remove peelings from stock and add apple slices. Simmer until soft, about 10 minutes.

4. Add ginger, lemon zest, and juice, along with sugar.

5. Boil, stirring occasionally, until spread thickens, or until a cooking thermometer reaches 220°F. (Remember to allow for thickening when spread is cooled.) Or you may use one of the tests for doneness found on pages 185–186.

6. Ladle into sterile jars, leaving ¼ inch headspace. Cap and seal.

7. Process 5 minutes in a boiling-water-bath canner.

YIELD: 10 ½-PINTS (EIGHTY 1-OUNCE SERVINGS)
NUTRITION PER SERVING

Calories	92	Total fat	<1g
% from fat	<1	Saturated	0g
Carbohydrates	23g	Cholesterol	1mg
Fiber	<1g	Sodium	1mg

Marion's Apple Butter

My friend Marion lives in the middle of an apple orchard. She makes many creative treasures out of her abundance of Rome apples. My very favorite is her recipe for apple butter. The ground spices and peelings give the mixture a dark, rich flavor and appearance.

10 large tart apples (about 5 pounds)

2 cups apple cider

3–5 cups sugar

¾ teaspoon ground cloves

½ teaspoon ground allspice

3 teaspoons ground cinnamon

½ teaspoon ground nutmeg

1. Wash, core, and quarter apples. No need to peel.

2. Cook apples slowly in cider until tender. Blend in a food processor. You should have about 12–14 cups of pulp.

3. Add ½–⅔ cup sugar, to taste, for each cup of apple pulp. Add spices.

4. Cook in 350°F oven or slow-cooker 6–8 hours, stirring often. Test for desired thickness by spooning mixture onto a cold plate. If no liquid oozes around the edges, it is thick enough.

5. Ladle into sterile jars, leaving ¼ inch headspace.

6. Process in a boiling-water-bath canner 10 minutes. This can also be frozen.

Note: The butter will keep up to 2 weeks in refrigerator after opening or after freshly made.

YIELD: 10 ½-PINTS (EIGHTY 1-OUNCE SERVINGS)
NUTRITION PER SERVING

Calories	59	Total fat	0g
% from fat	0	Saturated	0g
Carbohydrates	15g	Cholesterol	0mg
Fiber	<1g	Sodium	1mg

Apple-Plum Butter

. . . .

A variation on an old favorite, this is sure to delight your family.

2½ pounds plums, washed and pitted (about 15 medium)

½ cup lemon juice

1 cup water

2½ pounds apples, peeled, cored, and sliced

5½ cups sugar

1 teaspoon ground cinnamon

¼ teaspoon ground cloves

¼ teaspoon ground nutmeg

½ teaspoon salt

1. Cook plums in ¼ cup lemon juice and ½ cup water in a covered 3-quart saucepan over medium-high heat until plums are soft, about 20 minutes.

2. Meanwhile, cook apples with ¼ cup lemon juice and ½ cup water in a covered 3-quart saucepan over medium-high heat until apples are soft, about 10 minutes.

3. Let both mixtures cool slightly; combine in blender or food processor and puree.

4. Pour into heavy 8-quart flameproof roasting pan along with the sugar, spices, and salt.

5. Preheat oven to 300°F.

6. Cook on top of the stove over medium heat until all sugar dissolves.

7. Transfer roasting pan to preheated oven.

8. Bake uncovered, stirring occasionally, until mixture thickens. This will take 1–3 hours.

9. Test by spooning some on a plate. If no liquid appears on the edges, it is ready.

10. Ladle into sterile jars, leaving ¼ inch headspace. Cap and seal.

11. Process 10 minutes in a boiling-water-bath canner.

YIELD: 6 ½-PINTS (FORTY-EIGHT 1-OUNCE SERVINGS)

NUTRITION PER SERVING

Calories	113	Total fat	<1g
% from fat	2	Saturated	0g
Carbohydrates	29g	Cholesterol	0mg
Fiber	<1g	Sodium	23mg

Apple-Zucchini Butter

* * * * * * * * * * * *

This is a delicious way to use abundant zucchini in late summer.
The brown sugar gives it a rich taste.

4 pounds zucchini, peeled and chopped

5 tablespoons salt

2 pounds cooking apples, peeled, cored, and chopped

3 medium onions, chopped (2 cups)

2⅔ cups firmly packed light brown sugar

5 cups distilled white vinegar

1 piece dried gingerroot (about 2 inches)

2 tablespoons pickling spice

1. Layer zucchini into a large ceramic bowl with the salt. Cover and leave 12 hours or overnight.

2. Rinse and drain zucchini and place in a 6-quart saucepan. Add apples, onions, sugar, and vinegar.

3. Tie whole spices in a cheesecloth bag and add to the pan.

4. Bring slowly to a boil, stirring often, until mixture thickens, simmering about 1–1½ hours uncovered. Be careful not to burn it. Remove spice bag.

5. Ladle into clean jars, leaving ¼ inch headspace. Cap and seal.

6. Process 10 minutes in a boiling-water-bath canner.

* *

YIELD: 6 PINTS (NINETY-SIX 1-OUNCE SERVINGS)
NUTRITION PER SERVING

Calories	34	Total fat	<1g
% from fat	2	Saturated	0g
Carbohydrates	9g	Cholesterol	0mg
Fiber	<1g	Sodium	3mg

* *

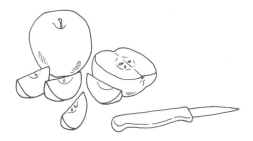

Basil-Apple Jelly

On a biscuit, with pork or chicken, or spread over pineapple cream cheese,
this herb jelly is a winner.

2 cups apple juice

⅓ cup dried basil

3 tablespoons fresh lemon juice, strained

¼ teaspoon butter or margarine

3½ cups sugar

3 ounces liquid pectin

1. In a 5-quart saucepan, heat apple juice to a boil. Add the dried basil, remove from the heat, and let it stand 2 hours.

2. Strain the apple-basil infusion through a paper coffee filter.

3. Rinse out the saucepan and return the mixture to it, along with the lemon juice, butter, and sugar.

4. Bring the new mixture to a boil over high heat, stirring constantly.

5. Add liquid pectin to the pan and return the mixture to a full boil. Boil exactly 1 minute, stirring constantly. Ladle the jelly into clean jars, leaving ½ inch headspace. Cap and seal.

6. Process in a boiling-water-bath canner 5 minutes.

YIELD: 2 PINTS (THIRTY-TWO 1-OUNCE SERVINGS)
NUTRITION PER SERVING

Calories	103	Total fat	<1g
% from fat	<1	Saturated	0g
Carbohydrates	27g	Cholesterol	0mg
Fiber	<1g	Sodium	7mg

Coriander and Honey Jelly

· · · · · · · · · · · ·

*Golden amber in color and subtle in flavor, this jelly stands up best
on delicate dinner rolls or breakfast breads.*

3 cups water

⅓ cup coriander seeds, bruised

¼ cup fresh lemon juice, strained

¼ cup mild honey

3 cups sugar

1 box (1¾ ounces) powdered fruit
pectin

1. Make an infusion of the water and
seeds by boiling 2 minutes in a 3-quart
saucepan. Let set 6 hours or overnight,
covered.

2. Strain the infusion through a coffee
filter and, measuring out 2½ cups liquid,
return to pan.

3. Add juice, honey, and sugar. Mix
together well. Boil hard and add pectin.

4. Bring to a boil again and boil exactly
1 minute. Remove from heat and skim off
any foam with a metal spoon.

5. Pour into four ½-pint sterile jars,
leaving ¼ inch headspace. Cap and seal.

6. Process 5 minutes in a boiling-water-
bath canner.

· ·

**YIELD: 4 ½-PINTS (THIRTY-TWO 1-OUNCE
  SERVINGS)**

NUTRITION PER SERVING

Calories	89	Total fat	<1g
% from fat	2	Saturated	0g
Carbohydrates	23g	Cholesterol	0mg
Fiber	<1g	Sodium	4mg

· ·

Nutmeg-Scented Geranium Jelly

You'll find this aristocratic concoction in specialty food stores. Now that you have the recipe, you can wow your family and friends.

4 cups apple juice

2 cups nutmeg-scented geranium leaves, washed and dried (always make sure plants have not been sprayed with insecticides)

5 cups sugar

3 tablespoons fresh lemon juice

3 ounces liquid pectin

¼ teaspoon freshly grated nutmeg

Drop of all-natural green food coloring (optional)

1. Make an infusion of the apple juice and geranium leaves by boiling them 2 minutes in an 8-quart saucepan. Let the mixture cool overnight. You can do this days ahead and refrigerate the results until needed.

2. Combine the strained infusion, sugar, and lemon juice in an 8-quart saucepan, and stir frequently over high heat 5 minutes.

3. Add the pectin. Bring the mixture back to a boil, timing it for exactly 1 minute.

4. Remove the pan from heat. Skim off any foam. Add the grated nutmeg.

5. Add a drop or two of all-natural green food coloring, if you wish.

6. Pour the jelly into clean jars, leaving ¼ inch headspace.

7. Process in a boiling-water-bath canner 5 minutes.

8. Let the jars cool, label, and then store them for about a week so the flavors can marry.

YIELD: 6 ½-PINTS (FORTY-EIGHT 1-OUNCE SERVINGS)

NUTRITION PER SERVING

Calories	96	Total fat	0g
% from fat	0	Saturated	0g
Carbohydrates	25g	Cholesterol	0mg
Fiber	<1g	Sodium	4mg

Mint Jelly

* * * * * * * * * * *

This subtle but delicious classic has endless possibilities.

2 cups apple juice or cider

2 bags peppermint tea, or 8 tablespoons (½ cup) fresh leaves

3 tablespoons lemon juice, strained

¼ teaspoon butter or margarine

1½ cups sugar

Few drops all-natural green food coloring (optional)

3 ounces liquid pectin

1. Make an infusion of the apple juice and tea bags, bringing it to a full boil and then letting it steep about 10 minutes in a heavy 5-quart saucepan. If you use fresh mint, strain liquid after cooking.

2. Remove the tea bags and add the lemon juice, butter, sugar, and food coloring, if desired. Bring to a boil over high heat, stirring constantly.

3. Add the liquid pectin and return the mixture to a boil, timing it for exactly 1 minute, stirring constantly.

4. Remove from heat and ladle into clean jars, leaving ¼ inch headspace. Cap and seal.

5. Process in a boiling-water-bath canner 5 minutes.

Note: Try using 2 tablespoons dried mint leaves instead of tea bags; strain the finished mixture through a coffee filter before ladling into jars for processing.

YIELD: 2 PINTS (THIRTY-TWO 1-OUNCE SERVINGS)
NUTRITION PER SERVING

Calories	53	Total fat	<1g
% from fat	1	Saturated	0g
Carbohydrates	14g	Cholesterol	0mg
Fiber	<1g	Sodium	6mg

Recycling "Failed" Fruit Spreads

* * * * * * * * * *

Sometimes the best efforts result in runny fruit spreads. If this happens to you, don't throw out your runny jams or jellies. Instead, use them as sauce for pound cake, waffles, pancakes, or ice cream. Or add them to plain yogurt for a treat. It tastes great.

Ginger Jam

This recipe gives new meaning to tea and toast.

2 lemons

8 medium-size tart apples, peeled, cored, and sliced (about 7 cups)

2½ cups water

1 teaspoon ground ginger

6 cups sugar

½ cup chopped crystallized ginger

1. Peel lemons, reserving skin. Cut lemons in half and squeeze for juice. Reserve.

2. In an 8-quart saucepan, cook the apples, water, lemon peel, juice, and ground ginger until the apples are soft. Add the sugar and stir until it is dissolved.

3. Boil the mixture rapidly 15 minutes, stirring frequently, until candy or cooking thermometer reaches 220°F.

4. Remove the pan from the heat and stir in the crystallized ginger. Skim off any foam and let the jam stand 10 minutes.

5. Pour it into clean jars, leaving ½ inch headspace. Cap and seal.

6. Process 10 minutes in a boiling-water-bath canner.

YIELD: 10 ½-PINTS (EIGHTY 1-OUNCE SERVINGS)
NUTRITION PER SERVING

Calories	68	Total fat	0g
% from fat	0	Saturated	0g
Carbohydrates	17g	Cholesterol	0mg
Fiber	<1g	Sodium	1mg

Carrot and Orange Marmalade

This spread is somewhat of a mystery — your family will never guess that it has carrots in it!

6 cups water

4 medium lemons, 2 rinds grated, then all 4 juiced and strained

2 medium oranges, 1 rind grated, then both juiced and strained

4 cups raw carrots, peeled and grated

4 cups sugar

⅛ teaspoon salt

1. In a 4-quart saucepan, add to 6 cups of water the rinds of 2 lemons and 1 orange and the carrots. Cook, covered, until tender, about 30 minutes.

2. Add the strained orange and lemon juices to the citrus rinds and carrots. Measure the mixture. There should be about 6 cups.

3. Add ⅔ cup sugar for each cup of the mixture. Stir over medium heat until sugar has dissolved.

4. Boil uncovered until mixture reaches 220°F on candy thermometer, or sheets off a spoon, 30–45 minutes. (See page 186.) Stir and watch the pot so the mixture does not burn.

5. Add salt and remove the mixture from the heat.

6. Pour the marmalade into clean hot jars. Leave ¼ inch headspace. Cap and seal.

7. Process in a boiling-water-bath canner 10 minutes.

YIELD: 4 ½-PINTS (THIRTY-TWO 1-OUNCE SERVINGS)
NUTRITION PER SERVING

Calories	107	Total fat	<1g
% from fat	<1	Saturated	0g
Carbohydrates	28g	Cholesterol	0mg
Fiber	<1g	Sodium	14mg

Summer Squash Conserve

When yellow squash are abundant, try this recipe. It is a great accompaniment to lamb, chicken, or pork.

2 pounds small, tender yellow squash, peeled and sliced

2 lemons, juiced

1 teaspoon grated lemon peel

1 can (13½ ounces) crushed pineapple in its own juice, drained

5 cups sugar

2 tablespoons chopped crystallized ginger

1 package (1¾ ounces) powdered pectin

1. Combine squash, juice, grated lemon peel, pineapple, sugar, and ginger in a heavy saucepan. Bring to a simmer, lower the heat, and cook uncovered about 15 minutes, stirring frequently.

2. Remove the pan from the heat and add the powdered pectin, stirring well. Bring the mixture to a boil again exactly 1 minute. Remove the pan from heat.

3. Pour hot mixture into clean jars, leaving ¼ inch headspace. Cap and seal.

4. Process 10 minutes in a boiling-water-bath canner.

YIELD: 5 PINTS (EIGHTY 1-OUNCE SERVINGS)
NUTRITION PER SERVING

Calories	57	Total fat	<1g
% from fat	<1	Saturated	0g
Carbohydrates	14g	Cholesterol	0mg
Fiber	<1g	Sodium	2mg

Horseradish Jelly

Serve this aromatic sweet-and-tart jelly with your next roast of beef — or mix it with low-fat cream cheese and eat it with vegetable sticks or crackers.

2 cups white wine vinegar

1 bottle (6 ounces) prepared horseradish (not cream style)

2 cups water

6 cups sugar

6 ounces liquid pectin

1. Heat the vinegar in nonreactive saucepan and pour it into a clean 1-quart jar.

2. Add the horseradish, cover the jar, and let it stand 24–48 hours at room temperature.

3. Strain through a wire strainer into a 2-quart saucepan. Mixture will measure 2 cups.

4. Add the water and sugar, stirring to dissolve the sugar. Bring to a full boil.

5. Add the liquid pectin and boil the mixture exactly 1 minute, stirring constantly.

6. Pour the jelly into clean jars, leaving ¼ inch headspace. Cap and seal.

7. Process in a boiling-water-bath canner 10 minutes.

YIELD: 7 ½-PINTS (FIFTY-SIX 1-OUNCE SERVINGS)
NUTRITION PER SERVING

Calories	95	Total fat	0g
% from fat	0	Saturated	0g
Carbohydrates	25g	Cholesterol	0mg
Fiber	<1g	Sodium	10mg

Quick Chile Pepper Jelly

Great with meats or as a sauce to mix with cream cheese for dipping crackers.

¼ cup seeded, chopped jalapeño peppers (4–6 medium) (wear rubber gloves)

1 medium-size green bell pepper, chopped

2½ cups cider vinegar

6 cups sugar

6 ounces liquid fruit pectin

1. Prepare jalapeños with rubber gloves then mince in a food processor.

2. Combine peppers, vinegar, and sugar in a heavy saucepan. Bring to full boil over high heat, stirring constantly.

3. Remove from heat and stir in liquid pectin. Return to heat and full boil. Boil exactly 1 minute.

4. Remove from heat and skim any foam with a metal spoon.

5. Ladle into sterile jars, leaving ¼ inch headspace. Cap and seal.

6. Process 5 minutes in a boiling-water-bath canner.

6½ PINTS

YIELD: ~~PINTS~~ (ONE HUNDRED TWELVE 1-OUNCE SERVINGS)

NUTRITION PER SERVING

Calories	47	Total fat	0g
% from fat	0	Saturated	0g
Carbohydrates	13g	Cholesterol	0mg
Fiber	0g	Sodium	3mg

Five-Pepper Jelly

Serve this jelly with corn bread or over cream cheese as an appetizer. Try prepared pineapple cream cheese, available at the supermarket.

1 large green pepper, seeded and chopped

2 large red bell peppers, seeded and chopped

1 small onion, peeled and chopped fine

4 jalapeños, seeded and chopped very fine (wear rubber gloves)

2 teaspoons salt

2½ teaspoons cumin seeds, toasted

1 whole, small red chile pepper

5 cups sugar

1½ cups red wine vinegar

½ cup fresh lemon juice

¼ teaspoon chili powder

¼ teaspoon cayenne pepper

6 ounces liquid pectin

6½ PINTS

YIELD: 7 PINTS (ONE HUNDRED TWELVE 1-OUNCE SERVINGS)

1. Combine the green and red peppers, onion, jalapeños, and 1 teaspoon salt in a colander about 3 hours. Drain well and press pepper mixture with the back of a spoon to remove moisture. (Wear rubber gloves.)

2. Make a spice bag of the cumin seeds and whole red chile pepper.

3. Combine peppers above with sugar, spice bag, vinegar, lemon juice, chili powder, cayenne, and remaining salt. Bring to a boil in a 6-quart saucepan. Stir and simmer 10 minutes.

4. Add pectin and return to a boil. Boil exactly 1 minute. Remove from heat. Remove the spice bag.

5. Ladle into sterile jars, leaving ¼ inch headspace. Cap and seal.

6. Process 5 minutes in a boiling-water-bath canner.

NUTRITION PER SERVING

Calories	42	Total fat	0g
% from fat	<1	Saturated	0g
Carbohydrates	11g	Cholesterol	0mg
Fiber	<1g	Sodium	42mg

Tomato Marmalade

After all, tomatoes are in the fruit family. When combined with citrus they make a remarkable marmalade.

1 medium orange, peeled (reserve peel in strips)

1 lemon, peeled (reserve peel in strips)

5 pounds tomatoes, peeled, cored, and chopped (about 8 cups)

¼ cup cider vinegar

1½ teaspoons ground cinnamon

1½ teaspoons ground allspice

½ teaspoon ground cloves

3 cups sugar

1. Carefully remove and discard membrane from citrus and chop the fruit.

2. Combine citrus with tomatoes in a heavy 8-quart nonreactive saucepan.

3. Add vinegar, spices, and sugar to saucepan and bring to a boil over high heat. Lower heat and simmer, uncovered, 1 hour or more or until mixture is reduced to about 4 cups. Stir frequently and be careful not to burn.

4. Ladle into sterile jars leaving ¼ inch headspace. Cap and seal.

5. Process 5 minutes in a boiling-water-bath canner.

YIELD: 4 ½-PINTS (SIXTEEN 2-OUNCE SERVINGS)
NUTRITION PER SERVING

Calories	93	Total fat	<1g
% from fat	1	Saturated	0g
Carbohydrates	24g	Cholesterol	0mg
Fiber	<1g	Sodium	6mg

Tomato Jam

Try this on a garlic bagel with cream cheese.

8 pounds tomatoes, peeled, cored, and chopped in a food processor

2 teaspoons salt

2 tablespoons sugar

4 tablespoons apple cider vinegar

4 tablespoons firmly packed light brown sugar

½ teaspoon ground white pepper

1 teaspoon ground cinnamon

1. Combine tomatoes, salt, and sugar in a 4-quart saucepan over medium heat. Bring to a boil and simmer about 30 minutes.

2. Skim foam with a metal spoon as it rises.

3. Add vinegar, brown sugar, and spices, and simmer until thick, about another 30 minutes or until mixture mounds up on a cold spoon.

4. Ladle into sterile jars, leaving ¼ inch headspace. Cap and seal.

5. Process 5 minutes in a boiling-water-bath canner.

6. Store 2 weeks before using, allowing flavors to marry.

YIELD: 4 ½-PINTS (THIRTY-TWO 1-OUNCE SERVINGS)

NUTRITION PER SERVING

Calories	37	Total fat	<1g
% from fat	4	Saturated	0g
Carbohydrates	9g	Cholesterol	0mg
Fiber	1g	Sodium	143mg

Yellow Tomato Jam

· · · · · · · · · · ·

This jam is delicious on a bagel, a warm piece of corn bread, or a bran muffin.

4 cups sugar

¾ cup water

6 cups tiny pear-shaped yellow tomatoes*

3 jalapeño peppers, seeded and chopped fine (wear rubber gloves)

3 tablespoons chopped fresh basil leaves

3 tablespoons fresh lemon juice

2 tablespoons white distilled vinegar

Note: Don't substitute red cherry tomatoes, as they are more acidic and less sweet.

1. In a 6-quart saucepan combine the sugar and ¾ cup water over medium heat. Bring to a boil and simmer until the syrup reaches 234°F on your cooking thermometer.

2. Remove from the heat and add tomatoes, mixing well. The syrup may change consistency, but continue stirring and eventually the tomatoes will be combined evenly.

3. Return to heat and add chiles, basil, lemon juice, and vinegar. Simmer uncovered on very low heat until mixture thickens, 1½–2 hours. Stir often, being careful not to burn. The jam will darken.

4. Ladle into clean jars, leaving ¼ inch headspace. Cap and seal.

5. Process 10 minutes in a boiling-water-bath canner.

· ·

YIELD: 4 ½-PINTS (THIRTY-TWO 1-OUNCE SERVINGS)

NUTRITION PER SERVING

Calories	108	Total fat	<1g
% from fat	<1	Saturated	0g
Carbohydrates	28g	Cholesterol	0mg
Fiber	<1g	Sodium	4mg

· ·

Ginger Shallot Marmalade

* * * * * * * * * * * *

Serve this remarkable condiment with steamed vegetables, grilled chicken, or pork.

10 shallots, sliced

2 tablespoons gingerroot, peeled and cut in julienne strips

2 tablespoons unsalted butter

1 clove garlic, sliced

½ cup chicken broth

⅓ cup balsamic vinegar

¼ cup honey

¼ teaspoon salt

¼ teaspoon freshly ground black pepper

1. In a heavy skillet, sauté the shallots and ginger in butter until they are tender, about 10–12 minutes. Add the garlic and sauté, stirring constantly, about 1 minute. Do not allow the garlic to brown.

2. Stir in the remaining ingredients and increase heat, stirring frequently, until the mixture thickens and most of the liquid has been absorbed.

3. Store in a clean refrigerator container up to 2 weeks.

YIELD: 1 CUP (EIGHT 1-OUNCE SERVINGS)
NUTRITION PER SERVING

Calories	85	Total fat	3g
% from fat	32	Saturated	2g
Carbohydrates	15g	Cholesterol	8mg
Fiber	<1g	Sodium	169mg

Garlic Jelly

* * * * * * * * * * *

Use this condiment as a flavorful accompaniment to lamb, pork, or chicken.

3 cups white wine vinegar

½ cup fresh garlic, peeled and finely chopped (about 50 cloves)

2 cups water

6 cups sugar

6 ounces liquid fruit pectin

1. In a 2½-quart saucepan, simmer the vinegar and garlic about 15 minutes. Remove the pan from heat and cool slightly.

2. Pour the liquid into a clean 1-quart glass jar. Cover the jar and let it stand at room temperature 24–48 hours.

3. Strain the vinegar and garlic through a wire strainer into a 6-quart kettle, making 2 cups of liquid. Add more uncooked white wine vinegar, if necessary.

4. Add water and sugar to the vinegar, stirring to dissolve the sugar. Bring to a full rolling boil over high heat.

5. Stir in the liquid pectin and bring the mixture back to a boil for exactly 1 minute, stirring constantly.

6. Skim off any foam.

7. Pour the jelly into hot clean jars, leaving ¼ inch headspace. Cap and seal.

8. Process in a boiling-water-bath canner 10 minutes.

YIELD: 3½ PINTS (TWENTY-FOUR 1-OUNCE SERVINGS)

NUTRITION PER SERVING

Calories	96	Total fat	0g
% from fat	0	Saturated	0g
Carbohydrates	25g	Cholesterol	0mg
Fiber	0g	Sodium	7mg

Preserved Lemons

* * * * * * * * * * * *

Serve these as a tangy flavor enhancer for fish, lamb, or chicken.

5 small organically grown lemons

⅔ cups canning salt

1 cup fresh lemon juice (about 6 lemons)

½ cup olive oil

1. Scrub lemons under cold water. Dry and cut into four wedges each.

2. Toss lemon wedges with the salt in a decorative airtight glass jar.

3. Add lemon juice and mix well.

4. Store at room temperature 7–10 days. Stir or shake the jar each day to remix salt and juice.

5. Add oil to cover the lemon mixture and store in the refrigerator up to six months.

6. Before using, rinse each slice under cold running water. Chop and sprinkle over baked fish or serve alongside roasted lamb or chicken. Delicious and beautiful.

Note: Lemons may darken as they age.

YIELD: 20 LEMON WEDGES (TWENTY SERVINGS)
NUTRITION PER SERVING

Calories	6	Total fat	0g
% from fat	0	Saturated	0g
Carbohydrates	3g	Cholesterol	0mg
Fiber	<1g	Sodium	3,411mg

Cranberry-Lime Curd

Spread it on breads or use it as a sauce for chicken, turkey, or pork. For more information on curds, see page 180. For a speedy shortcut, try the canned cranberry version.

2 cups whole cranberry sauce, or
   1 can (16 ounces) cranberry sauce

4 large eggs

2 teaspoons grated lime peel

½ cup fresh lime juice (juice of about
   4 medium limes)

½ cup sugar

½ cup butter, softened (1 stick)

1. Process all ingredients in a food processor until smooth.

2. Pour mixture into a double boiler over hot, not boiling water. Stirring constantly, cook until the mixture is thick, smooth, and shiny. This should take about 20 minutes. Do not overcook.

3. Ladle sauce into hot, clean jars, leaving ½ inch headspace. Cap and seal.

4. Process in a pressure canner at 10 pounds pressure for 10 minutes.

Whole Cranberry Sauce

To make your own cranberry sauce, combine:

1 cup sugar
1 cup water
½ pound whole cranberries

Boil 5–7 minutes in an uncovered saucepan, stirring constantly, until thick and clear.

YIELD: 3–4 ½-PINTS (TWENTY-FOUR TO THIRTY-TWO 1-OUNCE SERVINGS)
NUTRITION PER SERVING

Calories	77	Total fat	4g
% from fat	44	Saturated	2g
Carbohydrates	10g	Cholesterol	35mg
Fiber	<1g	Sodium	45mg

Pear Butter

Here is a great new way to enjoy an old-fashioned favorite.
Energy saving and speedy, this pear butter will delight all who try it.

12 ripe pears, peeled and chopped (Bosc or Bartlett)

1 lemon, juiced

¾ cup sugar

1 vanilla bean

3 2-inch strips lemon zest, ¼ inch wide

¼ cup water

1. Combine all ingredients in a heavy 8-quart saucepan. Cook over low heat 2½ hours, until fruit is very soft. Be careful not to burn. Stir frequently.

2. Remove vanilla bean and lemon zest.

3. Put mixture through a food mill. Pour into sterile jars. Cap and seal.

4. Refrigerate immediately. This will keep 2 weeks in the refrigerator.

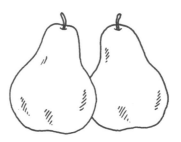

Yield: 2 ½-pints (sixteen 1-ounce servings)
Nutrition per Serving

Calories	95	Total fat	<1g
% from fat	4	Saturated	0g
Carbohydrates	25g	Cholesterol	0mg
Fiber	2g	Sodium	0mg

CHAPTER 6

PICKLES, RELISHES, AND CHUTNEYS are like jewelry — they accessorize the meal, adding zest and interest to the main course. Chutneys and relishes are kissing cousins to conserves and preserves and go well with such spicy foods as meat curry and grilled chicken with Cajun seasoning. A sandwich is never just a sandwich if a homemade sweet pickle is on the side. Chicken salad and tuna salad take on entirely new characters with 2 tablespoons of artichoke relish added.

In colonial America, particularly in Pennsylvania Dutch country, making relish, chutney, and pickles preserved the extra fruits and vegetables from the harvest. By chopping the fruits and vegetables, adding vinegar, spices, and perhaps sugar as available, they mixed the ingredients together until everything was "pickled." Commercially, as early as 1800, the H. J. Heinz Company bottled relishes and pickles, at the time a great new convenience food.

Today, although the preserving processes have sometimes changed, we can count on enjoying our own concoctions of pesticide-free, additive-free condiments for a fraction of the cost of store-bought ones.

VARIETIES

Pickles and relishes are, alas, a far cry from nutritious, but they serve a spicy purpose: making food that *is* nutritious even more appealing. Many favorite recipes are included here: refrigerator pickles, freezer pickles, fruit pickles, and brined pickles; relishes and chutneys using cranberries, tomatoes, peaches — and almost anything else you can imagine. I have also included recipes for low-salt, low-sugar pickles for those people on special diets. Choose from among the four basic types:

Fresh-pack pickles. This kind of pickle is the least labor intensive. Essentially, the produce is pared, soaked, drained, packed, and processed with vinegar and spices. The vinegar, as well as the processing, acts as a preservative.

Fruit pickles. Fruit for pickling usually requires paring, then simmering in a sugar and vinegar syrup, packing, and processing.

Chutneys and relishes. These condiments are usually mixtures of fruits and vegetables, pared and cooked with vinegar and/or sugar, packed, and then processed.

Salt-cured or brined pickles. This method takes longer and requires daily tending and skimming of foam or scum as it forms. The vegetables are pared and soaked (or cured) in brine. The salty brine encourages fermentation and, therefore, acid levels become high enough to prevent spoilage. Pack and process in a boiling-water-bath canner as a recipe dictates.

INGREDIENTS

For the best pickles, relishes, and chutneys, start with the freshest produce: firm, ripe, and solid, with no yellowing or tough skins, no damaged or moldy spots. Remove blossom ends and *cut* cucumbers from the vines rather than *pulling* them. It is a great rainy-day activity to put up pickles, but save the harvesting for a sunny day. Rain can drown the whole garden, waterlogging the cucumbers especially. Wait a day after a heavy rain to harvest. Handle the produce carefully to prevent bruising and wash it thoroughly, leaving no grit behind. Peaches and cucumbers especially need careful handling to prevent bruising.

Start with the best produce available.

Refrigerate the produce after picking and use it within 24 hours to ensure freshness and proper fermentation of pickles. To guarantee even pickling and cooking, it's a good idea to use produce similar in size, whether it's whole, chopped, or sliced.

SPICES AND HERBS

Spices and herbs have finally taken their rightful place again as valued medicines and cosmetics, as well as for cooking. In the last 50 years modern science seemed to replace the significance and usefulness of herbs and spices with technology and pharmacology. Thankfully, the current thinking seems to combine the science of medicine and the art of herbal knowledge.

The value of herbs and spices lies in more than their medicinal applications, of course. Who hasn't smelled the strong perfume of fresh lemon balm when accidentally brushed against by the lawn mower? How about the essence of dried oregano wafting up to your nose when you open a jar of this season's recently dried leaves? Herbs and spices have the power to evoke everything from strong memories of childhood to anticipation of just plain mouth-watering goodness.

To make sure your labors are worthwhile, always use fresh herbs and spices purchased or preserved especially for that season. Never use anything more than a year old when beginning any pickling project. When adding the flavors of spices and herbs, tie them in a cheesecloth bag, and unless otherwise noted in your pickling recipe, remove them when you're packing the finished product. Leave spices and herbs in the jar only if the recipe specifies it. Leaving them in will darken the foodstuffs and intensify the flavor.

Sweeteners

Use granulated white sugar for making relishes, pickles, and chutneys unless your recipe states otherwise. Brown sugar darkens the finished product and significantly changes the flavor.

Light-colored or flavored honey can be substituted for sugar. Remember that honey has *twice* the sweetening power of sugar. After boiling the vinegar, taste your pickle syrup as you sweeten with honey; you may need considerably less than you expect. Unlike recipes for fruit spreads, you can alter the amount of sugar or honey in a pickle recipe because, generally speaking, the sugar does not act as a preservative but is included for taste.

TIP

Remember to add the substituted honey to the syrup *after* boiling. Honey that has been boiled for long periods of time may break down and cause significant flavor changes.

Help for Too-Tart Pickles

Pickles that are too tart might seem to have too much vinegar in them, but that's not the ingredient to change the next time you make the recipe. Never alter the amount of vinegar called for in a pickling recipe, since the vinegar prevents the growth of bacteria. Instead, make your pickles less tart by adding sweetener, either sugar or honey.

VINEGARS

Vinegar, referred to in the Bible, has been used for hundreds of years in a variety of helpful ways. As well as a cosmetic, a healing tonic, and a skin preparation, it is also the main ingredient in pickling. The word "vinegar" is French in origin and means "sour wine."

Actually, vinegar is made from any liquid that can be fermented into alcohol. Yeasts change the sugar in a liquid into alcohol. Afterward, bacteria present in the alcohol solution change the alcohol to acetic acid, the primary acid in vinegar.

Read labels carefully when buying vinegar. The best vinegars should be aged and should state this on the label. If it isn't mentioned, it means it was made by an inferior process. Also stated on the label will be the percent acidity, essential to know when pickling food. Cider vinegar is usually about 4 percent acidity. Wine vinegar is usually about 6 percent. This range, from 4 to 6 percent, is perfect for pickling.

While both red and white wine and cider vinegar work well for pickling, fancy salad vinegars such as balsamic are not appropriate for pickles, relishes, and chutneys because they don't contain enough acetic acid. Cider vinegar can discolor or darken a light-colored vegetable like cauliflower, so you might wish to use another variety. Whatever kind of vinegar you choose, do not deviate from the amount specified in the recipe. Refer to chapter 7 (page 281) for more about vinegar.

OTHER INGREDIENTS

Don't overlook the quality of the other ingredients for pickling just because they are commonplace.

Water. Use only drinking-quality water. If it isn't potable before pickling, it won't be better after pickling. If your water is too hard and full of minerals, use bottled distilled water.

> **TIP**
>
> • • • • • •
>
> The chemical interaction of vinegar or salt on metals can impart off flavors and discolor foodstuffs. Use only stainless steel or unblemished enamel for cooking pickling liquids.

Salt. Salt-brined pickles rely on salt as a *preservative.* Canning salt is plain and pure, coarse or fine, and is available in most supermarkets. Avoid using sea salt, solar salt, kosher salt, and iodized or table salt in pickling. (See chapter 1, page 11 for a discussion of salt in canning.) For those on sodium-restricted diets, fresh-pack method pickles are quick and salt-free or salted sparingly for taste only. These can be just as crisp and are good for people on low-salt diets.

EQUIPMENT

Having all the equipment on hand and ready to use before you begin will make canning easier and help you feel more confident. If you have duplicates of kitchen equipment, keep them on the counter just in case you need them. It's

Equipment for Pickling

● ● ● ● ● ● ● ● ● ● ● ● ● ● ● ● ● ● ● ●

Before you begin pickling, have the following equipment in an accessible spot, ready for use.

Canning jars with screw-rings
New rubber-edged vacuum
  lids
Jar lifter or tongs
Boiling-water-bath canner
Widemouthed canning
  funnel
Kitchen timer
Teakettle
Clean kitchen towels
Large wooden and slotted
  spoons

Nonmetallic spatula or
  wooden chopstick
Scrub brush
Sieve
Colander
Paring and chopping knives
Measuring cups and spoons
Large glass or ceramic bowls
Food processing equipment
  (grinder, blender, slicer, or
  food processor)
Heavy potholders or mitts

great to be able to reach for a clean set of measuring spoons instead of fumbling in the drawer in the middle of a recipe. Be organized and read over your recipe and the list of equipment in the box on the previous page in advance of your pickling session.

Never use aluminum, brass, or copper bowls, pots, or utensils for pickling because of the off flavors or discoloration of the food resulting from the chemical interactions of the metal with the vinegar or salt. Cooking pans should be of stainless steel or unblemished enamel, and mixing bowls should be made of ceramic or glass, stainless steel, or enamel.

Jars and Containers

The same cleaning and sterilization rules and requirements for jars and lids that apply to other kinds of canning apply to pickling as well. All canning jars must be short enough for the water bath to cover them by 1 to 2 inches before the water boils. They need an additional 2 inches of "boiling room" at the top of the pot after the water begins to boil, so plan to use jars that are at least 4 inches shorter than the height of your canner.

In pickling, as in other forms of canning, the screw-ring holds the vacuum lid in place, and unlike the vacuum lid, a screw-ring, kept in pristine condition, can be used year after year. Twenty-four hours after the pickling process, when the jars have cooled, remove the metal screw-rings before you store your pickles in the pantry. Metal screw-rings left on jars may rust. If a screw-ring is stuck or stubborn, don't force it and risk breaking the seal, but rather leave the ring in place.

Other canning jars include European varieties, which can be quite attractive. But for safety's sake, don't buy any of these unless they include specific processing instructions that meet USDA guidelines.

Appropriate jars for pickling

TIP

● ● ● ● ● ●

Under no circumstances should you tighten down the screw-ring further after processing, as this might break the canning seal.

Antique jars with porcelain-lined zinc caps, requiring rubber rings, are available at flea markets, and you can purchase new rubber rings to fit them. However, rather than risk your hard work being foiled by jars not sealing, I recommend that you use these antique jars for dry storage for foods such as beans, pasta, and the like. The same goes for antique glass jars with bailed-wire seals. They look great, but use them for dry storage or short storage in the refrigerator for some of the fancy sauces or refrigerator jellies and pickles listed herein.

Crocks

For a brining or fermenting process, use a clean stoneware widemouthed jar, sometimes called a crock. A less glamorous but practical choice would be a glass or nonporous plastic bowl. You will also need a clean plate, which must fit inside the container and press directly against the food. Use a clean, unopened glass jar of last year's pickles — or any heavy, clean, nonmetallic object — to hold the plate down against the food in the crock.

PROCESSING PICKLED FOODS

The boiling-water bath is the canning process used for pickling foods. Because of the high acidity level, foods that are pickled do not require the higher temperatures produced by the pressure canning method to stay safe.

The boiling-water-bath method involves submerging the properly filled jars in a kettle of rapidly boiling water for a specified amount of time, ensuring that that a vacuum forms inside the jar, thereby sealing the lids. See chapter 2 (page 27) for more information about this method of canning.

BOILING-WATER-BATH EQUIPMENT

Ideally, a newly purchased 21- or 33-quart boiling-water-bath canner with lid and jar rack is the equipment

A boiling-water-bath canner

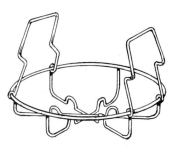

Wire rack for holding jars in a boiling-water-bath canner

of choice. The better ones are made of aluminum or porcelain-covered steel. The most expensive but durable ones are made of stainless steel. There are also many appropriate alternatives. Any large pot with a lid can be substituted as long as it is at least 4 inches higher than the jars — deep enough to allow 1 to 2 inches of water to cover the jars plus the 2 inches of boiling room. Use towels between the jars to prevent breakage during the canning process. You will need a wire rack for the bottom to hold jars away from the direct heat and to preventing cracking. In lieu of a rack, you can connect metal screwrings with twist-ties to place on the bottom of the canner.

Prewashing Jars and Lids

If the processing time is going to be more than 10 minutes, wash the empty jars in the dishwasher, or you may submerge them in hot, soapy water. Thoroughly rinse the jars after you remove them from the dishwasher or dishpan. No soapy residue can remain. Keep the jar lids hot in gently boiling water. If you are re-using screw-rings put them in the boiling water, also. You should always read the manufacturer's instructions and follow them to the letter when washing and sterilizing jars for canning any kind of food.

Sterilizing the Jars

For processing times under 10 minutes, sterilize clean prewashed jars. Fill the clean jars with hot water and lower them onto the rack in the water-filled pot, making sure that there is at least 1 inch of water above the rims of the jars. At sea level, the jars should boil for 10 minutes. At higher elevations, boil 1 additional minute for each 1,000 feet of altitude. Using the jar lifter, remove and pack the sterilized jars one by one. (Save the boiling water for the canning process.)

Packing the Jars

Immediately after you remove each sterilized jar from the boiling-water-bath canner, fill it with the relish, chutney, or other food to be pickled. A widemouthed funnel and ladle are invaluable for this stage. Be careful of drips when you remove the funnel from the filled jar. Drips, if not wiped off, can spoil the seal.

If you're making pickles, be sure to pack the jar loosely enough for the liquid to circulate around the food, leaving the headspace indicated in the recipe. To get rid of bubbles that appear in the liquid, tap the side of the jar with a knife handle to help settle the contents. You can also run a clean plastic spatula along the sides in several places to help remove bubbles. Don't stir, which creates more bubbles.

Use a thin, clean, wet dish towel pulled over your index finger to rub around the rim of each jar. It picks up the smallest drip of liquid, and you can feel the slightest chip on the rim as well. (If you find a flaw, either put the ingredients in a new sterilized jar, or place the damaged jar in the refrigerator for immediate use.) A wet paper towel works for this job, also. Place the lid and metal screw-ring on the jar and secure the ring to the jar.

Then fill the next jar until all are filled and ready for processing. Be sure to observe the proper headspace called for in the recipe.

Processing Pickled Foods

Because of their acidity, pickled foods never require the pressure canning method of processing. Follow these guidelines for successful boiling-water-bath processed pickles. The information is based on a bulletin from North Carolina State University.

1. Fill the canner halfway with water.

2. Preheat water to 200°F, a simmer with bubbles.

3. Load filled jars, fitted with lids, into the canner rack and use the handles to lower the rack into the simmering water; or fill the canner, one jar at a time, with a jar lifter.

4. Add boiling water, if needed, so the water level is at least 1–2 inches above jar tops.

5. Cover the canner with the lid.

6. Set a timer for the minutes required for processing the food and begin timing immediately. Be sure to allow for altitude.

7. Adjust the heat setting to maintain a simmer throughout the processing schedule.

8. Add more boiling water, if needed, to keep the water level above the jars.

9. When jars have been boiled for the recommended time, turn off the heat and remove the canner lid.

10. Using a jar lifter, remove the jars and place them on a towel, leaving at least 5 to 6 inches of space between the jars during cooling.

Pickle-Processing Time

• • • • • • • • • • • •

Processing time for pickles begins as soon as you submerge the jars in the boiling-water bath. This ensures a crisp, processed pickle that is not over-cooked.

STORAGE

Storing home-canned foods requires just a shelf in a cool, dry, dark place. You can tuck canned pickles in all sorts of nooks and crannies in your house or apartment — just don't forget where you stored them. Keep a location chart taped to the inside of a cabinet or pantry door. Mark the jars off the list as you use them. As with other canned goods, the best storage temperature is between 50° and 70°F. Store your newest batches of pickles toward the back of the shelf so you will use the oldest pickles first. Any jar kept for longer than one year is probably too old to eat.

Refrigerate homemade pickles after opening, just as you would store-bought pickles.

SAFETY FIRST

Never can enough be said about canning safety. *Clostridium botulinum,* the bacterium that causes botulism, grows in the absence of air, making the vacuum in a jar of canned food the ideal environment. Vinegar is a preservative, and botulism is less of a threat in pickles than in low-acid canned foods, but *never* bend the rules when spoilage is suspected. *Clostridium botulinum* is deadly. Never taste even a tiny bit of canned food you suspect may be spoiled.

First, check the seals after 12 to 24 hours. Use your thumbs to test the seal of the metal lid. Press hard on the center. If the lid does not move downward or "give," your jar is intact. If a jar or two in the batch isn't sealed, you can save it in the refrigerator and consume it over the next day or two.

Another method is to try lifting your newly canned jar by its lid after the screw-ring has been removed. Use the weight of the jar to test the weakness of the seal. (Protect yourself and the jar by doing this over the sink prepared with a towel to pad a possible fall.)

Questions to Ask Yourself After Pickling

To reduce your chances of ending up with jars that don't seal, don't try to cut corners, and make it a practice to be organized in advance.

1. Did I clean, pack, and process the jars exactly according to the recipe directions as well as the general directions for canning?

2. Did I fail to use the specified vinegar measurement in the recipe to prevent too tart a flavor, or did I correctly add a little sugar to overcome this problem instead?

3. Did I use clean equipment and have clean hands?

4. Did I regularly attend the brining solution, faithfully removing all traces of scum each day?

5. Was my water too hard or full of minerals?

6. Did I prepare all the produce approximately the same size to ensure even processing?

7. Did I remove the spice bag from the jars before processing?

8. Did I observe my finished cooling jars 24 hours after processing and check for incomplete seals and signs of spoilage? When in doubt or when you spot mold, spurting, or cloudy liquids, gases, change in color, or change in texture — throw it away. Use the safe method of disposal described on page 47 of chapter 2.

9. Did I store the canned pickles in a cool, dark place?

Pickle Making

1. Scrub the cucumbers with a soft brush and slice off the blossom end.

2. Pack the cleaned cucumbers loosely in the sterilized jars.

3. Using a widemouthed funnel, pour the hot brine over the cucumbers, allowing the proper headspace.

4. Using a nonmetallic spatula or wooden chopstick, press against the cucumbers to release all air bubbles.

5. Wipe the rim with a clean cloth to ensure a good seal.

6. Place the lid on the jar and tighten the screw-ring.

7. Preheat water to 200°F, a simmer with bubbles. Place filled jars in the preheated canner. Add more boiling water until it is 1 to 2 inches above the jars.

8. Process for the time and at the temperature given in the recipe. Add more boiling water, if necessary, to keep it 1 to 2 inches above jars.

(continued on page 252)

Pickle Making (continued)

9. Remove the jars and place on a towel or rack to cool for 24 hours.

10. Remove the screw-rings and test the seals. The center of the lid should be depressed. You can lift the jar by the lid and it should hold.

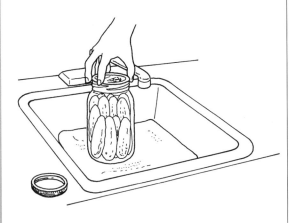

11. Wash the jars, label, and store unopened in a cool, dark place for at least six weeks before using.

RECIPES FOR PICKLES, RELISHES, & CHUTNEYS

Bread and Butter Pickles

Fresh-Pack Refrigerator Dill Pickles

Old-Fashioned Brined Dill Pickles

Mixed Pickling Spice

Refrigerator Super-Sweets

Two-Day Mustard Pickles

Watermelon Rind Pickles

Spicy Frozen Cucumbers

Green and Gold Refrigerator Pickles

Pickled Garlic

Pickled Brussels Sprouts

Pickled Cauliflower

Pickled Asparagus

Sweet Pickle Relish

Red Refrigerator Relish

Sweet Onion Relish

Refrigerator Corn Relish

Black-Eyed-Pea Refrigerator Relish

Green Tomato Chutney

Basil-Shallot Mustard

Raisin Refrigerator Relish

Colorful Pear Relish

Rhubarb Chutney

Refrigerator Plum Chutney

Southwestern Cranberry Sauce

Pickled Mixed Vegetable Chunks

Baby Carrots with Honey and Dill

Bread and Butter Pickles

This is an old-fashioned favorite. Use these pickles to dress up a plain sandwich!

Boiling-water-bath canner; seven 1-pint jars

6 pounds medium-size cucumbers, scrubbed and sliced ⅛ inch thick (about 4 quarts)

1½ cups small white onions, sliced and peeled (about 1 pound)

2 cloves garlic

⅓ cup salt

Ice cubes

4½ cups sugar

1½ teaspoons ground turmeric

1½ teaspoons celery seeds

2 tablespoons yellow mustard seeds

3 cups white distilled vinegar

1. In a large mixing bowl combine cucumbers, onions, and garlic. Add salt and mix thoroughly. Cover with ice cubes. Let stand 3 hours.

2. Rinse well, thoroughly drain the mixture, and remove garlic cloves.

3. Combine sugar, turmeric, celery and mustard seeds, and vinegar, and heat to boiling in an 8-quart saucepan. Add drained cucumber mixture and heat 5 minutes.

4. Pour in sterilized jars, leaving ½ inch headspace. Cap and seal.

5. Process 5 minutes in a boiling-water-bath canner.

YIELD: 7 PINTS (FIFTY-SIX 2-OUNCE SERVINGS)
NUTRITION PER SERVING

Calories	74	Total fat	<1g
% from fat	2	Saturated fat	0g
Carbohydrates	19g	Cholesterol	0mg
Fiber	<1g	Sodium	611mg

Fresh-Pack Refrigerator Dill Pickles

Great for a small family, these pickles stay crisp 6 weeks in the refrigerator if you can keep from eating them that long.

10–14 whole pickling cucumbers, approximately 2 inches, scrubbed

3 sprigs dill

2 cloves garlic

½ cup fresh lemon juice

Cold water

1. Pack sterilized jar with the cucumbers, dill, and garlic alternating in layers, leaving ¼ inch headspace.

2. Pour lemon juice over cucumbers. Fill jar with cold water.

3. Seal and refrigerate. These will keep at least 6 weeks. Serve and enjoy!

YIELD: 1 QUART (SIXTEEN 2-OUNCE SERVINGS)
NUTRITION PER SERVING

Calories	33	Total fat	<1g
% from fat	7	Saturated fat	<1g
Carbohydrates	7g	Cholesterol	0mg
Fiber	2g	Sodium	6mg

Old-Fashioned Brined Dill Pickles

*Here is another of my favorites. While these pickles need to sit in the crock
3 weeks, plan ahead, and maintaining these pickles will only take
a few minutes each day. They're worth it.*

Boiling-water-bath canner; ten 1-quart jars

20 pounds pickling cucumbers, 3–6 inches long, scrubbed (about ½ bushel)

¾ cup mixed pickling spice

3 large bunches fresh dill weed

2½ cups cider vinegar

1¾ cups salt

2½ gallons water

10 cloves garlic

1. In a 5-gallon crock, place half of the cucumbers and spice and dill, then layer again to within 3–4 inches of the top of the crock.

2. Mix the vinegar, salt, and water and pour over cucumbers. Cover with a ceramic plate that fits inside the crock and weight it down.

3. Make certain cucumbers are completely under the brine. Cover crock loosely with a clean towel.

4. Keep pickles at room temperature (80°–85°F). I use my laundry room sink for this purpose.

5. In about 3 days begin skimming off the foam. Do not stir pickles. Keep them completely covered with brine throughout this process.

6. Check daily, removing scum and foam. In 3 weeks cucumbers should be an olive green color. White spots inside the cucumbers will disappear when processed.

YIELD: 10 QUARTS (ONE HUNDRED SIXTY 2-OUNCE SERVINGS)

NUTRITION PER SERVING

Calories	10	Total fat	<1g
% from fat	15	Saturated fat	0g
Carbohydrates	2g	Cholesterol	0mg
Fiber	1g	Sodium	1,122mg

7. Pour the cucumbers in sterile quart jars. Add 1 clove garlic to each jar and divide the dill sprigs evenly into the jars.

8. Strain the brine through a coffee filter into the jars, leaving ½ inch headspace. Cap and seal.

9. Process 15 minutes in a boiling-water-bath canner.

Note: Start timing the canning process as soon as jars are put in boiling water instead of waiting for the water to boil again. This will ensure a crisp, processed pickle without actually cooking.

Mixed Pickling Spice

● ● ● ● ● ● ● ● ● ● ● ● ● ●

Use this in the same quantity as you would store-bought pickling spice.

2 tablespoons yellow mustard seeds

2 teaspoons whole allspice

2 teaspoons dill seeds

2 teaspoons coriander seeds

2 teaspoons whole black peppercorns

2 bay leaves, crumbled

2 dried red chile peppers
(2 inches long), crumbled
(wear rubber gloves)

1. Mix all ingredients and store in an airtight jar in a cool, dark place.

2. Use in any pickle recipe.

YIELD: ⅓ CUP

Refrigerator Super-Sweets

This is quick and easy and good for beginners and experienced cooks alike.

1 gallon cucumbers, scrubbed and sliced (about 10–12 large cucumbers)

2 quarts white distilled vinegar

6 cups sugar

1 teaspoon whole mixed pickling spice

1 teaspoon salt (optional)

1. Place cucumber slices in an 8-quart crock. Cover with vinegar. Be sure cucumbers are completely under the vinegar.

2. Cover cucumbers with a ceramic plate and place a heavy jar of last year's pickles on it to weight it down. Let stand 24 hours.

3. Drain and discard vinegar. Add sugar, spices, and salt (if desired) to cucumber slices.

4. Mix gently to allow sugar to dissolve somewhat. After several hours stir again. Pickles are ready to eat when all the sugar has dissolved.

5. Pack pickles in sterile canning jars and refrigerate before eating. These will keep 2 months in the refrigerator.

An adaptation of the NC Agricultural Extension Service recipe.

YIELD: 8 PINTS (SIXTY-FOUR 2-OUNCE SERVINGS)
NUTRITION PER SERVING

Calories	80	Total fat	0g
% from fat	0	Saturated fat	0g
Carbohydrates	21g	Cholesterol	0mg
Fiber	<1g	Sodium	34mg

Two-Day Mustard Pickles

This recipe is best made in early fall, when cauliflower is plentiful but before frost nips the tomatoes, green peppers, and cucumbers. Enjoy it all winter as an accompaniment to meat or sandwiches.

Boiling-water-bath canner; five 1-quart jars

- 1 head cauliflower, broken into florets (about 1½ quarts)
- 1 quart small white onions, peeled
- 1 quart small cucumbers, sliced
- 1 quart small green tomatoes
- 2 large green bell peppers, seeded and chopped (about 2 cups)
- 2 large red bell peppers, seeded and chopped (about 2 cups)
- ½ cup pickling salt
- 3 quarts cold water
- 2 quarts cider vinegar
- 6 tablespoons prepared mustard
- 1½ cups firmly packed light brown sugar
- ⅓ cup flour
- 2 tablespoons ground turmeric

1. Prepare vegetables; place in a large crock, or glass or ceramic bowl. Mix salt and water, then pour over cucumbers. Cover and let sit 24 hours.

2. Drain brine from vegetables, catching vegetables in a colander and solution in a saucepan. Heat solution to boiling and pour over vegetables in colander. Drain.

3. Combine vinegar, mustard, brown sugar, flour, and turmeric in a large nonreactive saucepan. Stir, then heat gradually, stirring constantly, until mixture is thick and smooth. Add vegetables and cook gently until they are tender but have not lost their individuality. Stir with a heavy wooden spoon to prevent scorching.

4. Pack into clean, hot quart jars, leaving ½ inch headspace. Cap and seal.

5. Process in a boiling-water-bath canner 10 minutes.

YIELD: 5 QUARTS (EIGHTY 2-OUNCE SERVINGS)
NUTRITION PER SERVING

Calories	29	Total fat	<1g
% from fat	3	Saturated fat	0g
Carbohydrates	8g	Cholesterol	0mg
Fiber	<1g	Sodium	658mg

Watermelon Rind Pickles

· · · · · · · · · · ·

A real old-fashioned classic, perfect with a turkey sandwich. As a child, my sister-in-law called this her "favorite green vegetable."

Boiling-water-bath canner; three 1-pint jars

3 tablespoons slaked lime*

2 quarts water

8 cups watermelon rind (1 large melon), peeled and cut in 1-inch squares

2 cups white distilled vinegar

3 cups firmly packed brown sugar

1 lemon, thinly sliced

1½ cinnamon sticks, 2–2½ inches long

1 teaspoon whole allspice

1 teaspoon whole cloves

2 drops all-natural green food coloring (optional)

1. In a large glass or ceramic bowl, add the lime to the water. Soak peeled watermelon rind in lime solution 8 hours.

2. Drain, then rinse well and drain again.

3. In a large saucepan simmer rind in clear water until tender, about 20 minutes.

4. Meanwhile make a syrup of vinegar, sugar, lemon, and spices (tied in cheesecloth). Boil 5 minutes in an 8-quart saucepan. Add rind to vinegar solution and cook until rind is clear and thin, about 10 minutes.

5. Pack clean jars with rind, and pour hot liquid over each one, leaving ½ inch headspace. Cap and seal.

6. Process 10 minutes in a boiling-water-bath canner.

· ·

YIELD: 3 PINTS (TWENTY-FOUR 2-OUNCE SERVINGS)
NUTRITION PER SERVING

Calories	124	Total fat	<1g
% from fat	1	Saturated fat	0g
Carbohydrates	32g	Cholesterol	0mg
Fiber	1g	Sodium	16mg

· ·

*Slaked lime or pickling lime is calcium hydroxide, found in health food and grocery stores.

Note: Watermelon rind can be pared and stored in the refrigerator "as eaten" up to 3 days. When you have accumulated 8 cups it's time to pickle.

Spicy Frozen Cucumbers

· · · · · · · · · · ·

Even after they've been thawed and stored in the refrigerator for up to a week, these pickles taste like Granny's homemade ones, but are a lot easier to make. This recipe is frequently requested by friends.

4 cups pickling cucumbers, 3–4 inches long (about 12–14)

2 large onions

1 tablespoon salt

1 cup sugar

½ cup cider vinegar

½ teaspoon ground turmeric

1 tablespoon whole white mustard seeds

1. Wash and thinly slice the cucumbers, unpeeled. Peel the onions and slice thin.

2. Combine the cucumbers, onions, and salt in a glass or ceramic bowl. Let them stand 2–4 hours to extract moisture.

3. Rinse and drain the vegetables well, blotting them with paper towels to absorb all the moisture.

4. Combine the remaining ingredients and mix well until the sugar dissolves completely, about 10 minutes.

5. Pour the cucumber mixture into clean freezer containers, leaving 1 inch of headspace for expansion. Cap and seal. These will keep up to 1 year in the freezer.

6. To use, thaw about 4 hours in the refrigerator. Serve chilled!

· ·

YIELD: 5 PINTS (TWENTY 4-OUNCE SERVINGS)
NUTRITION PER SERVING

Calories	54	Total fat	<1g
% from fat	4	Saturated fat	0g
Carbohydrates	13g	Cholesterol	0mg
Fiber	<1g	Sodium	321mg

· ·

Green and Gold Refrigerator Pickles

Easy-to-make refrigerator pickles, these will disappear rapidly.

2 cups sugar

1 cup cider vinegar

3½ cups yellow summer squash, thinly sliced

3½ cups zucchini squash, thinly sliced

1 cup onions, thinly sliced

1 cup green bell peppers, chopped fine

1 cup red bell peppers, chopped fine

1 tablespoon salt

1 tablespoon dill seeds

1. Heat sugar and vinegar in a nonreactive 4-quart saucepan until sugar dissolves.

2. Add remaining ingredients and chill overnight.

3. Transfer pickles to sterile quart canning jars. Cover with vinegar mixture, cap and seal. These will keep in the refrigerator 2 months.

YIELD: 2 QUARTS (SIXTEEN 4-OUNCE SERVINGS)
NUTRITION PER SERVING

Calories	116	Total fat	<1g
% from fat	1	Saturated fat	0g
Carbohydrates	30g	Cholesterol	0mg
Fiber	1g	Sodium	402mg

Pickled Garlic

Not only is this good for what ails you and low in calories, but it's also a mellow and delicious appetizer. Old Bay Seasoning can be found in most grocery stores in the seafood section as a "crab boil" seasoning.

6 ounces distilled white vinegar

4 ounces water

2 teaspoons coarse salt

⅛ teaspoon Old Bay Seasoning

6 large bulbs of garlic, separated, blanched, and skinned

Rind of 1 lemon, peeled in one continuous spiral

1 dill head, or ½ teaspoon dill seeds

1 small red chili pepper, whole

1. In a saucepan combine the vinegar, water, salt, and Old Bay Seasoning and bring to a boil. Add the garlic and let it steep 10 minutes over very low heat.

2. Line a clean 1-pint jar with the lemon rind and add the dill head and red pepper.

3. Ladle in the garlic and enough liquid to cover it. Cap and seal.

4. Cool at room temperature.

5. Allow the flavors to marry for 3–4 days before using. Refrigerate up to 4 weeks.

Substitute for Old Bay Seasoning

If Old Bay Seasoning is not available, make your own, using a pinch each of celery seeds, cayenne pepper, ground cinnamon, ground ginger, allspice, ground yellow mustard, and paprika, plus ½ bay leaf.

YIELD: 1 PINT (EIGHT 2-OUNCE SERVINGS)
NUTRITION PER SERVING

Calories	46	Total fat	<1g
% from fat	3	Saturated fat	0g
Carbohydrates	11g	Cholesterol	0mg
Fiber	<1g	Sodium	486mg

Pickled Brussels Sprouts

*Low in calories, high in taste and nutrients, this recipe can be used as a salad base
for mixed lettuces or eaten alone on toothpicks as an appetizer.*

Boiling-water-bath canner; four 1-pint jars

  6 cups Brussels sprouts (about 2 pounds)

2½ cups water

2½ cups vinegar

  3 tablespoons salt

  1 teaspoon cayenne pepper

  4 cloves garlic

  4 heads dill, or 2 teaspoons dill seeds

1. Boil Brussels sprouts until tender, leaving them whole but trimming off old foliage. Drain and pack into clean jars.

2. Mix the water, vinegar, salt, and pepper in a heavy saucepan, and boil 5 minutes.

3. Pour vinegar mixture over the sprouts, leaving ¼ inch headspace.

4. Distribute dill heads and garlic evenly among the jars.

5. Cap, seal, and process 15 minutes in a boiling-water-bath canner.

YIELD: 4 PINTS (SIXTEEN ½-CUP SERVINGS)
NUTRITION PER SERVING

Calories	32	Total fat	<1g
% from fat	7	Saturated fat	0g
Carbohydrates	8g	Cholesterol	0mg
Fiber	2g	Sodium	1,215mg

Pickled Cauliflower

Pickle cauliflower in cool weather when it is plentiful.
This recipe is easy and low in calories.

Boiling-water-bath canner; six 1-quart jars

3 heads cauliflower, cut into small florets
    and washed (about 10 pounds)

8 cups white distilled vinegar

8 cups water

¼ cup salt

¼ cup yellow mustard seeds

12 cloves garlic

12 dill heads

12 small chile peppers

1. Steam cauliflowerets over boiling water 1 minute.

2. Simmer vinegar, water, salt, and mustard seeds in a 5-quart saucepan 5 minutes.

3. Pack each sterile jar with 2 cloves garlic, 2 dill heads, and 2 chile peppers. Pack warm cauliflower in each jar, leaving ¼ inch headspace.

4. Cover with vinegar solution, leaving ¼ inch headspace. Cap and seal.

5. Process 15 minutes in a boiling-water-bath canner.

6. Store jars 3 weeks to allow flavors to develop.

YIELD: 6 QUARTS (NINETY-SIX 2-OUNCE SERVINGS)
NUTRITION PER SERVING

Calories	8	Total fat	<1g
% from fat	14	Saturated fat	0g
Carbohydrates	2g	Cholesterol	0mg
Fiber	<1g	Sodium	268mg

Pickled Asparagus

Remember spring as you serve these on lettuce leaves in the middle of winter; garnish with hard-boiled egg slices and a mustard mayonnaise.

Boiling-water-bath canner; two 1-quart jars

 3 cups distilled white vinegar

 3 cups water

 2 teaspoons salt

 4 tablespoons sugar

 3 pounds asparagus spears, trimmed and washed (about 8 cups)

 2 teaspoons pickling spice

12 whole black peppercorns

 4 cloves garlic, peeled

1. Combine the vinegar, water, salt, and sugar in a 2-quart saucepan and heat to a boil.

2. Pack asparagus in two 1-quart jars, leaving ½ inch headspace.

3. Divide the spice between the two jars. Pour hot vinegar mixture over the asparagus, leaving ½ inch headspace. Cap and seal.

4. Process 20 minutes in a boiling-water-bath canner.

YIELD: 2 QUARTS (SIXTEEN 4-OUNCE SERVINGS)
NUTRITION PER SERVING

Calories	45	Total fat	<1g
% from fat	5	Saturated fat	<1g
Carbohydrates	12g	Cholesterol	0mg
Fiber	2g	Sodium	272mg

Sweet Pickle Relish

* * * * * * * * * * *

Colorful and delicious, this remarkable relish will delight your picnic guests.

Boiling-water-bath canner; nine 1-pint jars

3 quarts cucumbers, scrubbed and chopped

3 cups green bell peppers, seeded and chopped

3 cups red bell peppers, seeded and chopped

1 cup onions, chopped

¾ cup salt

4 cups ice cubes

8 cups water

4 teaspoons yellow mustard seeds

4 teaspoons ground turmeric

4 teaspoons whole allspice

1 tablespoon whole cloves

2 cups sugar

6 cups white distilled vinegar

1. In a 12-quart saucepan, combine vegetables, salt, and ice in the water 4 hours. Drain and re-cover with fresh ice and water 1 additional hour. Drain thoroughly.

2. Combine spices in a cheesecloth bag. Place spice bag, sugar, and vinegar in a nonreactive 4-quart saucepan and heat to boiling.

3. Pour vinegar syrup over vegetables and refrigerate 24 hours.

4. Heat mixture to boiling and ladle into sterile jars, leaving ½ inch headspace. Cap and seal.

5. Process 10 minutes in a boiling-water-bath canner.

Note: A food processor can be used to chop vegetables in batches by pulsing motor on and off.

* *

YIELD: **9 PINTS (SEVENTY-TWO 2-OUNCE SERVINGS)**
NUTRITION PER SERVING

Calories	31	Total fat	<1g
% from fat	4	Saturated fat	0g
Carbohydrates	8g	Cholesterol	0mg
Fiber	<1g	Sodium	1,068mg

* *

Red Refrigerator Relish

This recipe can serve as a garnish for the standard hamburgers and hot dogs, but it's also delicious as a slaw with barbecue.

½ cup cider vinegar

⅓ cup sugar

1 tablespoon yellow mustard seeds

1½ teaspoons celery seeds

½ cup water

⅛ teaspoon cayenne pepper

1 small head green cabbage, shredded

½ small head red cabbage, shredded

1 large green bell pepper, seeded and chopped

6 medium tomatoes, chopped and drained

1 cup chopped dill pickles

1 large red onion, diced

1. Combine vinegar, sugar, mustard seeds, celery seeds, water, and cayenne pepper in an 8-quart saucepan. Simmer uncovered 5 minutes. Cool.

2. Add remaining ingredients to pan, cover, and refrigerate 8 hours. Serve chilled. Keeps 3–5 days in the refrigerator.

YIELD: 10 CUPS (TEN 1-CUP SERVINGS)
NUTRITION PER SERVING

Calories	89	Total fat	<1g
% from fat	8	Saturated fat	<1g
Carbohydrates	20g	Cholesterol	0mg
Fiber	3g	Sodium	331mg

Sweet Onion Relish

Make a hot dog a festive occasion with this relish. It is easy to prepare and adds zest to any meat.

Boiling-water-bath canner; five 1-pint jars

5 pounds sweet onions, chopped (about 10 cups)

1 cup sugar

2¼ cups white distilled vinegar

2 tablespoons salt

2 tablespoons celery seeds

1. Combine all ingredients in a heavy 8-quart saucepan. Bring to a boil.

2. Reduce heat and simmer 10 minutes, stirring occasionally.

3. Ladle relish into clean jars, leaving ½ inch headspace.

4. Cap and seal.

5. Process 10 minutes in a boiling-water-bath canner.

YIELD: **5 PINTS (FORTY 2-OUNCE SERVINGS)**
NUTRITION PER SERVING

Calories	40	Total fat	<1g
% from fat	3	Saturated fat	0g
Carbohydrates	10g	Cholesterol	0mg
Fiber	<1g	Sodium	322mg

Refrigerator Corn Relish

*A quick version of Granny's corn relish, this is a great favorite
on hot dogs and hamburgers.*

¼ teaspoon Tabasco sauce

¾ teaspoon mustard seeds

¼ teaspoon celery seeds

2¼ teaspoons salt

¾ cup sugar

1½ cups distilled white vinegar, 5% acidity

1 small green bell pepper, seeded and chopped

1 small red bell pepper, seeded and chopped

3 green onions, sliced

12 large ears corn, or about 8 cups of kernels

1. Combine spices, sugar, and vinegar in a heavy 8-quart nonreactive saucepan. Boil over medium heat, uncovered, about 5 minutes.

2. Combine vegetables. Distribute equally into four sterilized pint jars. Pour vinegar mixture over vegetables.

3. Cover tightly and refrigerate. Consume within 1 month. Delicious!

YIELD: 4 PINTS (THIRTY-TWO 2-OUNCE SERVINGS)
NUTRITION PER SERVING

Calories	42	Total fat	<1g
% from fat	5	Saturated fat	0g
Carbohydrates	10g	Cholesterol	0mg
Fiber	1g	Sodium	154mg

Black-Eyed-Pea Refrigerator Relish

In the South, black-eyed peas are traditionally served on New Year's Day to bring good fortune. What a great New Year's gift for friends. But don't forget, this relish is delicious served all year long.

½ pound dried black-eyed peas, cooked barely tender (al dente)

½ pound dried black beans, cooked barely tender (al dente)

½ onion, chopped fine

2 ears yellow corn, blanched, kernels removed

1 red bell pepper, seeded and chopped fine

½ red onion, chopped fine

2 green onions, chopped fine (including green tops)

½ orange, sectioned and seeded

Simple Vinaigrette

1 cup extra-virgin olive oil

⅓ cup red wine vinegar

⅛ teaspoon freshly ground black pepper

¼ teaspoon salt

¼ teaspoon dry mustard

1 teaspoon chopped fresh parsley

1 teaspoon chopped fresh tarragon

1. Combine all ingredients in a 4-quart ceramic bowl. Pour Simple Vinaigrette dressing over warm vegetables.

2. Cover bowl and refrigerate overnight.

3. Ladle relish into six sterile canning jars. Cap and seal. This will keep 3 days in the refrigerator.

YIELD: 3 PINTS (TWENTY-FOUR 2-OUNCE SERVINGS)
NUTRITION PER SERVING

Calories	163	Total fat	9g
% from fat	50	Saturated fat	1g
Carbohydrates	16g	Cholesterol	0mg
Fiber	3g	Sodium	27mg

Green Tomato Chutney

This chutney can be heated and thickened with cornstarch to complement Chinese vegetables or rice.

Boiling-water-bath canner; seven 1-pint jars

- 16 cups green tomatoes, cored and chopped
- ½ cup salt
- 8 cups coarsely chopped green cabbage
- 2 cups coarsely chopped green peppers
- 1 cup chopped onion
- 3 cloves garlic, peeled and sliced
- 1½ cups firmly packed brown sugar
- 4½ cups cider vinegar
- 2 tablespoons mustard seeds
- 4 teaspoons celery seeds
- 1 tablespoon prepared horseradish (not cream style)

1. Choose tomatoes that are slightly pink.

2. Sprinkle the salt over the chopped vegetables and let them stand 4–5 hours.

3. Transfer the salted vegetables to a colander. Press them with the back of a broad spoon, removing as much moisture as possible. Drain well.

4. Combine the garlic, sugar, vinegar, spices, and horseradish. Simmer 15 minutes in a heavy nonreactive 12-quart saucepan.

5. Add the drained vegetables to the saucepan and bring the mixture to a boil.

6. Pack into clean jars, leaving ¼ inch headspace. Cap and seal.

7. Process 10 minutes in a boiling-water-bath canner.

YIELD: 7 PINTS (FIFTY-SIX 2-OUNCE SERVINGS)
NUTRITION PER SERVING

Calories	45	Total fat	<1g
% from fat	5	Saturated fat	0g
Carbohydrates	11g	Cholesterol	0mg
Fiber	1g	Sodium	926mg

Basil-Shallot Mustard

* * * * * * * * * * *

Turn a plain sandwich into a feast with this mustard.

¼ cup light mustard seeds

½ cup dry mustard

⅔ cup apple juice

⅔ cup red wine vinegar

⅓ cup water

2 tablespoons minced shallots

2 tablespoons packed light brown sugar

1 teaspoon salt

¼ teapoon allspice

3 tablespoons fresh basil, chopped

1. Combine the seeds, dry mustard, apple juice, vinegar, and water in a glass or ceramic bowl and stir, mixing well.

2. Let sit 4–6 hours, stirring occasionally. (Cover the bowl with plastic wrap.)

3. Process the mixture in the bowl of a food processor until the seeds are coarsely ground.

4. Cook the mixture in a double boiler over simmering water, adding the shallots, sugar, salt, allspice, and basil. Cook 20–25 minutes. The mustard will thicken as it cools.

5. Pour into sterile jars. Cap and seal.

6. Allow flavors to marry 2–3 days before using. Will keep in refrigerator 2–3 months.

YIELD: 5 ½-PINTS (FORTY 1-OUNCE SERVINGS)
NUTRITION PER SERVING

Calories	15	Total fat	1g
% from fat	33	Saturated fat	0g
Carbohydrates	2g	Cholesterol	0mg
Fiber	<1g	Sodium	54mg

Raisin Refrigerator Relish

It wouldn't be Thanksgiving without this relish on our table. But we love it with pork and ham as well.

½ cup white wine vinegar

1½ tablespoons sugar

3 cloves garlic, minced

¼ teaspoon salt

2 teaspoons fresh gingerroot, peeled and minced

½ teaspoon yellow mustard seeds

½ teaspoon cayenne pepper

1 cup dark raisins

1 cup golden raisins

1. Heat vinegar and sugar. Add garlic, salt, and remaining spices.

2. Pour warm vinegar over raisins in a 1-pint sterile canning jar.

3. Cap, seal, and refrigerate. Will keep 3–5 days in the refrigerator.

YIELD: 1 PINT (EIGHT 2-OUNCE SERVINGS)

NUTRITION PER SERVING

Calories	131	Total fat	<1g
% from fat	2	Saturated fat	<1g
Carbohydrates	35g	Cholesterol	0mg
Fiber	2g	Sodium	72mg

Colorful Pear Relish

* * * * * * * * * * *

*This recipe is a perfect way to save the delicious taste of fresh pears
when they are plentiful.*

**Boiling-water-bath canner; fourteen
1-pint jars**

12½ pounds ripe pears, peeled, cored,
     and chopped

8   jalapeño peppers, seeded and
     chopped (wear rubber gloves)

6   red bell peppers, seeded and
     chopped

6   green bell peppers, seeded and
     chopped

6   medium onions, chopped

1   tablespoon salt

1   tablespoon celery seeds

5   cups sugar

5   cups white distilled vinegar

1. In a heavy 10-quart saucepan combine
all ingredients. Mix well and bring to a boil.
Reduce heat.

2. Simmer uncovered 20–30 minutes,
stirring frequently and being careful not
to burn.

3. Ladle hot relish into clean pint jars
leaving ½ inch headspace. Cap and seal.

4. Process in a boiling-water-bath canner
20 minutes.

*Note: You may use the food processor to chop the
fruit and vegetables in batches, pulsing the motor on
and off.*

Yield: 14 pints (one hundred twelve 2-ounce
servings)

Nutrition per Serving

Calories	70	Total fat	<1g
% from fat	3	Saturated fat	0g
Carbohydrates	18g	Cholesterol	0mg
Fiber	2g	Sodium	58mg

Rhubarb Chutney

* * * * * * * * * * *

Try this chutney with poultry, pork, or lamb.

Boiling-water-bath canner; eight ½-pint jars

2	large oranges
2½	pounds rhubarb, washed and cut in 1-inch pieces
2	medium onions, peeled and chopped
5⅓	cup firmly packed light brown sugar
2	cups golden raisins
4	cups cider vinegar
1	tablespoon yellow mustard seeds
12	black peppercorns, whole
12	allspice berries, whole

1. Grate the peeling from both oranges. Set aside.

2. Halve and then section both oranges as you would a grapefruit, removing the white membranes. Place in a 2-quart bowl.

3. Chop the orange sections coarsely. Squeeze any remaining juices out of the orange halves into the chopped sections.

4. Combine the rhubarb, oranges, onions, sugar, raisins, and vinegar in a 4-quart saucepan.

5. Tie the whole spices in a cheesecloth bag and add to the pan. Bring mixture slowly to a boil, stirring to dissolve sugar.

6. Simmer uncovered until thick, about 1–1½ hours, being careful not to burn and stirring often. Remove spice bag.

7. Ladle into hot, clean jars, leaving ¼-inch headspace. Cap and seal.

8. Process 10 minutes in a boiling-water-bath canner.

* *

YIELD: 8 ½-PINTS (THIRTY-TWO 2-OUNCE SERVINGS)

NUTRITION PER SERVING

Calories	199	Total fat	<1g
% from fat	2	Saturated fat	<1g
Carbohydrates	52g	Cholesterol	0mg
Fiber	2g	Sodium	20mg

* *

Refrigerator Plum Chutney

* * * * * * * * * * *

Baste grilling pork or chicken with this rich chutney during the last stages of cooking.
Then serve the rest as a side dish. Delicious.

2½ cups red plums, washed, pitted, and chopped (about 1 pound)

¼ cup sugar

¼ cup chopped red onion

3 tablespoons orange juice

3 tablespoons golden raisins

2 tablespoons white distilled vinegar

2 cloves garlic, minced

½ teaspoon ground allspice

¼ teaspoon salt

1. Combine all ingredients in a 2-quart saucepan with lid. Bring to a boil, covered, then reduce heat to medium. Simmer covered 20–30 minutes.

2. Uncover and cook 8–10 minutes more until moisture disappears, being careful not to burn.

3. Pour into 3 ½-pint sterile canning jars, leaving ¼ inch headspace. Cap and seal.

4. Refrigerate and consume within 1 week.

* *

YIELD: 3 ½-PINTS (TWELVE 2-OUNCE SERVINGS)
NUTRITION PER SERVING

Calories	60	Total fat	<1g
% from fat	5	Saturated fat	0g
Carbohydrates	15g	Cholesterol	0mg
Fiber	1g	Sodium	45mg

* *

Southwestern Cranberry Sauce

*A variation on a theme, this cranberry sauce tastes fresh even
after being frozen or refrigerated. Serve with lamb or a turkey cutlet.*

1 package (12 ounces) fresh cranberries, rinsed and picked over

¾ cup sugar

1 medium jalapeño, seeded and quartered (use rubber gloves)

1 green onion, coarsely chopped

3 teaspoons fresh cilantro

¼ teaspoon ground cumin

1. Coarsely chop all ingredients in a food processor, pulsing the motor on and off.

2. Pour into 3 sterile 1-cup canning jars, leaving 1 inch headspace.

3. Allow flavors to develop in the refrigerator overnight. This will keep 1 week in the refrigerator or 2 months in the freezer.

4. To use frozen cranberry sauce, thaw in the refrigerator.

Note: For a quick version of this recipe, combine one 16-ounce can of whole cranberry sauce with ½ cup Five-Pepper Jelly, page 228. Melt together in a saucepan over medium heat until combined. Cool, then serve. This will keep 2 weeks in the refrigerator.

YIELD: 3 ½-PINTS (TWELVE 2-OUNCE SERVINGS)
NUTRITION PER SERVING

Calories	67	Total fat	<1g
% from fat	1	Saturated fat	0g
Carbohydrates	17g	Cholesterol	0mg
Fiber	2g	Sodium	3mg

Pickled Mixed Vegetable Chunks

A great accompaniment to all meats and sandwiches.

Boiling-water-bath canner; ten 1-pint jars

- 4 pounds pickling cucumbers, washed and thickly sliced
- 2 pounds small onions, peeled and quartered
- 4 cups celery, sliced in 1-inch pieces
- 2 cups carrots, peeled and thickly sliced
- 2 cups red bell peppers, sliced in 1-inch pieces
- 2 cups cauliflowerets
- Ice cubes
- 6 cups white distilled vinegar
- ¼ cup prepared mustard
- ½ cup salt
- 3½ cups sugar
- 3 tablespoons celery seeds
- 2 tablespoons yellow mustard seeds
- ½ teaspoon whole cloves
- ½ teaspoon ground turmeric

1. Combine vegetables in an 8-quart ceramic bowl and cover with ice cubes. Refrigerate 4 hours.

2. Combine vinegar, mustard, salt, sugar, seeds, and spices in a heavy 8-quart saucepan. Bring to a boil.

3. Drain vegetables, saving vinegar solution.

4. Pack vegetables into sterile jars, leaving ½ inch headspace.

5. Ladle vinegar syrup over vegetables, leaving ½ inch headspace. Cap and seal.

6. Process 5 minutes in a boiling-water-bath canner.

YIELD: 10 PINTS (EIGHTY 2-OUNCE SERVINGS)
NUTRITION PER SERVING

Calories	50	Total fat	<1g
% from fat	4	Saturated fat	0g
Carbohydrates	12g	Cholesterol	0mg
Fiber	<1g	Sodium	657mg

Baby Carrots with Honey and Dill

Try this with poultry or fish or as a low-calorie appetizer.

2 packages (1 pound each) peeled baby carrots (4 cups)

⅔ cup white wine vinegar

½ cup honey

2 tablespoons whole light mustard seeds

1 teaspoon salt

2 tablespoons minced fresh dill

1. Cook the carrots in a large pot of salted boiling water until tender but still crisp, about 5 minutes. Drain.

2. Combine the vinegar, honey, mustard seeds, and salt in a 2-quart bowl. Add the hot carrots to the vinegar mixture. Stir to cool.

3. Cover and store these in the refrigerator for 3–5 days. Serve at room temperature sprinkled with fresh dill.

YIELD: 5½ CUPS (ELEVEN ½-CUP SERVINGS)
NUTRITION PER SERVING

Calories	91	Total fat	1g
% from fat	9	Saturated fat	<1g
Carbohydrates	21g	Cholesterol	0mg
Fiber	2g	Sodium	225mg

CHAPTER 7

Vinegars & Seasonings

I REMEMBER, YEARS AGO, the first time I visited Harrod's food hall in London. It was, and remains today, the granddaddy of all food halls in the world. The aisles overflowed with pyramids made of tins of dry mustard and other foods. Overhead displays were laden with sassy bunches of dried herbs tied with ribbon and raffia bows. And a mosaic mural of dried cloves, allspice, dried beans, and other spices adorned the walls. It was an art gallery of food!

In the midst of all this, I found culinary magic in bright, crystal-clear bottles of vinegar, which had suspended inside fruit larger than the bottleneck. I pondered this for years, wondering how they had gotten the fruit into the bottle. Later, I learned that they had threaded the bottleneck over a small, immature, growing peach. They had chosen fruit from a bottom branch, somewhat shaded from the sun, easy enough to reach. Then they removed all the leaves from the branch and tied the bottle over the immature fruit.

After learning how those fruited vinegars at Harrod's had been created, my husband and I tried this process. We tied our bottles over peach and apple branches and checked them often as the fruit grew. Of course, you don't want to do this with fruit trees that have been sprayed. It took us many bottles tied to many branches to actually get one completed peach inside. At that stage, all we had to do was shake the branch and the fruit fell off, caught in the bottle. We then followed a recipe for fruit vinegar and ended up with a real conversation piece. In fact, we almost had more fun talking about it than we did eating it.

Looking back, we had many failures but great fun. It's no wonder the fruited vinegar in Harrod's was so expensive. But you can make your own flavored vinegar using much simpler methods and ingredients. Give it a try. Flavored vinegars make a meal interesting by providing a little of the unexpected to an otherwise ordinary dinner. Look upon these condiments and seasonings as your help mates in making good food delicious.

Vinegar

Is it a medicine, cosmetic, preservative, flavor enhancer, cleanser, disinfectant, beverage, or digestive aid? While modern science has had to prove vinegar's antibacterial and antiseptic powers, inhabitants of the ancient Mediterranean already knew its qualities. In the Old Testament, reference is made to the medicinal qualities of wine and vinegar. The many flavored, refined vinegars of today are used mostly to enhance and enliven different cuisines around the world.

Vinegar, which contains acetic acid, is the natural outcome of fermented fruit juices and grains. Oxygen and the alcohol of wine combine with organisms known as acetobacters to produce vinegar. Each grain or fruit used imparts its own special flavor to the vinegar. The flavor range seems endless. Appreciating the subtle and not-so-subtle vinegar flavors is a full-time occupation. Age, flavoring, and the acidity contribute to the taste and character of vinegars.

Modern vinegar production has been speeded up greatly by mechanization — although aged balsamic vinegars are still being produced today, as they were in ancient Italy.

Vinegar is the single most effective vehicle for low-calorie flavoring of meats and vegetables. Sometimes vinegar is identified as containing a certain "grain," which specifies the amount it is diluted by water. A 40-grain vinegar means one that is 40 percent acetic acid. Read the label carefully to determine acidity when you purchase vinegar. For cooking purposes, 4 to 6 percent acidity is ideal. Once you have

Vinegar Varieties

●●●●●●●●●●●●●●

Balsamic. Once produced as an art form family by family for private use; true *aceto balsamico* is made only in the Emilia-Romagna region of Italy near Modena. It has been fermented and sometimes aged for hundreds of years. Today's balsamic vinegar, controlled by the Italian government, is aged at least 12 years. It is fruity and thick, rich and dark brown, and ideal for meats, marinades, and salads.

Champagne. Technically speaking, this vinegar is made only in the Champagne district of France. Delicate in flavor and expensive in price, it is best used in seafood sauces or with mild herbs.

Cider. Made from apples and aged from pure apple cider, it is best used with strong, pungent herbs or spices. Great for pickling, it can also be used as salad dressing and marinade.

Malt. The intense flavor of malt vinegar, which is fermented from beer (grains), stands up best in pickles and other relishes. Malt vinegar is sprinkled over fried potatoes and fried fish in the United Kingdom to create the classic fish-and-chips.

White rice. Very distinct in taste and fairly sweet, this Japanese vinegar complements rice and makes an excellent sauce base, combining well with seafoods and vegetables. Chinese white rice vinegar, which is a mild sweet vinegar, enhances sweet-and-sour dishes.

Sherry. Slightly sweet and nutty, sherry vinegar comes from Spain. It can be used lavishly in cooking with strong herbs and spices. It stands up well in cream- and tomato-based sauces and has a more intense flavor than rice vinegar.

White wine. Pair this delicately flavored vinegar with other subtle flavors, such as mild herbs and seafoods.

Red wine. Stronger in character, this vinegar stands up well to dark meats, heavier vegetable salads, and dark marinades that may contain soy sauce or Worcestershire sauce.

learned about the differences in flavors, aged versus non-aged, and variations in acidity, you will want to choose the full-bodied, aged vinegars over the pale grocery store varieties every time. White distilled vinegar is perfect for pickling, but not for making flavored concoctions to enhance your menu.

While homemade vinegar is great for flavoring your meals, do not use homemade vinegar in canning. Usually the acidity of homemade vinegar is much lower than that of commercial varieties, and measuring the exact acidity percentage of your homemade brew is difficult to do. Another

Store flavored vinegars in decorative glass bottles or cruets.

After the steeping process, filter the vinegar into clean, narrow-necked bottles for final bottling.

problem with using homemade vinegar in canning is that it often contains the "mother" of vinegar, a jellylike, cloudy substance that contains the bacteria used for making vinegar. You don't want the mother clouding your pickles.

WINE VINEGAR

Wine vinegar contains no alcohol, which is oxidized in the process of turning wine into vinegar. All the vinegars listed here are suitable in flavor and acidity for our purposes, but always read labels carefully to check acidity before buying.

FLAVORED VINEGAR

Is it a kitchen decoration, gift-giving idea, culinary essential, or the perfect suspension medium for those summer herbs that grow in such abundance? Flavored vinegar does it all. In addition to herbs and spices, you can flavor vinegar with fruits, flowers, and vegetables singularly or in combination.

For today's cook it is easy to buy a good-quality vinegar and use your energy and ideas for creative flavor combinations. Remember, poor-quality vinegar cannot be elevated by adding a few herbs to it — always choose the best in the beginning.

MAKING FLAVORED VINEGAR

The process of bottling flavored vinegars is simple compared to that of canning fruits or vegetables. Because of its high acidity, vinegar prevents the growth of bacteria, eliminating the need for processing with heat. Nevertheless, all the usual rules of cleanliness apply.

Make sure you are prepared and organized before you begin bottling. Use hot soapy water to wash the bottles and utensils, removing all the soap with hot water. Drain all the washed equipment on clean tea towels. Pour boiling water into the clean bottles and let stand for 10 minutes. Your individual recipe will give instructions for steeping or otherwise combining ingredients.

I find it most convenient to steep the vinegar ingredients in a clean, widemouthed jar. Many recipes call for removing the spices and herbs before the final bottling, and this kind of jar allows you to do that easily. If you steep the ingredients in a narrow-necked bottle, you may find it difficult to remove the spices and herbs later. Spices and herbs that remain in the vinegar after bottling continue to impart their flavors. Sometimes this is desirable, as with Lemon-Thyme Vinegar (page 300). Sample your wares after a few days of steeping and decide for yourself. It is a matter of taste. You may choose to leave the seasonings intact. Sometimes the suspended seasonings are quite beautiful and add to the effect of your creation. Often it is a judgment call by the cook. Herbs such as garlic, when left in the vinegar, could eventually overpower the other flavors. So after the herbs and spices have steeped in the vinegar, filter the vinegar through a coffee filter into clean, narrow-necked bottles for final bottling.

EQUIPMENT

Most of the equipment you need for flavoring vinegar can be found in your kitchen (see box at right). The bottles

Basic equipment for making flavored vinegars

for steeping and storing the vinegar are possibly the only things you will have to search for. Keep your eyes open throughout the year for interesting re-usable bottles and jars. Rosé and white wine bottles are best, as they are clear. Pick up a package of generic corks in different sizes the next time you see them at the hardware store and have them on hand for "bottling season." Of course, you can always buy ornamental glass bottles as well. The upscale home-furnishings stores carry quite an array of them.

STORAGE

Always store your finished product in a cool, dark place. Some light, but certainly not direct light, is okay while the solution is steeping. It is tempting to store vinegars in plain view of guests because the fancy varieties can be quite attractive, but unless you keep your living room dark and cool, don't do it. Your fancy flavored vinegar will keep for six months, fruit vinegar for three months.

MAKING HERB-FLAVORED VINEGAR

Herbal vinegars are delightfully attractive, wonderfully flavorful, and extremely easy to make. Experiment with different herbs and vinegars to create a diversity of flavors for use in cooking and for salads. All vinegars can be paired with herbs, but red wine vinegar and white wine vinegar are the most versatile. More-delicate varieties, such as champagne vinegar, are best suited for lemony herbs. Apple cider vinegar and malt vinegar pair well with oniony herbs like chives and garlic.

1. Gather the herbs before the midmorning sun hits the leaves but after the dew has evaporated. Clean off all the grit and blot the herbs dry with clean towels or paper towels.
2. Remove the leaves from the stems to measure 1 cup leaves for 2 cups vinegar. If you are using dried herbs, choose one-half the amount or ½ cup herbs to 2 cups

Clean the herbs and then blot them dry on clean towels.

vinegar. It may seem to be too strong a ratio of herbs to vinegar, but don't be put off. The solution must be strong enough to be effective even after steeping and straining.

3. Put the leaves into a clean jar and fill with the vinegar. Cover the jar and store it in a dark, cool place. Shake or stir the solution every few days and taste it after about one week. If the flavor is intense enough and to your liking, it is ready.

4. Strain the vinegar infusion into a clean bottle using cheesecloth, muslin, a clean jelly bag, or a coffee filter. Cork or cap, label, and store in a dark, cool place.

MAKING SPICE-FLAVORED VINEGAR

While heat is not recommended for other kinds of flavored vinegars, it enhances the flavor of spiced vinegar by releasing the essential oils in the spices. All types of vinegar work well with spices. Experiment to find your favorite combinations by trying allspice, cardamom, cinnamon, ginger, juniper, peppercorns, peppers, and nutmeg. Use the seeds of herbs such as dill, anise, caraway, celery, mustard, coriander, and cumin.

1. Use whole spices, not the ground form, which could cloud the finished product. You may wish to bruise them slightly or crush them, using a mortar and pestle or food processor.

2. Heat 2 cups vinegar to 110°F, being careful not to let it overheat. Remove the pan from the heat and let it cool slightly.

3. Put up to 4 tablespoons of the bruised spices in a clean widemouthed jar along with the 2 cups of vinegar. Cover the jar and store it in a dark, cool place. Shake or stir the solution every few days and taste it after about one week. If the flavor is intense enough and to your liking, it is ready.

4. Strain the vinegar infusion into a clean bottle using cheesecloth, muslin, a clean jelly bag, or a coffee filter. Cork or cap, label, and store in a dark, cool place.

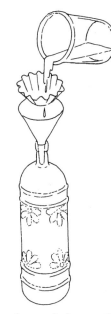

Use a cheesecloth or coffee filter to strain the vinegar infusion.

TIP

For the sparkling vinegar concoction you give as a gift, include the recipe on a card tied to the bottleneck. The only problem is that your friends will see how easy flavoring vinegar is!

Making Fruit-Flavored Vinegar

The hardest part of making fruit-flavored vinegar is deciding your fruit preference. The possibilities are nearly endless. Most fruit vinegars fare well with milder red or white wine vinegar as a base to match the delicacy of the fruit flavors. Make sure the vinegar has at least 5 percent acidity.

1. Wash and blot the fruit dry, pit it if necessary, and peel if desired.

2. Mash slightly or cut up the fruit, and place the prepared fruit in a clean jar with the vinegar. Don't heat the vinegar for flavoring with fruit; it's too hard on the fruit, as a rule. The two-to-one ratio of vinegar to fruit is good here. Cover with vinegar and place in a cool, dark place for the flavors to marry.

3. After a few days to a week, taste the solution. At this point, you can strain out the fruit, adding newly prepared fruit for a more intense flavor. Let the mixture steep for another week or two. Repeat the steeping process until the taste is to your liking.

4. Strain the mixture into a nonreactive saucepan. For each 2 cups of flavored vinegar, add ⅛ cup to ½ cup of sugar, or use 1½ tablespoons to ⅓ cup of honey. Simmer but do not boil the mixture, stirring as the sweetener dissolves, for about three minutes. If foam develops, skim it off.

5. Let the vinegar cool and pour it into a clean bottle. Add a fruit slice to the bottle for beauty. Cork or cap, label, and store in a cool, dark place.

Making Floral-Flavored Vinegar

The main item to remember in floral vinegar making is to use nonpoisonous flowers and only those that have not been sprayed with dangerous chemicals. Never use florist flowers. Know your sources or use your own flowers.

Using herbs that have "bolted" in the hot sun of late summer is a great way to flavor vinegars, because the flowers

Flowers to Use

● ● ● ● ● ● ● ● ● ● ● ●

Anise	Marjoram
Basil	Mint
Borage	Nasturtium
Calendula	Oregano
Carnation	Pinks
Chamomile	Primrose
Chive	Rose
Dill	Rose-scented
Elder	geranium
Fennel	Thyme
Lavender	Violet
Lovage	

add delicate flavor. If you're flavoring with roses, though, use only the petals, never the whole rose, and use the inner petals, not the sepal or outer green petals. No matter what kind of flower you use, make sure the petals are clean, dry, and free of insects.

1. Choose a mild white vinegar such as champagne, white rice, or white wine. Use 1 cup of petals to 2 cups of vinegar. With some flowers, such as violets, this could end up requiring a huge supply of plant material. Combine the ingredients in a clean, widemouthed jar, then cap and store in a cool, dark place.

2. As with other flavored vinegars, steep for about a week and then taste. Continue to steep a few more weeks if you want a stronger taste.

3. Strain the vinegar into a clean, small-necked bottle, add a fresh flower if desired; cork or cap, seal, and label.

Seasoning Mixes

Keep on hand your own mix of herbs, spices, and other seasonings. What a luxury to enliven your fresh, steaming-hot produce with a vegetable seasoning right before serving, or to add sparkle to that pot of soup with a spoonful of soup-seasoning blend. How easy it is to turn all your everyday dishes into something spectacular with herb blends and seasonings. Most of these recipes add no calories to your dishes, and they are easy to combine and keep on hand.

TIP
. . . . . .

Use your own pesticide-free flowers for cooking.

Steep the petals in a mild vinegar in a sealed container.

Flavored Oils
. . . .

Flavored oils are wonderful for adding zest and body to a recipe. Use them instead of butter on breads and in recipes.

But to be safe, they must be refrigerated as soon as the flavoring is added and must be used within one day of flavoring. Clostridium botulinum, *the deadly bacterium that causes botulism, can quickly develop in oil. Never use flavored oils that have been left standing on a table or shelf.*

Recipes for Flavored Vinegars and Seasonings

Herbes de Provence

Popcorn Shaker Mix

Dill Blend

Vegetable Seasoning Mix

Southwestern Spice Mix

Asian Seasoning Blend

Seasoned Butters

Spiced Sherry Vinegar

Provençal Vinegar

French-Blend Herb Vinegar

Spiced Vinegar

Ginger-Pepper Rice Vinegar

Mint Vinegar

Tarragon Vinegar

Basil Balsamic Vinegar

Spicy Dill Vinegar

Fresh Herb Vinegar

Lemon-Thyme Vinegar

Lime Vinegar

Cranberry Vinegar

Strawberry Vinegar

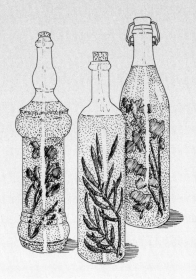

Herbes de Provence

* * * * * * * * * * *

This is my version of the famous French herb blend. But if you are feeling patriotic, rename it for your local area! This is especially excellent for grilling meats. Sprinkle on lamb chops, chicken, or beef on the grill.

2 tablespoons dried fennel seeds

2 tablespoons dried lavender leaves

¼ cup dried marjoram

¼ cup dried oregano

½ cup dried rosemary

¼ cup dried savory

½ cup dried thyme

1. Combine all ingredients and store in an airtight container in a cool, dark place.

2. This will stay fresh 2 months.

YIELD: 2 CUPS

TIP

* * * * * *

Save your grocery store spice jars with shaker-style lids. They are convenient dispensers for many of these blends.

Popcorn Shaker Mix

* * * * * * * * * * * *

Sprinkle about ½ teaspoon of this spicy seasoning on each cup of buttered popped corn, adjusting to taste. The butter helps it stick to the popcorn, but if you wish to eliminate the fat, sprinkle the blend on hot unbuttered popcorn and stir often to keep it mixed together.

¼ cup ground cumin

1 tablespoon cayenne pepper (or less to taste)

3 tablespoons dried oregano

1. Combine ingredients and pour into a salt shaker. Sprinkle over hot buttered popcorn to taste.

2. This will keep 6 weeks in a cool, dark place. Keep tightly sealed.

YIELD: ½ CUP

Dill Blend

. . . .

*Dried herbs keep this recipe uncomplicated. This blend is terrific with fish or as
a seasoning for fresh tomatoes and cucumbers. Try it on baked potatoes or in
soups for a change of pace.*

¼ cup dried dill weed

2 tablespoons dried lemon balm leaves

1 tablespoon garlic powder

1. Combine all ingredients and store in an airtight jar away from heat and light.

2. Sprinkle on foods according to taste.

YIELD: ½ CUP

Vegetable Seasoning Mix

. . . .

*This mix of your favorite dried summer herbs is good for seasoning fresh vegetables,
and when you sprinkle a little on pasta, it becomes a special-occasion meal.*

8 tablespoons dried parsley

4 tablespoons dried chives

1 teaspoon dried sage

1 teaspoon dried oregano

1 teaspoon dried thyme

1 teaspoon dried basil

½ teaspoon celery seeds

1 teaspoon garlic powder

1. Combine all ingredients and store in an airtight container away from heat and light. The garlic can sink to the bottom of the container, so stir well before each use.

2. Sprinkle on vegetables, buttered pasta, salads, or soups as desired.

YIELD: ¾ CUP

Southwestern Spice Mix

Dried red pepper flakes give this spice mix an extra kick. Use this blend anytime you want a southwestern flavor for cream cheese dip, chicken salad, tangy soup, or chili. Good with any recipe calling for chili powder.

3 tablespoons chili powder

2 tablespoons ground cumin

1 tablespoon ground black pepper

1 tablespoon salt

1 tablespoon garlic powder

1½ teaspoons dried red pepper flakes

1. Mix all ingredients thoroughly in a small bowl.

2. Store in an airtight container in a cool, dry place up to 3 months.

YIELD: 8½ TABLESPOONS

Asian Seasoning Blend

This combination gives rice a hot, complex, wonderfully seasoned Thai flavor. Use it for stir-fried vegetables as well.

4 tablespoons dried mint leaves

2 tablespoons dried lemon zest

3 teaspoons ground white pepper

2 teaspoons dried lemon verbena leaves

¼ teaspoon ground cumin

½ teaspoon cayenne pepper

1. Combine all ingredients in a blender and pulverize to a fine powder.

2. Store in an airtight container away from heat and light. Add to rice or stir-fried vegetables according to taste.

YIELD: ABOUT ½ CUP

Seasoned Butters

· · · · · · · · · · · ·

Herbs and spices give vegetables and other foods a new dimension. Start with ½ cup of softened butter, and add the combinations below. Seasoned butters will keep for several days in the refrigerator.

ROSEMARY-THYME BUTTER SEASONING

1 teaspoon dried rosemary, crushed

1 teaspoon dried thyme, crushed

¼ teaspoon ground white pepper

ALL-PURPOSE BUTTER SEASONING

2 teaspoons dried basil, crushed

¼ teaspoon freshly ground black pepper

¼ teaspoon onion powder

SPICY BUTTER SEASONING

¼ onion, finely minced

½ teaspoon ground cumin

½ teaspoon dried oregano, crushed

¼ teaspoon cayenne pepper

ITALIAN BUTTER SEASONING

2 teaspoons dried oregano, crushed

2 cloves garlic, peeled and minced

¼ teaspoon freshly ground black pepper

Seasoned Butter on French Bread

· · · · · · · · · · ·

1. *Slice 1 loaf French bread lengthwise.*

2. *Mix the ingredients with ½ cup softened butter and spread on each slice of bread.*

3. *Reassemble loaf and wrap in foil.*

4. *The buttered French bread can be stored in the freezer 1 week.*

5. *To use, remove the bread from the freezer, defrost it in the refrigerator, and bake it at 425°F for 15 minutes or until it's heated through.*

Note: Make one loaf of bread for dinner that night and one for the freezer.

· ·

YIELD: ½ CUP (EIGHT 1-TABLESPOON SERVINGS)

NUTRITION PER SERVING

Calories	100	Total fat	11
% from fat	99	Saturated fat	7g
Carbohydrates	0g	Cholesterol	31mg
Fiber	0g	Sodium	116mg

· ·

Spiced Sherry Vinegar

This hearty vinegar stands up well to grilled pork and beef when used as a marinade ingredient.

1 teaspoon whole black peppercorns

1 teaspoon whole cloves

1 small whole red chile pepper

1 1-inch piece dried gingerroot

2 cups sherry vinegar

1. Combine all ingredients except vinegar in a large widemouthed jar.

2. Heat the vinegar just to boiling in a non-reactive 2-quart saucepan over medium heat.

3. Pour vinegar into the spice-filled jar and let steep until cool.

4. Tightly cover the jar and store in a cool, dark place.

5. Check the flavors after 1 week. Decant from the widemouthed jar through a coffee filter into narrow-necked bottle. Cork or cap and store in a cool, dark place.

Yield: 1 pint

Provençal Vinegar

This herb vinegar has a wonderfully light, fresh flavor imparted by a bit of orange peel. Use as is over fresh raw summer vegetables, or add a dash of olive oil.

1 pint red wine vinegar

1 sprig fresh thyme

1 sprig fresh rosemary

1 bay leaf

1 large garlic clove, peeled

1 strip orange peel, 1 inch by 4 inches

1. Combine all ingredients in a clean 2-cup jar.

2. Seal jar and store at room temperature in a dark place about 1 month before using.

3. Filter into a clean 1-pint bottle.

4. Store at room temperature, tightly sealed, up to 6 months.

Yield: 1 pint

French-Blend Herb Vinegar

Serve this lovely vinegar drizzled over sliced fresh tomatoes or cucumbers.

2 sprigs fresh rosemary

4 sprigs fresh oregano

3 large stems fresh basil

2 sprigs parsley

1 whole clove garlic, peeled

2 teaspoons whole black peppercorns

1 quart red wine vinegar

1. Combine all ingredients in a large widemouthed jar.

2. Tightly cover the jar and store in a cool, dark place. Check the flavors after 1 week.

3. Decant from the widemouthed jar through a coffee filter into a narrow-necked bottle.

4. Cork or cap, and store in a cool, dark place.

YIELD: 2 PINTS

Spiced Vinegar

This recipe makes a large quantity, so plan to give some as gifts.

6 quarts cider vinegar

2 cups sugar

¼ cup fresh gingerroot, peeled and sliced

6 tablespoons whole black peppercorns

¼ cup yellow mustard seeds

3 tablespoons celery seeds

2 tablespoons mace

¼ cup whole allspice

¼ cup whole cloves

3 tablespoons turmeric

1. Combine all ingredients in a nonreactive 10-quart saucepan.

2. Heat slowly, stirring until all sugar dissolves.

3. Pour into two 1-gallon jars, dividing spices evenly. Cover and let steep about 3 weeks in a cool, dark place.

4. Strain through a coffee filter into 6 sterile quart jars. Cap, seal, and store in a cool, dark place.

YIELD: 6 QUARTS

Ginger-Pepper Rice Vinegar

This vinegar is a wonderful ingredient in stir-fry sauces.

1 cup fresh gingerroot, peeled and sliced

1 tablespoon whole black peppercorns

1½ cups rice wine vinegar, heated to 110°F

1. Place the ginger and peppercorns into the steeping container. Press them with the back of a spoon to release the flavor.

2. Add the vinegar. Screw on the lid tightly and put in a cool, dark place. Stir the mixture or shake the jar every other day.

3. Check the flavor after 1 week. Let sit longer if desired. When the ginger flavor is to your liking, strain the vinegar and use. It will keep for 3–6 months.

YIELD: 1½ CUPS

Using Fresh Ginger

Look for smooth-skinned ginger. Wrinkled or cracked skins indicate older ginger.

To peel ginger: *Holding the gingerroot firmly, use a paring knife to peel the tough skin, being careful not to remove much of the flesh.*

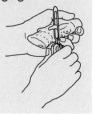

Mint Vinegar

Marinate fresh tomatoes in this vinegar concoction.

6 cups white wine vinegar

½ cup honey, or 1 cup sugar

Zest of 3 lemons

1½ cups fresh mint leaves

1. Bruise mint leaves in a ½-gallon container with the back of a spoon.

2. Add remaining ingredients and stir.

3. Store in two 1-quart jars, capped and sealed, at room temperature about 2 weeks.

4. Filter into three clean containers and add a fresh mint sprig for beauty. Store tightly sealed in a cool, dark place up to 6 months.

YIELD: 6 CUPS

Tarragon Vinegar

A base for almost any sauce or dressing, tarragon vinegar is a tried-and-true favorite. Combine 1 part vinegar with 3 parts olive oil for a delicious salad dressing.

20 sprigs fresh tarragon

4 cups white wine vinegar

1. Bruise tarragon in a widemouthed, 1-quart jar, using the back of a spoon.

2. Pour the vinegar over the herbs and seal the jar.

3. Store in a dark place 2–4 weeks, or until the flavor has reached desired intensity.

4. Remove the herbs by straining the vinegar (or use a coffee filter) into a 1-quart decorative bottle. Cork or cap and seal airtight.

YIELD: 1 QUART

Basil Balsamic Vinegar

Sprinkle this over fresh sliced tomatoes and cucumbers.

1 teaspoon whole black peppercorns

4 sprigs fresh basil

1 clove garlic, peeled

1 pint balsamic vinegar

1. Combine all ingredients except vinegar in a large widemouthed jar.

2. Pour vinegar into the jar and tightly cover.

3. Store jar in a cool, dark place. Check the flavors after 1 week.

4. Decant from the widemouthed jar through a coffee filter into narrow-necked bottle.

5. Cork or cap, label, and store in a cool, dark place.

YIELD: 1 PINT

Spicy Dill Vinegar

Try with fish or boiled potatoes.

6 sprigs fresh dill

2 fresh dill heads, or ½ teaspoon dill seeds

1 clove garlic, peeled

1 tablespoon yellow mustard seeds

1 quart white wine vinegar

1. Combine all ingredients except vinegar in a large widemouthed jar.

2. Heat the vinegar to 110°F.

3. Pour vinegar into the jar and let herbs steep until cool. Tightly cover the jar and store in a cool, dark place. Check the flavors after 1 week.

4. Decant from the widemouthed jar through a coffee filter into narrow-necked bottle.

5. Cork or cap, label, and store in a cool, dark place.

YIELD: 2 PINTS

Fresh Herb Vinegar

This large quantity is perfect to make when the garden is rampant, to give as welcome gifts.

8 sprigs fresh thyme

8 sprigs fresh rosemary

1 dozen shallots, peeled

2 dozen black peppercorns

¾ cup fresh tarragon leaves

½ cup fresh parsley leaves

¼ cup chopped fresh chives

3 gallons cider vinegar

3 cloves garlic

1. Combine the herbs and divide the mixture into three 1-gallon jars.

2. Pour vinegar into each jar. Add 1 clove garlic to each jar and let steep 24 hours.

3. Remove garlic. Seal jar and place in a cool, dry place 2 weeks.

4. Strain or pour through a coffee filter into twelve 1-quart bottles. Cap, seal, and label. Store in a dark, cool place.

YIELD: 12 QUARTS

Lemon-Thyme Vinegar

* * * * * * * * * * *

Try to peel the lemon in one continuous spiral. "Thread" it into the bottle in a spiral fashion. Beautiful!

2 sprigs fresh thyme

1 lemon, peeled in one spiral

2 teaspoons white peppercorns

2 cups white wine vinegar

8–10 fresh cranberries (optional)

1. Combine all ingredients in a sterile decorative bottle.

2. Seal and store for 1 month in a cool, dark place before use.

YIELD: 1 PINT

Note: I like to thread about 8–10 fresh cranberries on a wooden skewer and inject the skewer into the neck of the bottle. It's challenging and fun to try to get the skewer in the center of the lemon spiral. Like building a ship in a bottle, your friends will wonder how you did it!

Lime Vinegar

* * * * * * * * * * *

This is remarkable on fresh fruit.

1 clove garlic, peeled

1 tablespoon coriander seeds

Zest of 1 lime

1 quart white wine vinegar

1. Combine all ingredients except vinegar in a large widemouthed jar.

2. Heat the vinegar to 110°F.

3. Pour vinegar into the jar and let cool.

4. Tightly cover and store in a cool, dark place. Check the flavors after 1 week.

5. Decant from the widemouthed jar through a coffee filter into a narrow-necked bottle. Cork or cap, label, and store in a cool, dark place.

YIELD: 2 PINTS

Cranberry Vinegar

. . . .

Use this vinegar as a dressing base for cole slaw. Add two chopped apples to your favorite slaw recipe. Different and delicious!

10 ounces white rice vinegar

3 tablespoons honey

1½ cups fresh cranberries, rinsed and picked over

1. Heat the ingredients in the top of a double boiler over simmering water 10 minutes.

2. Cool and store in a clean pint jar 3 weeks in a cool place.

3. Strain the vinegar through a coffee filter, pressing out all the fruit juices.

4. Funnel it into a clean 1-pint bottle.

YIELD: 1 PINT

Strawberry Vinegar

. . . .

Use in slaw, as a base for pork marinade, or heated slightly with olive oil for a different salad dressing.

2 pints strawberries, rinsed, stemmed, and halved, ¼ cup reserved

1 quart cider vinegar

1 cup sugar

1. In a large 4-quart nonreactive saucepan combine the berries and vinegar. Let sit 1 hour.

2. Add sugar to saucepan and heat to a slow boil to dissolve sugar. Simmer 10 minutes.

3. Use a coffee filter to strain into three sterile 1-pint bottles. Press out as much juice from the berries as possible.

4. Add reserved strawberries to each bottle. Cap, seal, and label. Store in a cool, dark place 2 weeks before use.

YIELD: 3 PINTS

Cold Storage

COLD STORAGE IS THE SIMPLEST FORM of preserving. It involves placing food in a cool, dark environment with varying amounts of humidity. Some foods require moist air, while others prefer dry; some need warmer temperatures and others, colder. All these factors must be taken into account when deciding on the proper form of cold storage for each food.

A root cellar takes advantage of the cool, moist temperatures of the earth to prevent food from decomposing. Old houses with dirt floors in their basements, for example, provide the ideal environment for storing food. The temperature in a root cellar needs to remain above 32°F but below 40°F. Humidity of at least 80 percent is important, too. Most house foundations have air ducts that can be opened and closed as needed to vary the temperatures and humidity. If your furnace is in the same area of your basement as your root cellar, the temperature may not stay low enough. Monitor it frequently during a cold spell to make sure the temperature stays low enough.

Keeping vegetables and fruits in a root cellar basically differs from refrigeration only in humidity. Refrigeration does provide a dark environment with controlled cool temperatures, but there the similarity stops. Air in a refrigerator dries food quickly — consider what happens to unwrapped cheese — while the humidity in a root cellar is higher. The added moisture works with the cool temperature to help produce to stay fresh.

Bruises can be the start of the rotting process. With gentle handling and proper storage, your cold-stored produce will nourish you throughout the winter months.

PRODUCE FOR COLD AND DRY STORAGE

As with any form of preserving, always start with unblemished, good-quality produce. Handle it gently as you harvest and prepare it for storage. While many varieties of produce adapt well to the root cellar, many do not. You can store the following produce without *any* processing.

PRODUCE	IDEAL STORAGE TEMPERATARE	HUMIDITY*	AIR CIRCULATION	SHELF LIFE (IN MONTHS)
COLD STORAGE				
Apples	32°F	medium moist	medium	4–6
Grapefruit	32°F	medium moist	low	1–1½
Grapes	32°F	medium moist	low	1–2
Pears	32°F	medium moist to moist	low	2–6
Beets	32°–40°F	moist	low	3–5
Cabbage	32°F	medium moist to moist	low	2–4
Carrots	32°–40°F	moist	low	6
Cauliflower	32°F	medium moist	low	1½–2
Celery	32°F	medium moist to moist	low	1½–4
Endive	32°F	medium moist to moist	medium	2–3
Horseradish	32°F	moist	low	4–6
Kohlrabi	32°–40°F	moist	low	2–3
Leeks	32°F	medium moist	medium	1–3
Parsnips	32°F	moist	low	4–6
Potatoes, white	35°–40°F	medium moist	low	4–6
Radishes	32°F	moist	low	2–4
Rutabagas	32°F	moist	low	3–4
Turnips	32°F	moist	low	2–4
DRY STORAGE				

These vegetables prefer drier conditions and should not be stored in the classic root cellar, which tends to be too moist. These good "keepers" like cool ambient temperatures but not moisture.

PRODUCE	IDEAL STORAGE TEMPERATARE	HUMIDITY*	AIR CIRCULATION	SHELF LIFE (IN MONTHS)
Onions	32°F	dry	medium	4–6
Pumpkins	55°F	medium dry to dry	medium	4–6
Squash, winter	55°F	dry	medium	4–6
Tomatoes, green	55°–70°F	medium moist	medium	1–1½

*dry = 70% or less; medium dry = 70–80%; medium moist = 80–90%; moist = 90–95%

Choosing a Location

Many places in a home can work for cold storage of produce. The requirements are higher-than-average humidity of 80 percent or more, temperatures of between 32° and 40°F, proper ventilation, and low light. The earth's unprotected surfaces freeze and thaw with the cold temperatures of winter to a depth of 18 inches or more, depending on the severity of the weather. An unheated basement or cellar protected by a house is deep enough to be unaffected by the changes in surface temperature and will remain above 32°F and below 40°F, which is perfect for root storage.

Brainstorm to find an area in or around your house that meets these requirements. Ask yourself:

1. Does your basement have a dirt floor? You can wet down a dirt floor periodically for added moisture if it's needed. Or you can keep pans of water in various locations.

2. Is your basement cool to cold, or does the furnace heat it up? Use a thermometer to test.

3. Does your basement have an outside entrance? The steps to the outside door are great for lining up baskets of produce.

Produce for Drier Conditions

Some produce won't last long in the cool, moist air of most root cellars. Pumpkins, squash, and onions prefer drier air and warmer temperatures — from 50°F to 55°F with humidity at about 70 percent. You can sometimes find these conditions near the ceiling of your basement root cellar, closer to the main floor of the house. Hang a thermometer and a humidity gauge from a beam in the ceiling of your basement to determine whether these vegetables will last if stacked above other produce in your root cellar.

Drier, warmer conditions can sometimes exist in an attic, too, but monitor the temperature there vigilantly because temperatures in an attic tend to exhibit a wider range than in a cellar.

TIP

• • • • • •

Store each kind of vegetable separately so that the gases and flavors of different foods won't mingle.

4. Could your garage be a good place with the right amount of moisture and cold-enough temperatures? Will exhaust fumes be absorbed by the fruits or vegetables that you intend to store there?

5. Do you have an old lightweight ice chest (Styrofoam with a lid) that could serve as a "mini" root cellar for a month or so? The unheated space of a garage is a good spot to store a cooler filled with the end-of-the-season green tomatoes, onions, pumpkins, or squash, all of which prefer a drier climate and slightly warmer temperatures than found in most basement root cellars. Use a thermometer first to test for below-freezing temperatures inside the garage.

6. Do you have a window well that could be adapted as a root cellar, in which you can take advantage of below-earth temperatures and moisture? Top off the window well with hardware cloth to discourage rodents, and a wooden cover to seal in the right conditions. If severe cold comes, you can open the basement window to allow "heat" from the basement to raise the ambient temperature of the well.

7. Does the area have proper ventilation to keep mold and bacteria from forming?

Classic Built-in Basement Root Cellar

Old houses had basements with dirt floors, which helped keep the temperatures low and steady, and the air moist. A built-in basement (about 8 feet by 10 feet) is plenty large for storage purposes for today's gardeners. You can use your basement even if it has a cement floor. If it's the right temperature, you can keep the floor moist by sprinkling water on it periodically, or by keeping pans of water in it.

Check the temperature frequently before selecting a final spot. To build a small storage area in your basement, select a spot away from the heat of the chimney and furnace, since air close to heat sources is warmer. The north

TIP
• • • • • •

A garage is usually a convenient location for storage of produce. When you're in a hurry to prepare dinner, you'll find it easy to access.

TIP
• • • • • •

Don't wash produce before storing in a root cellar. Even if it then dries before storage, the added moisture is sometimes enough to encourage mold and therefore spoiling. Instead, wipe each dirty piece gently with a clean cotton-gloved hand. Treat all produce tenderly.

Old industrial packing pallets are great for elevating containers from a dirt or gravel basement floor.

TIP

• • • • • •

When it's first harvested, store produce in the refrigerator to remove the ambient heat. This takes the cooling "load" off your root cellar. The cool shade of a north-facing porch or garage works well, too.

wall, I usually find, is best. The northeast corner walls are the very coldest, and if your partition is in the corner, you need only construct two walls to make your storage room.

Be sure to include a foundation vent in the room to regulate the temperature. In the fall or spring, when outside temperatures shoot up during the day, keep the vent to the outside closed to prevent warm air from raising the temperature too much. When outside temperatures suddenly drop to freezing, close the vents immediately. Obviously, a thermometer is a necessity in a root cellar.

Train yourself to check the temperatures outside and inside the root cellar frequently.

The walls and ceiling should be made of nonporous materials so you can clean them easily.

Bins and storage shelves should be removable for cleaning. Take them outside on a dry summer day and dry brush them, or scrub them with soapy water. Be certain they are completely dry before replacing them in the root cellar. Open all the air vents and the door and let the breeze blow through the entire room.

OTHER KINDS OF COLD STORAGE

If you don't have a root cellar and aren't in a position to build one, try another method of storing your produce. There are many easy and economical ways to keep food during the winter months that don't require elaborate measures.

OUTSIDE STAIRWAY

The outside basement steps can be a simple storage area for root crops. Construct an inside basement door at the bottom of your steps to prevent the heat from your basement from warming the stairwell area. As long as you make room to walk up and down them, the steps themselves make great shelves for storing containers of produce. If the outside air gets too cold, you can open the basement door at the bottom of the steps to warm up the stairwell. As you go down the steps to the basement, and away from the outside door, the temperature will be warmer. Set pans of water on the steps to keep the air moist, if necessary. This works well for most vegetable root crops and for apples and pears. Remember, however, not to store apples, pears, cabbage, or turnips near other produce. The fruit will emit gases that will spoil other produce, and the vegetables give off odors that spoil other produce.

Ice Chest

A Styrofoam ice chest is a perfect cooler for crops such as apples and green tomatoes. As long as you have an unheated place that does not actually freeze, these coolers can work well for short periods of time.

The benefit of using something as portable as an ice chest is the ease of moving it. This is especially helpful when you want to keep foods in separate areas.

Window Well

A window well is protected by the house itself and the ground. Beets store particularly well in this kind of space. Store food in covered baskets, buckets, wooden boxes, coolers, or cans and place the container in the window well. Although it is not as constant in temperature as a cellar storage room, you can vary the temperature by opening and closing the window, allowing the heat from the basement to warm up a snow-covered well in the most severe weather. I like to cover the well with pieces of wood, although screening works, also. Wood usually keeps out sunlight and large pests and helps buffer the outside temperatures. However, wood will not keep field mice or other rodents out.

An outside basement stairwell makes an excellent root cellar, as long as access is not blocked.

UNDERGROUND STORAGE

Burying produce is another way to preserve food over the winter, and is successful even in areas with harsh winters. The buried or partially buried produce containers should be kept separate from one another, and if snow is likely to make them hard to find, you should mark their location. It's also important that water drain away from the containers. Sturdy covered wooden boxes, barrels, or plastic garbage containers provide good protection for underground storage. A large, cylindrical piece of tile or drainage pipe can also be used.

When you dig the hole remove any large stones that would touch your underground storage container, as stones conduct frost.

Regardless of what kind of container you choose, put 3 inches of clean sand in the bottom and a finishing layer on top for insulation. Layer produce between 3-inch layers of clean sand. Produce of different types can be stored in the same containers in a pinch, except for cabbage, turnips, apples, and pears.

Partially bury a wooden barrel, sloping the ground away to prevent groundwater from running in, then cover with plastic sheeting to keep rain out. Top with 6 inches of straw for insulation.

A wooden box wrapped in hardware cloth to keep pests out can be completely buried, creating a protected pit for the produce. Slope the ground away to avoid groundwater runoff. Cover the box with a secure wooden lid.

Buried galvanized garbage cans also provide effective storage. These metal cans are pest-proof and work well as long as you treat the produce kindly, store it with layers of clean sand, and keep groundwater away. Cover the top with plastic sheeting and 6 inches of straw, depending on how cold your climate is. You may need to cover it with more straw for colder winter weather. Use the straw later in the spring for mulch.

Straw-Bale Storage

Without the protection of the earth, storing produce aboveground requires another method of insulation. Straw-bale storage does just that while allowing easy access to food. Straw bales can be a wonderful insulating material for aboveground storage. However, this method is practical only in areas that have fairly mild winters. The insulation straw provides is not enough to protect produce from consistent very cold temperatures. Straw is superior to hay, because bales of hay have seeds in them that will germinate and cause problems later in the spring.

When using straw bales for food storage, choose a well-drained location. Play it safe by digging a trench around your straw-bale aboveground storage site to prevent rain water from running in. Build a rectangle of straw bales approximately two bales long and one bale wide. Lay the bales end to end, and line the "floor" with about 3 inches of loose straw. Line the hole created by the bales with hardware cloth or place the food to be stored in covered wooden boxes to keep small animals from making a meal of your produce. Carefully place the produce in the hole or boxes, separating each layer with about 3 inches of loose straw. Top off the produce with another layer of loose straw. Close the pit or box with either more hardware cloth or a wooden top. Place two straw bales over the top, propped up with bricks or stones to let a little air circulate. If the weather turns severely cold, remove the bricks or stones and close down the extra air vent created by the elevated bales. The baled straw will provide enough ventilation as is. When the warmer weather of spring arrives, you can again prop up the top bales with stones or bricks for added ventilation.

The straw-bale storeroom is simple to construct and makes it very easy to remove needed produce. It is ideal for carrots, beets, potatoes, and turnips. Use the straw for mulching your garden in the spring.

Look for containers that are sturdy enough to withstand pressure but not so large as to cause the bottom layer to be crushed by the weight of the produce above it.

Containers

Wooden boxes or crates
Sturdy cardboard cartons
Styrofoam coolers
Barrels
Baskets
Plastic and metal trash cans and buckets — no lid — shallow enough so the weight of the top produce does not crush the bottom layer
Mesh bags — the kind grocery store produce such potatoes and oranges comes in
Slatted bins

Packing Material

Newspaper
Fresh sawdust
Clean, dry leaves
Straw
Clean sand
Peat moss

Materials for Cold Storage

Fortunately, root-cellaring requires no expensive or specialized equipment. The beauty is that you can use what you already have — your home, commonly found containers, produce from your garden — and creatively choose a natural way of preserving simply by putting your food to rest after harvest in just the right spot.

Consider how much produce you'll need to store, first of all, and be aware of the size restrictions of your storage sites. You don't want to save more than you'll be able to accommodate. Then get in the habit of collecting containers and packing materials throughout the year, wherever you come across them. Wooden fruit crates or banana cartons can stack in out-of-the-way corners for use in the fall, and most can be re-used from year to year.

Make sure the storage container you choose is free of any substance that would affect the quality of the food you store. Contamination from diseased vegetables will spoil your produce, and the odor and scent of gasoline, cedar, or any other strong-smelling substance can be absorbed by vegetables. Wash plastic and metals containers before your use for storage, making sure they are dry before you pack produce in them.

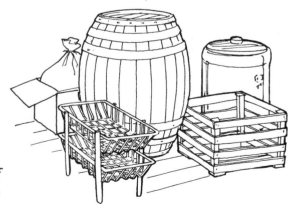

Many types of containers are appropriate for cold storage.

Cold Storing Fruits and Vegetables

I have listed the vegetables that I have had the best experience with for storing in a root cellar. If you don't see a fruit or vegetable listed, it probably is not a good keeper for root cellars. No need wasting valuable produce or your energy on items that will have an unsatisfactory outcome. Start small the first year and keep notes on successes and failures for the next year.

Never bring a big load of just-harvested produce into your root-cellar area. The warmth of all that extra bulk will certainly change the temperature of the root cellar. If at all possible, chill the produce first. Refrigerators will do this quickly, of course, but it's impractical for some folks to use up all their refrigerator space with produce for a day. Instead, try cooling the produce by stages. Store it in a cool garage for a day or so, then move it to the root cellar. Two drawbacks are that the garage can have gas and oil fumes, and the temperature in a garage can't always be controlled, but for a day or so, if the temperature remains cooler than outdoors, precooling there can work quite well. Find other spots around your home that remain cooler than the average outdoor temperature, for instance a porch on the north side or a shaded spot.

Preparing Fruits for the Root Cellar

If at all possible, keep the fruit in your root cellar well away from your vegetables. Apples and pears give off ethylene gas, which causes potatoes to sprout.

The fruits listed here are the best for storing in a root cellar. Refer to the index in this book for alternative preservation methods if you don't see your fruit of choice listed here.

Apples. Wrap apples in newspaper or nest them in straw or clean dry leaves. Apples "breathe" more than most other fruits and give off a pungent aroma, so keep them away from other produce. Store in boxes or barrels, trash cans or buckets. Cover with 2 inches of packing material on top.

Nest apples in layers of clean straw.

Grapefruit. No wrap is needed for grapefruit. Store them in boxes, cartons, baskets, or coolers with no covering.

Grapes. Use very small bunches and cushion them with straw between layers. Use cartons, boxes, or bins and cover with a top layer of packing material. Be sure to use a shallow storage container — too many grapes on top of each other can crush the bottom layer.

Pears. Store while still green. Wrap pears in newspaper or nest them in straw or clean dry leaves. Store in boxes or barrels, trash cans or buckets, covering with 2 inches of packing material on top. Store pears away from other fruits and vegetables.

Preparing Vegetables for Cold Storage

If you're a beginner to cold storage, start with the most commonly stored root vegetables: beets, carrots, potatoes, turnips, and rutabagas. If a particular fruit or vegetable is not listed here, check the index for its other methods of preservation.

Remember to keep vegetables separate from the fruits in your root cellar if at all possible. Cabbage and turnips can have permeating odors for fruits like apples and pears.

Beets. Harvest after nights reach 30°F. Cut off most of the green tops and leave the tails intact. Use boxes, cans, baskets, coolers, or buckets, all lined with a plastic bag. Layer the beets with sawdust or moist sand; use peat moss or straw for outside storage, as in window wells. Beets prefer higher humidity, as much as 95 percent. You can also leave the beets in the ground covered with 6 inches of straw and harvest as needed.

Cabbage. Remove the outer leaves and roots and wrap in newspaper. Store in boxes or cartons in your basement, or leave the roots on and store in damp sand in an outside area, such as a window well.

Carrots. Cut off most of the green tops. Use boxes, cans, or buckets lined with a plastic bag. Layer the carrots with sawdust or moist sand; use peat moss or straw for outside

Layer beets with sawdust or moist sand.

window-well storage. You can also leave carrots in the ground covered with 6 inches of straw and harvest as needed.

Cauliflower. Cut off the roots and leave the leaves intact. Use covered boxes or baskets with moist sand layers.

Celery. Leave on roots and leaves; stand upright in very moist sand.

Endive. Leave on roots and leaves; stand upright in very moist sand.

Horseradish. Harvest after nights reach 30°F. Cut off most of the green tops and leave the tails intact. Use boxes, cans, or buckets lined with a plastic bag. Layer the horseradish with sawdust or moist sand; use peat moss or straw for outside storage, as in window wells.

Kohlrabi. Harvest after nights reach 30°F. Cut off most of the green tops and leave the tails intact. Use boxes, cans, or buckets lined with a plastic bag. Layer the kohlrabi with sawdust or moist sand; use peat moss or straw for outside storage, as in window wells.

Leeks. Harvest after nights reach 30°F. Cut off most of the green tops and leave the tails intact. Use boxes, cans, or buckets lined with a plastic bag. Layer the leeks with sawdust or moist sand; use peat moss or straw for outside storage, as in window wells. You can also leave leeks in the ground covered with 6 inches of straw and harvest as needed.

Onions. Condition onions by letting them dry after digging. Put them outside in the shade on newspaper, turning them several times, for about 10 to 14 days. If the weather should turn wet, bring the onions inside on newspapers. Let them "harden off" or dry somewhat. As the tops dry, braid them together for hanging or store them in old stockings, tying a knot between each onion, in a cool, dry place. Hang near the ceiling of the root cellar (the driest place) or in the attic, where it's cool but dry.

Parsnips. Harvest after nights reach 30°F. Cut off most of the green tops and leave the tails intact. Use boxes, cans, or buckets lined with a plastic bag. Layer the parsnips with sawdust or moist sand; use peat moss or straw for outside storage, as in window wells. Parsnips love

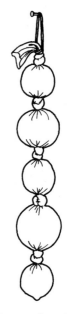

Hang onions in old stockings.

the frozen ground of a dormant garden (no wonder they are so popular in northern Europe). Try leaving them in the ground and digging as you need them. Beware of a warm spell, though, because you don't want them to thaw and then freeze again.

Potatoes. Dig after the vines have been dead about two weeks, or dig when it's no hotter than 70°F and not raining. Allow the potato skins to toughen up in moist 70°F air in a nonwindy place (not in the sun) for about two weeks. Store at about 40°F with dirt and all on the skins in covered boxes or cartons in a dark, very moist place. The cover will keep out light and, therefore, prevent green skins or sprouting, which indicate the presence of poisonous alkaloid that has formed due to exposure to light. (Dispose of these potatoes.) Storage at 40°F helps prevent sugars from forming and thereby changing the taste. Store potatoes away from other produce, especially apples. You can also leave potatoes in the ground covered with 6 inches of straw and harvest as needed.

Pumpkins. Harvest when very mature, before frost, with stem attached. Let them cure for about two weeks in 70°F temperatures so the skins will toughen. Wash pumpkins with a mild bleach solution to prevent mold from forming during storage. Another method that works well is to wipe them with a soft cloth moistened with vegetable oil to deter molds. Store on a shelf in a dry, 55°F place. Don't pile them up, as their weight may crush the bottom layer. Try storing them on the top shelf near the ceiling of the root cellar as long as it's dry.

Radishes. Cut off most of the green tops and leave the tails intact. Use boxes, cans, or buckets lined with a plastic bag. Layer the radishes with sawdust or moist sand; use peat moss or straw for outside storage, as in window wells.

Rutabagas. Cut off most of the green tops and leave the tails intact. Use boxes, cans, or buckets lined with a plastic bag. Layer the rutabagas with sawdust or moist sand; use peat moss or straw for outside storage, as in window wells. You may also keep rutabagas in an inside root cellar

Store potatoes in a covered box in a dark, very moist location.

TIP

• • • • • •

If produce begins to sprout, it is too warm in your root-cellar.

wrapped in plastic wrap to prevent their strong odor from permeating other produce. (This takes the place of the layer of wax almost always found on supermarket rutabagas.)

Winter squash. Harvest when very mature, before frost, with stem attached. Let them cure for about two weeks in 70°F temperatures so the skins will toughen. Wash squash with a mild bleach solution to prevent mold from forming during storage. Another method that works well is to wipe them with a cloth oiled with vegetable oil to deter molds. Store on a shelf in a dry, 55°F place. Don't pile them up, as their weight may crush the bottom layer. Try the top shelf near the ceiling of the root cellar as long as it's dry.

Green tomatoes. Harvest before the first frost without stems attached. Wash and dry thoroughly; store in shallow cartons or boxes packed with straw, leaves, or shredded paper to prevent weight of top layer from crushing the bottom layer. Put in a cool place like the attic or an enclosed back porch where the temperature range is between 55° and 70°F.

Turnips. Cut off most of the green tops and leave the tails intact. Use boxes, cans, or buckets lined with a plastic bag. Layer the turnips with sawdust or moist sand; use peat moss or straw for outside storage, as in window wells. You may also keep turnips in an inside root cellar wrapped in plastic wrap to prevent their strong odor from permeating other produce. (This takes the place of the layer of wax almost always found on supermarket turnips.)

CLEANING AND MAINTENANCE OF ROOT CELLARS

Clean and air out your storage area before each season begins. Scrub all containers with hot, soapy water and place them in the open air for a few days in the warm sun.

During the winter, check your cellar frequently. Remove overripe produce and use immediately if possible.

To keep out rodents, stuff cracks or holes in a cellar wall with steel wool.

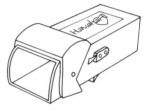

You may wish to try a live mouse trap.

TIP

• • • • • •

To discourage smaller pests such as insects, sprinkle bay leaves on the storage shelves.

If it shows signs of spoiling — such as soft spots, drainage, shriveling, mold, mildew, off odor, or other decay — dispose of it at once. It makes a good addition to your compost pile.

A Word About Pests

Be certain to watch out for rodents and other critters that would like to feast on your "rooty booty."

Mice can be a real problem. Obviously, you'll want to fill in every crack and cranny of your root cellar's walls with steel wool. Try not to exterminate mice, since rodents are the favorite entrée of many wild birds, reptiles, and other animals, and do serve a useful purpose on the food chain. What a disappointment, though, when rodents eat away at your cellar bounty — not to mention the safety and health hazards of runaway breeding mice.

The kindest way of dealing with this problem is a live trap. For capturing an occasional creature that comes in from the cold in fall's first freeze, this is great.

Mouse bait also works for a larger infestation, but, of course, is not as environmentally kind. The poison makes the rodent very thirsty and, theoretically, it leaves the premises looking for water before dying. But the mouse could simply wander to a dark corner or find shelter in your walls before expiring, resulting in the pungent odor of decomposition.

Folklore has it that borax sprinkled around the shelves and floors of root cellars can help control pests. However, the Environmental Protection Agency has not approved borax for this purpose and therefore does not recommend using it.

My recommendation for keeping your root cellar free of pests is to get a mousetrap on legs — a cat. A country cat can be a real joy. When hunting rodents, cats are following their intended purpose in life!

CHAPTER 9

Gifts of Preserved Food

A HOMEMADE JAR OF FOOD given in love is one of the finest gifts available. And the pleasure when you take the time to decorate it creatively rewards both the maker and receiver. Use the ideas that follow as a springboard for your own creations. Creativity is really the art of seeing. Teach yourself to look at different containers, for example, and not be locked into only putting beans in a bean pot, or only serving tea or coffee in a cup and saucer.

Once you learn to think this way, you'll never view life in the same way again. You are broadened and expanded by creative thinking rather than diminished. The more expansive your thinking, the more you share with others, then the more that begins to come back to you. It is like priming a pump. I used to marvel at how my dad could add just a little water to the hand pump at his fish camp and, after a few tries, the water would come gushing out of the spout. I realize now that this is a metaphor for life. Give and you will receive — but save a little for yourself so the water will come out of the pump the next time!

PLANNING FOR GIFT GIVING

I start at the beginning of the calendar year, right after the holidays, to organize my ideas for the coming season. I set aside a special closet in which to store ideas, containers, and decorations as I come across them. When you set aside items as the year unfolds instead of doing crisis-intervention

Save items you can use for decorating gifts.

shopping in December or the middle of canning season, creating gifts becomes a joy, not a drudgery.

When it is too cold to garden, you can learn a lot about produce by reading the colorful seed catalogs that begin arriving right after Christmas. It's fun, when there's snow on the ground, to begin planning your springtime garden and anticipating the harvest. Think how rich you will feel to have jars ready for filling when the harvest season comes. Then think how marvelous it will be to have your Christmas shopping completed long before the deadline! When the next holiday season rolls around, you may have more leisure time to celebrate with your family, to consider the real meaning of the holidays, or to just plain relax and enjoy yourself.

Not only is it rewarding to share, I believe it also must be just as rewarding to receive, judging from the reactions of people who receive the produce or gift of prepared food. Of course, you wouldn't want to give a basketful of zucchini to a fellow gardener in August. And you might not want to give a basket of homemade jams to a neighbor who makes fruit spreads. However, there are plenty of folks who don't garden or preserve their food who would love to receive some as a gift.

Gift giving can become a way of life. Because I am a cyclical-thinking person, nothing pleases me more than growing the food, harvesting it, cooking it, and then giving it away to friends or preparing it for my family. Nature is my biggest ally when I'm searching for suitable decorations for gift packages of food. You can ask my friends in my walking group, because I rarely walk without stopping to pick up something — a cone, an acorn, a thistle — that can be used to decorate a gift package. I'll admit that it takes storage space to save all the items, but the pleasure of collecting and the savings in storing far outweigh the disadvantages.

Collecting Containers

Store jars you collect in a cardboard box in the garage or attic. As you finish your canned goods from last season, clean the jars and place them in the box for the coming season. Neighbors frequently return canning jars after they have consumed your food offerings. Flea markets and garage sales have all kinds of containers available.

Don't limit yourself to canning containers. Look at potential containers with other preserving processes in mind, such as storage for dried foods or no-process preserving such as pickles or chutneys. Even the simplest baby-food jar can be spruced up for gift giving.

Train your eye to spot unusual containers that can be recycled — a maple syrup bottle with distinctive handles, a purchased preserves jar in that octagonal shape with a "gingham"-printed lid, a cheese crock. These make good containers for gifts that need only refrigeration.

After you've collected your containers, soak off the labels, clean them thoroughly, and sterilize.

Here are some other ideas for attractive containers for your preserved-food gift:

Decorate jars and bottles to make wonderfully unique gift packages.

- Be on the lookout in hardware stores for cork assortments to use as stoppers for small-necked bottles you have saved.
- Use cheese crocks for herbal butters or other flavored butters.
- Long-necked bottles with attached lids, such as Grölsh bottles, make perfect containers for flavored vinegars or other homemade dressing.
- Spray the lids of junior baby-food jars a colorful shade of nontoxic paint and use the jars for spicy mustards.
- Save the aluminum pie plates that are given to you or that come with grocery store goods. Recycle them for a freezer casserole to give to an under-the-weather friend, tied up in colorful wrap.

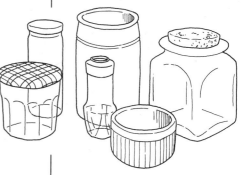

You can use a variety of containers for packaging preserved foods.

Save Fabrics and Other Items

I never throw away even a small piece of ribbon left over from the end of a project. Sometimes it's just the right size to tie around the neck of a bottle of flavored vinegar. Who says the ribbon has to have a bow? A knot is just as effective when it has a dried flower tucked in it.

Fabric scraps can be a great source of decoration for food gifts. If you don't sew, ask a friend who does. Most folks who sew have more scraps than they know what to do with and are grateful to recycle them for creative use.

What follows are other ideas you can use to spur your creativity with things that are left over or no longer usable for their original purpose.

Glue dried acorns or other seedpods to a lid and spray lid and acorns gold. Add a matching bow.

- Save a dried flower or cut a piece of holiday greens from your garden to incorporate in a bow.
- For an old-fashioned lid cover, recycle those hand-crocheted coasters or doilies Aunt Lil made years ago.
- Cut out circles of brown paper bags, then carve a pattern in a potato, dip it in paint, and press it firmly onto the paper for a fun decoration. Tie raffia around the lid to hold down the circle.
- Brown lunch bags can be decorated and used to hold your gift. Dress up the bag by pasting cutout photos from magazines that relate to what's inside.
- Glue alternating colors of yarn around the lid of a jar, and use the same colors to attach a gift tag. Glue yarn into a pattern on top of the lid.
- If you have the time, you can sew lace or other edging on your cloth covers for a frilly finished look.
- Have a scrap party with friends to get a good assortment of fabrics. Everyone can bring one or two pieces of clothing that are being discarded and share for a variety of fabric circles to decorate food jars.

CREATIVE LABELS

No matter what you give, be sure your preserved food is clearly labeled with the contents, the date preserved, your name, the date by which it should be consumed, and how it should be stored. If the food needs to be used in a particular way or is especially good in a specific recipe, be sure to include instructions for it as well.

Hunt for colorful labels in stationery, gardening, and hardware stores. Sometimes the labels that are the most fun are not intended to be labels at all. Keep your eye pealed during the year in stationery stores and card and hardware stores for remarkable labels. Whatever you use for a label, I recommend attaching it with rubber cement. Here are some other creative ideas for labeling.

Cut a circle of fabric 2 inches wider than the jar top in diameter. Use pinking shears for a finished look.

Secure the fabric circle with a rubber band.

Add a ribbon and a bow to cover the rubber band.

- How about a manila old-style tag found in office supply stores to use as a label? Write with a colorful marker or glue it on a colorful sticker. Suspend the tag with colored string that comes with the tag or add your own ribbon.
- Use your local copy store for photocopying snapshots of the family for use as labels for gifts of food.
- Don't underestimate the appeal of a plain brown paper bag torn into an interesting shape used as a label. This is inexpensive and convenient as well.
- Include recipes for a meal that features the food gift. This can provide extra enjoyment for someone you know who loves to cook.
- Use stencils as borders around labels, varying the colors.
- You may want to print your own labels; a number of computer programs generate these for an inexpensive solution. Cut them out and use rubber cement to attach to the jar. Color them with magic markers if you wish.
- If you have access to a color copier you can use magazine pictures to create labels.

Gifts of Food

Last winter in Spain I saw a proverb on a restaurant wall that, loosely translated, means: "Wine is better in a beautiful glass." How true that is of many gifts of food, as well. Presentation can be half the fun. Let the ideas that follow get your imagination going.

- When you make that special mustard and ladle it into a decorative recycled crockery jar, tie a wooden spreader or spoon for serving it to the lid with a decorative ribbon or raffia. For that really special someone, include a homemade picnic sausage along with the mustard. Elaborate on this theme and place it in a picnic basket packed for two to celebrate a special anniversary.

Give a picnic basket filled with homemade food as an anniversary gift.

- Sealing wax, available in stationery and gift stores, will make your bottle of flavored vinegar look very expensive. It's great fun to use, and it smells good as well. If you can't find sealing wax, you might want to try dripping candle wax over the cork topping the bottle.
- Ribbon ideas are endless. Try raffia, green garden twine, or the short end of another project. Even a 6-inch piece of leftover grosgrain ribbon can usually do for the neck of a small bottle.
- Dig up a living tossed salad out of your garden as a special treat. Use a large clay pot and replant it with several heads of bibb lettuce, roots and all, a parsley plant, and a parcel of fresh chives or an oregano plant. Include a bottle of mustard vinaigrette and a couple of fresh tomatoes. For the finishing touch, copy the dressing recipe on an index card. What a welcome surprise this will be!

A living tossed salad makes a novel gift.

- Fill a basket with lettuce from the garden for your neighbor's dinner. Stack it root-end down in a recycled peach basket. Be sure to cut it just before you give it, for it will wilt in an hour or so. Include a jar of herbal vinegar to go with it.

- That decorative jar that bubble bath came in, once it has been thoroughly cleaned, will make a wonderful container for your favorite herbal-blend tea. You can enjoy the container twice as long and save money as well.

- When you dry your Italian tomatoes, pack some in oil as a gift. Although flavored oils must be used immediately, a jar of Italian dried tomatoes in oil and a box of angel-hair pasta could make the basis of a delicious dinner that very day the oil was made.

- My friend Marion packs her dried apples in a quart jar for use as a gift the whole family enjoys. I left the filled jar out on the counter and the apples disappeared very quickly as snacks. Of course, other dried fruits would work just as well. Marion just happens to live in an apple orchard. Add a refrigerator magnet in an apple motif to the metal top of the jar.

- Save the little spice and herb bottles that come from the grocery store. These little containers make great resources for your own dried herbs the next season.

- One use for stale bread is to make giant plastic bags of herb-flavored croutons for salads or soups. Tie the bags with a bow of your choice. Croutons can freeze, but they also keep on the shelf a week or so. To make the croutons, sauté the bread cubes in oil of your choice and sprinkle with garlic powder plus a variety of dried herbs, such as parsley, thyme, oregano, and rosemary.

- Layer colorful beans in that quart jar that is decorative but not safe for the canning process and create a wonderful New Year's gift. Be sure to include black-eyed peas and follow the recipe for Eight-Bean Soup (page 100).

- Try a frozen fruit apple pie (page 172) as a gift the whole family will enjoy.

TIP
. . . . . .

Recycled aluminum pans are wonderful for storing frozen gifts. Re-using the aluminum pans makes it easy for the receiver. No need to return the dish later on: The receiver can recycle the already-recycled aluminum pan if it is in good shape.

APPENDIX A

· · · · · · · · · · ·

BUILDING AN ELECTRIC FOOD DEHYDRATOR

Editor's Note: We studied diagrams and plans for several electric food dehydrators before selecting this one, which appeared to be best because of its design and its size. We built it at Storey Publishing, tested its operation, then shipped it to Phyllis Hobson, an authority on food drying, for her to test.

The following information was written by three people. The first article, describing the construction of the dehydrator, was written by Dale E. Kirk, agricultural engineer at Oregon State University, and published in USDA Home and Garden Bulletin 217. The next section was written by Roger Cota, a former Storey Communications staff member, who built and tested this dehydrator. Finally, the results of the food tests were written by Phyllis Hobson, author of *Making & Using Dried Foods*.

PLANS FOR A DEHYDRATOR

By Dale E. Kirk

A SMALL DEHYDRATOR can be used in the home to preserve many types of fruits, blanched vegetables, meats, and nuts and to make specialty confections from fresh, natural products.

This dehydrator provides 8½ square feet of tray surface, which can accommodate approximately 18 pounds of fresh, moist produce. The necessary heat for evaporating the moisture is supplied by standard household lightbulbs, which are efficient and relatively safe heating elements. An 8-inch household electric fan can be used for air circulation, or a 6- or 8-inch-diameter air-duct circulating fan may be purchased from an electrical supply house.

The dehydrator box described here is easy to build. It requires only two forms of wood building materials: ½-inch plywood and ¾-inch-square wood strips. Construction can be done with a handsaw, coping saw or compass saw, drill, countersink, screwdriver, and knife. A square or tape is needed for measurements.

The drying trays may be built of wooden slats or metal mesh. We recommend, however, that you purchase prefabricated aluminum window screens for use as trays. They are lightweight, sturdy, easily cleaned, and relieve the builder of much of the more difficult construction. Sometimes under heavy use, however, screening tends to pull out of aluminum frames with the weight of the food.

Construction Materials

· · · · · · · · · · · · · · · · · · · ·

You'll need these materials to build the dehydrator described:

1 sheet of ½-inch, 4 x 8-foot, A-C exterior plywood

Nine 4-foot pieces of 1 x 1-inch nominal (¾ x ¾-inch actual) wood strips

One 8-inch household electric fan

1 set of 5 aluminum screens* for trays: 16¾ x 20, 16¾ x 19, 16¾ x 17¾, 16¾ x 16¾, and 16¾ x 15 ½ inches

1 pair of 2-inch, metal butt hinges

1 ball chain or equivalent door latch

9 porcelain surface-mount sockets

Nine 75-watt lightbulbs

15 feet of S.F. #14 copper wire

6 feet of #14 wire extension cord with male plug

One 36-inch length of heavy-duty household aluminum foil

116 1-inch No. 8 flathead wood screws (nails and glue may be used instead)

Eighteen ⅝-inch No. 7 roundhead wood or sheet-metal screws

One 10-amp-capacity thermostat, 100°–160°F approximate range (a baseboard heater thermostat may be used)

One 4-inch electrical surface utility box with blank cover

Two ½-inch utility box compression fittings

2 wire nuts

*Fiberglass treated with nylon or Teflon or wood trays may be substituted for aluminum. Do not use galvanized screening material.

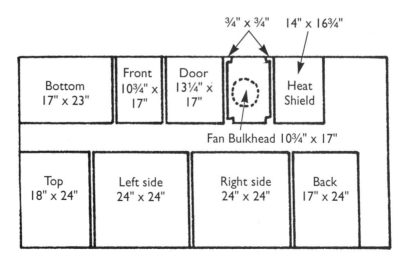

Cutting plan to obtain the necessary plywood parts with a minimum of saw cuts

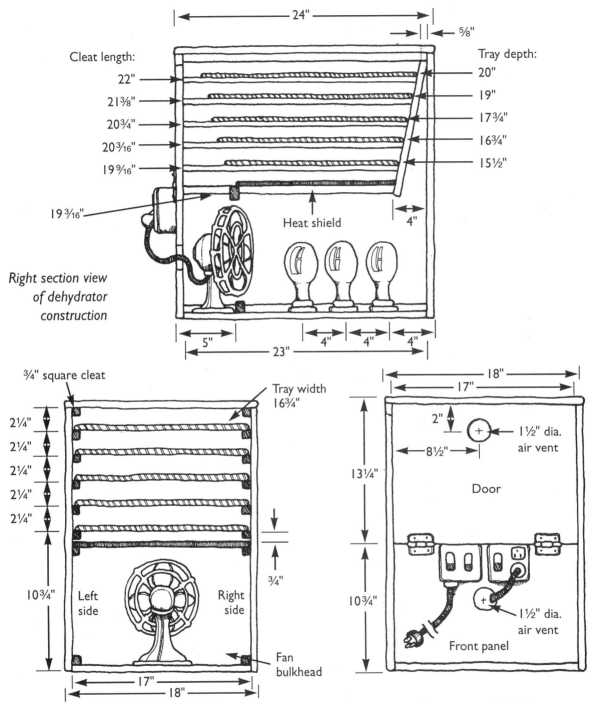

Right section view of dehydrator construction

Cleat length:

22"

21⅜"

20¾"

20³⁄₁₆"

19⁹⁄₁₆"

19³⁄₁₆"

24"

⅝"

Tray depth:

20"

19"

17¾"

16¾"

15½"

Heat shield

4"

5"

4"

4"

4"

23"

¾" square cleat

Tray width 16¾"

2¼"

2¼"

2¼"

2¼"

2¼"

10¾"

¾"

Left side

Right side

Fan bulkhead

17"

18"

Front section view of dehydrator construction

18"

17"

2"

1½" dia. air vent

8½"

13¼"

Door

10¾"

1½" dia. air vent

Front panel

Front view of dehydrator

Cutting and assembly. The cutting diagram shows how all of the ½-inch plywood pieces can be cut from the single 4 x 8-foot sheet. It is usually most satisfactory to measure from the factory-cut edges as shown. Allowances for saw kerfs must be made between adjacent pieces.

Cut the plywood sections to size and the 1 x 4-foot strips to the lengths shown. Then assemble the side panels as shown in the illustration

Next, lay out the porcelain sockets and fasten to the base, as shown. Fasten the S.F. wire to the porcelain sockets. Connect the wire that goes to the yellow screws on the sockets to the thermostat, mounted near the rear on the left side panel. (The yellow screws on the sockets connect to the center pole, rather than the threaded wall of the socket.) Connect the wire that goes to the

white screws to the white wire in the extension cord. The third wire (green) in the extension cord should be connected directly to the junction box, mounted on the front panel.

If you use a household electric fan with the base left attached, fasten it in place on the dehydrator base and cut the hole in the fan bulkhead to fit. If you use a duct-type fan, cut the necessary-size hole (approximately 8½ inches in diameter for an 8-inch fan or approximately 6½ inches in diameter for a 6-inch fan) in the bulkhead and fasten the fan-mounting frame directly to the bulkhead. Now set the bulkhead in place (approximately 5 to 5½ inches from the front panel) and fasten it temporarily in position by two screws through the left side panel as shown. Center the 1½-inch-diameter air-vent hole in the front panel directly in front of the fan motor, approximately 1 inch away from the motor. This will allow the cold air to enter and pass over the motor to cool it.

Next, fasten the right side, back, and top in place.

Cover the heat shield with heavy-duty household aluminum foil. This provides a reflective surface to protect the plywood heat shield and also provides a smooth surface on the top of the shield for easier removal of juices that may drip from the drying trays.

You could build the drying trays, but we suggest you purchase aluminum window screens made to the sizes listed. You can order these through your local lumber or building supply dealer. If they do not have a

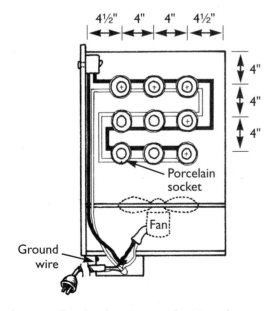

Layout of socket locations and wiring plan

ready source of supply, further information about suppliers may be obtained through your local county extension office. If you prefer to build the trays, we suggest you make a light, wooden frame and aluminum screen. Most plastic screens will sag badly under load and heat. Black metal screens will rust and leave stains on the food product.

You'll need some type of adjustable latch to hold the door in a partially opened position during the early stages of drying, when the moisture is being removed rapidly.

As a check on the thermostat setting, some type of thermometer capable of service in the 100° to 160°F (37.8° to 71.1°C) temperature range should be available. The dial type should be rugged and easily read. A kitchen meat thermometer also will serve. The sensing part of the thermometer should project through the box into the space above the trays for accurate indication of the drying temperature. Placing the sensing element in the heating chamber with the lightbulbs will give a misleading, high reading.

Operation. For most moist fruits and blanched vegetables, the trays may be loaded at the rate of 1 to 2 pounds of fresh produce per square foot of tray surface. The door may be kept closed for the first 30 to 60 minutes to bring the produce and the dehydrator box up to the desired drying temperature. Once this temperature is reached, the door should be opened about ½ to ¾ inch at the top to allow easier escape of the moisture-laden air. The moist air will exhaust at the top, and additional fresh air will be taken in along the sides of the partially opened door.

Test to see when the first high-moisture stage is over. Hold your hand at the opening at the top of the door.

When moisture no longer tends to condense on your hand or on your metal watchband, close the door. The air exchange provided by the two 1½-inch-diameter vents should be enough to complete the drying process.

Maintenance. The electric fan motor is supplied by a stream of fresh air from the lower vent, positioned in front of the motor, but it will still operate at a higher temperature than in normal, open-room service. Lubricate the motor bearings with 30-weight engine oil. Lighter-grade household or sewing machine oil may tend to gum and stall the fan motor after extended service.

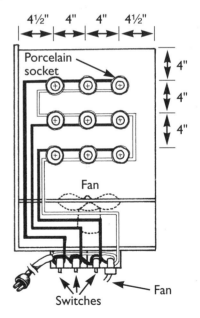

Socket location and wiring plan for use with three-switch control

Wash the trays with hot soapy water when they become soiled with dried-on juices. If you purchased the recommended aluminum window screens with an aluminum wedge strip to hold each screen in place, you can put them in a dishwasher without damage.

Alternate construction and operation. The dehydrator can be built without a thermostat. Temperature can be controlled by the use of switches to operate various numbers of lightbulbs. The diagram shows such a unit, with three separate switches, each controlling three bulbs in the heating chamber.

All three switches should be turned on for at least the first hour or two when the dehydrator is loaded with moist produce. As soon as the temperature comes up to the desired level and the extra heat is not needed to warm large amounts of incoming fresh air, one or two switches may be turned off and the drying completed at the reduced heating rate.

BUILDING THIS DEHYDRATOR

By Roger Cota

I LIKE THIS DEHYDRATOR. It's a good basic design — easier to build than I thought it would be when I first glanced at the plans. The directions plus the illustrations are easy to follow.

Before you decide to build, however, let me tell you two things you should consider:

1. *Parts may be difficult to find.* The most difficult thing to find was the thermostat. Usually a thermostat is available from an electrical supply company. A baseboard heater thermostat may be possible to mount in the dehydrator.

2. *The parts are not cheap.* I bought everything except the bulbs. You could cut costs if you scrounge parts, such as the plywood, the fan, the thermometer, or any of the others. If you value your time and have to purchase all of the materials, a commercial model might be a good buy for you.

And here are a few thoughts I had while building this:

The fan that I found turns at 3,000 RPM. I don't think that speed is necessary. About 1,700 RPM might be fine. If I were building again, I might even mount a rheostat on the fan, so that I could control those RPM.

We had a surprise with the fan motor. On the first test everything was going smoothly — until the fan quit. We waited. The bulbs, of course, heated the box quickly, and the thermostat shut them off. Within a minute, the fan kicked back in, cooled the box, and the lights came on again. The cycle was repeated a few minutes later. That's when we learned that this motor (and most of the electric motors built today) turns itself off when it shows signs of overheating. This temperature level was reached only when the thermostat was turned to give the hottest conditions in the box. It seemed to make no difference in the functioning of the dehydrator — our test apple dried at just about the same speed as the one in a commercial dryer.

We added one refinement to our dehydrator — a piece of the tray screen tacked above the fan at the level of the heat shield. You'll see in the illustrations that there's a space there. Food might drop down from a tray being moved and hit the fan, or a finger might stray down and get spanked by the fan.

The thermostat we bought came with-out a box. We had to fashion a utility box to hold it.

The door on ours fits very smoothly (he said with some pride), but you might want to add a magnetic catch to yours to hold it in place. They're available at most hardware stores.

Finally, I painted a polyurethane coating over the exterior of the box to give it a protective coating.

If I were going to build another, I wouldn't build the trays. They can be built of wood, as mine were, but any repair shop that handles screen doors and windows can quickly turn out five aluminum trays that would be dandy — and maybe easier to clean than the ones with wooden sides.

Dale Kirk did a fine job on this design. A lot of thought went into it to produce a workable dehydrator that even the person with little experience can build.

Tests of This Dehydrator

By Phyllis Hobson

THIS DEHYDRATOR was larger and heavier than any commercial models I've tested. But it did fit nicely on a low table in a well-ventilated utility room, which I had already decided was a better location than the kitchen for an electric dehydrator. I liked this dryer, because it has two features — deep, sturdy trays and a snug-fitting door. These are two of the most consistent problems I've encountered in commercial models.

This dryer performed beautifully. On as dry a day as you're likely to find in Indiana in early spring, apple slices and banana chips were crisp in five hours. Without any pre-treatment, there was no darkening of pear slices and no loss of flavor in grapes. Unlike many of the commercial dehydrators, it was not necessary to turn the fruit or rotate the trays. All areas of every tray dried evenly.

With the dial set on low and the trays empty, the interior temperature reached 100°F (37.8°C) in 10 minutes. With the dial turned to the 110°F (43.3°C) mark, it reached precisely 110°F (43.3°C) in another 10 minutes. It took 10 minutes more to reach 120°F (48.9°C).

With the trays filled, it took longer to reach maximum temperature, but the thermostat worked well, adjusting the temperature by turning the lights off, then on again.

I especially liked the trays. With almost 1 inch of depth, they were easy to handle, even when fully loaded. But I had some problems with the open-weave wire mesh, because the rough surface made it difficult to remove sticky foods at almost any stage of drying. Not only were the dried foods hard to peel off, but the trays were also hard to clean and almost impossible to soak.

In spite of that, I still would use the open-weave wire mesh, because it allows for better circulation of air and quicker drying of foods than fine screen. Not only are the trays sturdier than those made of screen, but they will last longer. Those are the reasons I would vote against using aluminum window screens as suggested, even though it would be a lot easier on the builder than making wood-framed trays. Under heavy use, screening tends to pull out of aluminum frames with the weight of the food.

I would suggest one change in the trays. Roger Cota followed the directions faithfully for the test model and graduated the length of the trays to fit the sloping tray slots. With every tray ½ inch longer than the tray below it, inserting five different lengths of trays into five different lengths of slots can be a shell game when you have five full trays to load at once. I'm sure the slope is necessary for air circulation, and it is possible to mark the trays, but it would simplify construction and use to make all the trays the shorter length.

APPENDIX B

• • • • • • • • • • •

TABLE OF EQUIVALENTS

Apples . . . . 1 pound = 3 medium = 2½ cups peeled and sliced

Apricots . . . . 1 pound fresh = 8 to 10 medium = 2 cups sliced
. . . . 1 pound dried = 3 cups

Asparagus . . . . 1 pound = 12 to 16 stalks = 3½ cups (in pieces)

Avocados . . . . 1 medium = 1 cup cubes

Bananas . . . . 3 to 4 = 2 cups sliced = 1½ cups mashed

Beets . . . . 1 pound = 2 cups sliced

Blueberries . . . . 1 pint = 2 cups

Broccoli . . . . 1-pound head = 2 cups florets

Cabbage . . . . 1 pound = 4½ cups raw, shredded or sliced
. . . . 1 pound = 2½ cups cooked

Carrots . . . . 1 pound = 6 or 7 = 3 cups sliced or shredded

Cauliflower . . . . 1½ pounds = 2 cups cooked

Celery . . . . 1 stalk = ½ cup sliced or chopped

Cherries (fresh) . . . . 1 pound = 2 cups pitted

Chicken . . . . 3½ pounds, whole = 3 cups cooked meat
. . . . 1 large boned breast = 2 cups cooked meat

Corn . . . . 1 plump ear = ½ cup kernels

Cranberries . . . . 1 12-ounce bag = 3 cups
(fresh or frozen) . . . . 2 ounces dried (by weight) = ¼ cup

Cucumbers . . . . 1 medium = 1½ cups sliced

Currants . . . . ¼ pound fresh = 1 cup
. . . . ⅓ pound dried = 1 cup

Eggplant . . . . 1½ pounds = 2½ cups diced

Garlic . . . . 2 medium cloves = 1 teaspoon minced

Grapefruit . . . . 1 medium = ½ pound = 1 cup sections

Grapes . . . . 1 pound = 2½ cups

Ginger (fresh) . . . . 1-inch piece = 2 tablespoons grated or chopped

Green beans . . . . 1 pound = 3 cups fresh = 2½ cups cooked

Herbs (general) . . . . 1 tablespoon fresh = 1 teaspoon dried

Lemons . . . . 1 medium = 3 tablespoons juice, 2 teaspoons grated zest

Lentils . . . . 1 cup dried = 3 cups cooked

Limes . . . . 1 medium = 1½ to 2 tablespoons juice, 1 teaspoon grated zest

Mushrooms (fresh) . . . . ½ pound = 2 cups sliced

Nectarines . . . . 1 pound = 3 or 4 = 2 cups peeled and sliced

Okra . . . . 1 pound = 22 to 28 small pods = 5 cups

Onions . . . . 1 medium = ¾ cup sliced or chopped

Oranges . . . . 1 medium = ⅓ cup juice, 2 to 3 tablespoons grated zest

Peaches . . . . 1 pound = 4 medium = 2 cups peeled and sliced

Pears . . . . 1 pound = 3 medium = 2 cups peeled and sliced

Peas . . . . 1 pound pods = 1 cup shelled
. . . . 1 cup or ½ pound dried split = 2½ cups cooked

Peppers (bell) . . . . 1 large = 1 cup chopped

Pineapple (fresh) . . . . 1 medium = 3 cups peeled and diced

Plums . . . . 1 pound = 8 medium = 2½ cups pitted

Pumpkin . . . . 1 pound = 1 cup cooked and pureed

Raisins . . . . 1 pound = 3 cups

Raspberries . . . . 1 pint = 1¾ to 2 cups

Rhubarb . . . . 1 pound = 2 cups cooked

Scallions . . . . 1 bunch = ⅓ cup chopped (whites only)

Shallots . . . . 1 large = 1 tablespoon minced

Squash (summer) . . . . 1 pound = 3½ cups sliced

Squash (winter) . . . . 1 pound = 1 cup cooked and pureed

Strawberries . . . . 1 pint = 2 cups sliced

Sugar, granulated . . . . 1 pound = 2¼ cups

Sugar, brown . . . . 1 pound = 2¼ cups (firmly packed)

Sweet potatoes . . . . 3 medium = 1 pound = 3 cups sliced

Tomatillos . . . . 1 pound = 10 to 12

Tomatoes . . . . 1 pound = 3 medium = 1½ cups peeled, seeded, and chopped

Zucchini . . . . 1 pound = 3½ cups sliced

APPENDIX C

• • • • • • • • • • • •

CONVERTING RECIPE MEASUREMENTS TO METRIC

Use the following formulas for converting U.S. measurements to metric. Since the conversions are not exact, it's important to convert the measurements for all of the ingredients to maintain the same proportions as the original recipe.

When the Measurement Given Is	Multiply It By	To Convert To
Teaspoons	4.93	milliliters
Tablespoons	14.79	milliliters
Fluid ounces	29.57	milliliters
Cups (liquid)	236.59	milliliters
Cups (liquid)	.237	liters
Cups (dry)	275.31	milliliters
Cups (dry)	.275	liters
Pints (liquid)	473.18	milliliters
Pints (liquid)	.473	liters
Pints (dry)	550.61	milliliters
Pints (dry)	.551	liters
Quarts (liquid)	946.36	milliliters
Quarts (liquid)	.946	liters
Quarts (dry)	1,101.22	milliliters
Quarts (dry)	1.101	liters
Gallons	3.785	liters
Ounces	28.35	grams
Pounds	.454	kilograms
Inches	2.54	centimeters
Degrees Fahrenheit	$\frac{5}{9}$ (temperature − 32)	degrees Celsius (Centigrade)

While standard metric measurements for dry ingredients are given as units of mass, U.S. measurements are given as units of volume. Therefore, the conversions listed above for dry ingredients are given in the metric equivalent of volume.

INDEX

Page references in *italic* indicate charts; those in **bold** indicate recipes.

Blueberries
    canning of, *51*
    and cherry preserves, **214**
    drying of, *81, 86–87*
    juicing of, *183*
    marmalade, **213**
    preserving methods for, *18*
    waffles, **96**
Boil blanching, 120, *121*
Boiling-water-bath canning
    altitude, adjustments for, 40, 41, 44
    discussion of, 27–28
    for fruit spreads, 182, 189
    and high-acid foods, *51*
    for pickles, 238, 244–47
    recipes, canning, **53–60, 67–69, 71, 73–77**
    recipes, pickles **254, 256, 259–60, 264–67, 269, 272, 275–76, 279**
    and tomatoes, 33
Borax and pests, 316
Borscht, Cabbage, **61**
Bottles, vinegar, 286
Botulism. *See also* Spoilage
    and canning, 24, 27, 31–33, 47
    and flavored oils, 289
    and pickling, 248
Bouquet garni, 92
Breads
    banana, **170**
    and butter pickles, **254**
    cranberry, **111**
    French bread and seasoned butters, **294**
Brined pickles, 238, 244
Broccoli, *10, 20, 121*
Brussels sprouts, *10, 20, 121*, **264**
Bubbles, removal of, 38, 43, 188, 246
Butternut Squash Soup Base, **151**

Butters. *See also* Fruit spreads
    apple, **216**
    apple-plum, **217**
    apple-zucchini, **218**
    definition of, 180
    freezing of, 133
    herb blend, **98**
    pear, **236**
    pear, spiced, **138**
    seasoned, **294**
    slow-cook method, 85

C

Cabbages
    borscht, **61**
    canning of, *10*
    cold storage of, *303*, 312
    freezing of, *121*
    preserving methods for, *20*
Cake, Apple Coffee, **112**
Calcium
    salt (dicalcium phosphate), 180
    tonic, **114**
    in water, 16
Canning. *See also* Boiling-water-bath canning; Pressure canning
    altitude, adjustments for, 40–42, 44, 49, 246
    equipment for, 27
    evaluation of, 46
    food, preparation for, 35, 42–43
    and headspace, 38, 39, 40, *50–51*
    high-acid foods, 27–28, 33–34, 37, 41, *51*
    history of, 22–23
    homemade vinegars, 283–84
    hot pack, 33, 36–38, 41–44, 49, *50–51*
    jars, choice of, 24–26
    jars, filling, 38–39, 42, 43

jars, preparation for, 35–36, 42–43
    lids, 24–26, 39, 186–87, 188, 243
    low-acid foods, 28–30, 33–34, 41, 48–49, *50*
    meats, 49
    and pasteurizing, 23–24, 32, 42
    poultry, 49
    pretreat methods, 35
    and processing times, 41, *50–51*
    raw pack, 36–37, 41–44, *50–51*
    recipes, **52**
    safe methods, importance of, 31–32
    salt, 11, 242
    and spoilage, 23, 47–48, 248
    storage, 47
    of tomatoes, 33–34
    unsafe methods, 29
Carrots
    canning of, *10, 50*
    cold storage of, *303*, 312–13
    with honey and dill, **280**
    in honey and vinegar, **69**
    and orange marmalade, **224**
    preserving methods for, *20*
Cauliflower
    canning of, *10*
    cold storage of, *303*, 313
    freezing of, *121*
    pickled, **265**
    preserving methods for, *20*
Caviar, Eggplant, **139**
Celery, *20, 303*, 313
Champagne vinegars, 283, 286, 289
Cheesecloth bag, for spices, 12, 240, 287
Cheeses, freezing, 133
Cherries
    canned, quantity per quart, *10*
    canning of, *10, 51*
    drying of, *81, 86–87*

OTHER STOREY TITLES YOU WILL ENJOY

The Well-Stocked Pantry Series: Preserving Fruits & Vegetables, by Carol Costenbader. Catering to both the novice and the more experienced cook, this suberbly illustrated guide provides a creative answer to preserving fruits and vegetables when they are most abundant, for the leaner months of the year. 96 full-color pages. Hardcover. ISBN 0-88266-852-8.

The Well-Stocked Pantry Series: Mustards, Ketchups & Vinegars, by Carol Costenbader. Use the fruits and vegetables of the season to create a veritable cornucopia of the freshest condiments for your pantry and refrigerator. 96 full-color pages. Hardcover. ISBN 0-88266-813-7.

The Busy Person's Guide to Preserving Food: Easy Step-by-Step Instructions for Freezing, Drying, and Canning, by Janet Chadwick. An indispensable guide to the fastest, easiest ways to stockpile and preserve the season's best fruits, vegetables, and herbs. 224 pages. Paperback. ISBN 0-88266-900-1.

Root Cellaring: Natural Cold Storage of Fruits & Vegetables, by Mike and Nancy Bubel. Suitable for city and country folks, with information on harvesting and creating cold storage anywhere, even closets! Includes 50 recipes. 320 pages. Paperback. ISBN 0-88266-703-3.

Making & Using Dried Foods, by Phyllis Hobson. Step-by-step instructions for drying almost everything with or without a commercial dehydrator. Includes more than 200 delicious recipes using dried foods. 192 pages. Paperback. ISBN 0-88266-615-0.

Cider: Making, Using & Enjoying Sweet and Hard Cider, by Annie Proulx and Lew Nichols. A new edition of the cider maker's bible covering all aspects from growing the trees to cooking with cider. Includes basic procedures, equipment, and materials and explains how to make cider blends, sparkling cider, applejack, apple brandy, and more. 224 pages. Paperback. ISBN 0-88266-969-9.

The Perfect Pumpkin, by Gail Damerow. A complete guide to growing and using pumpkins, including growing and harvesting techniques, step-by-step craft and carving projects, mouth-watering recipes, and tips on successful winter storage. 224 pages. Paperback. ISBN 0-88266-993-1.

These books and other Storey books are available at your bookstore, farm store, garden center, or directly from Storey Publishing, Schoolhouse Road, Pownal, Vermont 05261, or by calling 1-800-441-5700. www.Storey.com